A BRIEF HISTORY OF
MUTINY

Richard Woodman

ROBINSON
London

Constable & Robinson Ltd
3 The Lanchesters
162 Fulham Palace Road
London W6 9ER
www.constablerobinson.com

This edition published by Robinson,
an imprint of Constable & Robinson Ltd, 2005

A copy of the British Library Cataloguing in
Publication data is available from the British Library

ISBN 1–84119–737–8

Printed and bound in the EU

1 3 5 7 9 10 8 6 4 2

Oh, whatever you do, never flinch from your King,
From your Country, your Parents and all
The best Blessings which from honest Duty do spring,
To join in a mutinous brawl:
For mind me, my Mates, and I say it in sooth,
To avert you from every dread evil,
That the one is the way of high Honour and Truth,
But the other the road to the Devil!

Anon, eighteenth century

CONTENTS

LIST OF ILLUSTRATIONS

Captain General Ferdinand Magellan
(*Courtesy of National Maritime Museum, London*)

Sir Francis Drake
(*Courtesy of Fotomas Index UK*)

Captain William Bligh
(*Courtesy of Fotomas Index UK*)

Richard Parker presenting a list of the seamen's demands to Admiral Buckner at the Nore.
(*Courtesy of National Maritime Museum, London*)

The crew of HMS *Surprise* recapturing HMS *Hermione* from the Spanish.
(*Courtesy of National Maritime Museum, London*)

Captain Thomas Worth
(*Courtesy of The Martha's Vineyard Historical Society*)

Captain A. S. Mackenzie
(*Courtesy of United States Naval Institute Photo Archive*)

The American brig-of-war, USS *Somers*, with her young
mutineers hanging from the main yardarm.
(*Courtesy of US Naval Academy Museum*)

The Imperial Russian battleship, *Potemkin*
(*Courtesy of John Morris*)

De Zeven Provincien
(*Courtesy of John Morris*)

The converted cargo-liner, HMS *Lothian*
(*Courtesy of John Morris*)

Marcus Arnheiter, commanding officer of USS *Vance*
(*Courtesy of Bettmann/CORBIS*)

INTRODUCTION

MUTINY is defined as 'open revolt against constituted authority; now chiefly on the part of a disciplined body, especially military or naval.' Despite a considerable number of military mutinies, the word is, in its modern connotation at least, almost invariably associated with ships' crews, and it is mutiny in this form with which this book is concerned.

Mutiny is a subject that exerts a strange and apparently enduring fascination. According to the book of Genesis the very establishment of the human race rests upon an act of disobedience, and a portion of the rebel exists in us all. Indeed, the *Oxford English Dictionary* quotes a passage of 1633 which might apply to most of us: 'Wee [*sic*] cannot quench hot and unruly desires in youth without some mutiny, and rebellious opposition.' Perhaps this is why the vicarious experience of a revolt against established authority engages our interest, for in our demotic age the notion of mutiny is seen as a series of historic incidents by which we, 'the people', liberated ourselves from tyrannical rule. This vague assumption all too easily leads us to favour the under-dog, often in defiance of the facts, for many mutinies did not follow this stereotype and, with the passage of time, legal determination of the act itself has become increasingly difficult.

The truth is that although many of these rebellions seem to us today to possess a measure of justification, no two mutinies were quite alike; fewer still conformed with the image presented by successive filmic attempts to represent the best-known of all such insurrections. By far the most famous, or perhaps one ought properly to write infamous, mutiny was that aboard the British naval transport *Bounty* in 1789, a year famous for revolution. Yet on a scale of either violence or justification, Fletcher Christian's mutiny against the allegedly tyrannical rule of William Bligh hardly registers. It is a cub among mutinies and has neither the furious, savage and bloody vigour of that of the crew of the frigate *Hermione* against the sadistic Captain Hugh Pigot in 1797 nor the justifiable anger of the rebellion of the crew of HMS *Culloden* against the hot-headed Captain Thomas Troubridge in December 1794. Though very different in their causes, these were red-blooded mutinies in the full sense of the word.

The Royal Navy was subject to a number of mutinies during the long wars with France between 1793 and 1815. Most significant were the serious 'fleet mutinies' of 1797 when the Channel squadron at Spithead and the North Sea squadron at the Nore effectively struck for better pay and conditions. Yet even these two insurrections, although they owned their incidence to a common cause, were quite different from each other in their progress and their outcome. But while the notion of the Royal Navy 'going on strike' might square itself with social historians of a later age, the naval authorities of 1931 were in no more doubt that the refusal of the sailors in the Atlantic Fleet to do their duty at Invergordon was due to open and defiant mutiny than were those of 1797 that the immobility of the Channel and North Sea Fleets was similarly attributable.

The Admiralty and its senior servants have never admitted the case for strikes – or 'industrial action' – in pursuit of righting a grievance. They have only admitted a subtle gradation of mutiny, which might be an offence committed by an individual as much as by a part or the whole of a ship's company, or a rather more spectacular eruption among an entire fleet. Naval law recognized 'mutinous assembly' and 'mutinous language' under one article, 'concealment of mutiny' under another, and mutiny itself under a third. A problem arises from this woolly definition in that striking a superior (and this might mean a bullying and unbearably dominating petty officer) was automatically a mutinous act. Single or collective acts of mutiny were carried out for reasons as diverse as political conviction (such as republicanism), demands for shore leave and the society of the opposite sex, acts of extreme prejudice to a man-of-war due to mental instability, or rumours that a ship was not to be paid off and the crew allowed home at the conclusion of hostilities.

Such tabulations, however, left no room for leniency. The punishment for mutiny, whatever its magnitude or extent, was either death or 'such punishment as a court-martial shall think fit to inflict'. Since mutiny was a serious matter, death was the usual sentence once guilt was established after the incident had been subjected to due process.

And due process in a naval court martial was never impartial. A naval court martial was not convened to establish the guilt or innocence of those charged with mutiny; its purpose was to maintain discipline within a fighting service, and all a court's judgments, which were by no means entirely unenlightened, were made with this end in view. For it to be otherwise would have entailed its members, commissioned officers all, acting to the prejudice of the king's service, and thus contrary to the rule of naval law. But this, though true, is to present a distorted view. Brutal though naval discipline could be it was often more compassionate than that pertaining in contemporary society at large, and since the Royal Navy and its associated infrastructure of Royal Dockyards formed for more than a century not only the largest institution in the world but one run by human beings, it embraced many paradoxes.

To comprehend naval mutiny it is important to see each example in this context, mindful that insofar as the Royal Navy

was concerned the word 'mutiny' enjoyed a fairly wide interpretation, not always as specific nor as reprehensible as is thought
today. Some cases of mass dissension, though technically mutiny,
were treated with lenience and understanding; others were not.
Moreover, the navy's attitude changed with time and circumstance: a refusal to obey orders in the face of the enemy was a
capital offence, a refusal to sail from a home port something
rather different. This was perfectly understood by the best among
the seamen, who rarely railed against the injustices in society but
only against specific tyrannies applied to themselves. Thus, when
the crews of the assembled ships anchored at Spithead refused to
go to sea, the great combination of seamen acted in all other
respects with great self-control and discipline and as we shall
see, presented its reasonable demands in a reasonable manner.
This restraint compelled the Admiralty and the Government, as
distinct from assorted peppery admirals, to consider not only the
seamen's demands but the consequences of acting against them.
Confronted as it was by the wild menace of Republican France,
for the Government to have moved against the entire Channel
Fleet could only have resulted in a disaster highly prejudicial to
the service of George III and to the British nation as a whole.

On the other hand, incitement to mutiny could be taken
extremely seriously, even in its most mild form. On 1 September
1804 a sailor was tried aboard the Portsmouth guardship, the
former Spanish line-of-battle ship *Salvador del Mundo*, for
distributing the words of seditious songs, which he was wont to
sing to himself. He was sentenced to be flogged round the fleet
and given 500 lashes as an example to all; he was then to serve
two years in the Marshalsea prison.

Most responsible officers – and most officers were responsible
– did what they could to avoid matters coming to a court martial.
Many of them also did what they could to avoid the formal
punishment of flogging which, depending upon the crime, could
disturb the tranquillity of a ship's company. Sadly there was no
formal scale of lesser sanctions. There was, as Nicholas Rodger
points out,

a real problem for officers to find suitable punishments for trivial offences, and it was this which led so many to use canes. It seemed to them, not unreasonably, to be more humane to give a quick blow and forget the affair, than to condemn a man [who might otherwise be valuable to the ship] to the delay and severity of a flogging. It was also far less inconvenient for all, it avoided disrupting the ship's routine, and it accorded with simple justice in matching the slightness of the offence with that of the punishment.

Rodger goes on to quote Captain Peyton of the *Prince,* who pointed out that it would be impossible to maintain discipline aboard ship if officers had to apply to him for a flogging rather than administer 'the lesser punishment of a stroke' with their canes at the time of the offence.

Unhappily, it was not always the lower ranks of put-upon ratings who revolted. Occasionally officers, even senior officers, disobeyed orders and risked charges of mutiny. Such affairs were a serious stain on the honour of the service, and were more often influenced by politics than by pure personal enmity or private conscience.

But there was another British 'fleet' which was more numerous and in many ways more influential of itself, both economically and politically, than His Majesty's Royal Navy. This was the mercantile marine. Diverse, privately-owned but nationally beneficial, its seamen were not merely identical to those in the Royal Navy but, during the age of sail, interchangeable. On the outbreak of hostilities a mobilizing navy sent its notorious press-gangs not to catch innocent farm boys, counting-house clerks and wig-makers' apprentices but to round up the crews of merchant ships, able seamen who knew how to 'hand, reef and steer'. Indeed, on the outbreak of war many seamen volunteered for the navy to avoid the obnoxious inevitability of being pressed at some time or another, a decision influenced by a meagre bounty of five pounds.

Little more than two years after the outbreak of war in 1793 the twin demands of manning both naval and merchant ships caused a shortage of competent seamen, whereupon the Royal Navy was compelled to cast its insatiable net wider. In March 1795 Parliament passed the first of the Quota Acts, requiring each county and borough to produce a specified number of men and laying the duty upon the magistrates who, it must be emphasized, could offer the inducement of a bounty of seventy pounds. Those men who offered themselves up under such generous terms were immediately unpopular with the long-service, professional seamen, who not only – and justifiably – considered themselves duped but found their new and invariably inexperienced shipmates a burden, many of them trouble-makers. Nor did the officers necessarily welcome an influx that often brought a worse consequence than under-manning, since magistrates were likely to resort to despatching vagrants, petty thieves, debtors and all manner of undesirable characters who were either a burden on the parish or simply undesirables in the local community. Often naval service was ordered instead of a gaol sentence: in 1780 two men of the 7th Light Dragoons were condemned by a military court-martial to serve in the navy. Many of these useless individuals were turned into seamen by *force majeure*, most fulfilled their basic duties, but many succumbed to the influence of 'lower-deck lawyers', political agitators and men with republican sympathies, or of simple trouble-makers eager to stimulate discontent and take advantage of the instability thus caused. Such men could, and often did, incite petty mutiny, but their influence has been over-emphasized. While it caused domestic disruption aboard individual ships, it is not thought to have had wider impact.

A dramatic example of the ultimate weakness of this system occurred in 1779 when a powerful Franco–Spanish fleet entered the English Channel and threatened invasion. Outnumbered, Admiral Sir Charles Hardy 'could only observe its movements', and panic, like high tide, ran along the south coast of England. One British man-of-war, the *Ardent*, 'had been hurried out of port with a raw crew . . . of the 500 [of which], 400 were landsmen . . . not one of whom had ever seen a gun fired. The 100 seamen, destitute of clothing and every necessary, were mutinously inclined.' The *Ardent* was surrounded by several French ships and surrendered; her captain, Philip Boeteler, was afterwards dismissed from the service.

Indeed, Their Lordships at the Admiralty did not automatically reinforce a captain's authority. On several occasions, learning of bad blood arising between captain and crew, they replaced the former. It was not merely expedient, for it was far easier to find a new captain than an entire crew; it was sensible. They might also threaten an unsuitable captain, as happened aboard the *Penzance* in 1758 when the admiral at the Nore reported dissension between Captain Ward and 'his people'. Without more ado Ward was informed of Their Lordships' disapprobation and threatened with supercession; there was no question of arraigning the mutineers.

That said, the Admiralty and its sea officers were well aware of the potential for disorder emanating from any combination of disaffected spirits, particularly in wartime, when they were less liberal. On board every man-of-war a detachment of marines messed between the seamen and the officers as a buffer. Theoretically their loyalty lay with the officers, though occasional individual lapses did occur, as we shall remark. Nor should it be assumed that a grievance nursed by a particular group of men inevitably infected a whole crew. Many of the long-service seamen held the Johnny-come-latelies in contempt, and would refuse to join any projected rebellion. This emphasizes the very real threat inherent in any combination that did lead to mutinous conduct. What made the mutiny at Spithead so dangerous, and distinguished it from that at the Nore, was the conduct of the long-service, professional able-seamen.

These men, if not actually bred to the sea, knew no other life, and in peacetime found employment in merchant ships. So too did many of the officers; even Nelson served briefly in a merchant ship as a young man. Discipline in merchantmen varied according to the trade in which a ship was engaged, and the regime on board. That on a large East Indiaman making an annual round-voyage to India or China was very similar to that pertaining on a naval vessel. Such a ship was officered by gentlemen and reflected a similar social hierarchy to that of a man-of-war. In contrast, a vessel engaged in the Baltic trade – of which, in say 1810, there were thousands – was run on more easy-going lines, the master ruling by ability and personality rather than the lash. Such vessels, from which the great James Cook came, employed the cream of British able-seamen and were prime targets for the Press.

In general, mutiny in merchant ships seems to have increased in incidence as change flattened the hierarchical pyramid in society as a whole. Initially a man entrusted with the command of a merchantman was invariably linked in some way with a vessel's owner, and might indeed be a part or even whole owner of the ship. Over time this link was eroded and men were promoted on ability, though nepotism remained and many merchant ships were incompetently commanded. By the mid-nineteenth century a series of disasters involving loss of the life of passengers had caused the government to appoint the Board of Trade as the regulating body of the mercantile marine, and the quality of masters, mates and, in due course, engineers improved. Matters were therefore clear-cut after the Merchant Shipping Act of 1854. Prior to that, a master enjoyed wide powers but his enforcement of them was devoid of powerful legal sanction, relying rather more on custom, usage and precedent. A merchant master indulged sadistic passions with less certainty, than his Royal Naval counterpart, of having them gratified, despite the fact that he might bring an action in a civil court against the rebellious members of his crew.

Unfortunately, ship-owning profits were and are made at the margins and owners are always anxious to keep costs to a minimum, a circumstance often inconsistent with safety. This particularly affected crew numbers and standards of food, shore-leave and accommodation. Nor in many nineteenth-century sailing ships were masters, whose personal remuneration depended upon the costs and profits of a voyage, unwilling to dupe the sailor. If a seaman could be induced to desert, seduced by some doxy or by the lure of a goldfield up-country, he forfeited his pay. Often this desertion was accomplished with the help of a dockside crimp. Instead of a whore's bed or the diggings, the hapless and penniless sailor found himself next morning comatose, hung-over and 'shanghaied' aboard another outward-bound ship, without proper clothes and heading for Cape Horn. A combination of such strictures and abuses scarcely provided a man with a subsistence income and frequently provoked outbreaks among merchant seamen of mutinous conduct often quite as bloody as anything the alleged brutalities of the Royal Navy a generation earlier had initiated.

In 1925, six years before the Royal Navy's last 'classic' mutiny at Invergordon, the crews of numerous merchant ships berthed in the ports of South Africa, Australia and New Zealand, many of them crack cargo and passenger liners rather than grubby trampships, either went on strike or mutinied in horrible emulation of the Bolshevik Revolution of 1917, depending upon the point of view. It was an industrial action that threatened to cripple the three economies, but it was of little benefit to the much put-upon seafarers, who like their naval cousins in 1931 found they could not maintain their families. Its chief effect was to strengthen the resolve of Government to resist when confronted with a General Strike in Britain the following year.

Forty years later, in 1966, the British National Union of Seamen called its members out on strike over issues of pay and conditions. It was an era bedevilled by such disruptions, but the shipowner was disinclined to submit to what he saw as unreasonable extortion in a world no longer tolerant of such unilateral behaviour. There were other bottoms to carry cargoes, and other seafarers willing to undertake the labour of their safe navigation. The Seamen's Strike of 1966 effectively reduced the British merchant fleet to a minor world player. It was not a mutiny but, as with so many mutinies, the seamen's action failed to achieve its objective.

In attempting a 'Brief History' I have had to be partial. The mutinies that follow are chiefly those in British ships, largely because over a period of several centuries Great Britain possessed enormous fleets of both naval and merchant vessels which she employed all over the globe. One so-called mutiny absent from these pages which has of late received some attention is the disturbance following the wreck of the Dutch East Indiaman *Batavia* which ran aground and broke up on Houtmann's Abrolhos off the west coast of Australia in 1628. Although there was a plot to take the ship and defraud the owners by seizing the Verrenigde Oost-indische Compagnie's representative or super-cargo, Francisco Pelsaert, the leaders of the plot included the vessel's master, Ariaen Jacobszoon. Thus this was not mutiny, but barratry. The proposed action would not have been a breach of discipline but a crime of greed aimed at defrauding the rightful owners of the ship and cargo. But before Jacobszoon and his accomplice, Pelsaert's assistant Jeronimus Corneliszoon, could carry out their intentions the ship was wrecked. What followed – the abandonment of the survivors by Jacobszoon and Pelsaert, who reached the Dutch colonial capital on Java, and the massacre of the majority of the crew left behind by Corneliszoon and his ruthless followers – is a bloody and terrible story, but it was not mutiny. Corneliszoon, an Antinomian psychopath, was a man of diabolical character, and if the prurient reader should feel cheated by his omission I have not ignored a later psychopath who led a thoroughly 'proper' mutiny aboard the American whaleship *Globe* two hundred years later.*

Although the historian tends to seek a causal chain in areas of social change, and although in the specific case of mutinies there is usually a specious attraction in discerning extremes of deprivation and a consequent dysfunction in ship-board life, the laws of cause and effect do not fit comfortably as generalizations here. The mariners' environment is a hermetic one, misunder-

* For an account of Cornelisz' crimes see *Batavia's Graveyard,* by Mike Dash, published by Phoenix, 2002.

stood by those unfamiliar with its subtleties yet easily subverted by over-simplified assumptions. A ship's crew are employed for a specific purpose and there are usually just enough of them for that purpose to be accomplished: destroy a part and you destroy the whole. The very act of mutiny therefore requires a motivation strong enough to set aside its consequences, for the risk the mutineer runs goes beyond retribution on the part of the usurped authority. The mutineers have to outwit the dangers of the sea and conduct their little world somewhere safe or sympathetic. To do so they must act in harmony, and harmony was scarcely a quality to be found among men confronting constitutional authority, no matter how tyrannical. In this the fate of the *Bounty* mutineers comes to mind but, as we shall see, they were not alone. The outcomes of mutinies were often as appalling as their causes.

Quite obviously the most influential factor in the conduct of all mutinies was the personalities of those involved. Since all humans are distinct individuals it should be no surprise to find that a brief history of mutiny is but a brief history of men constrained within the curious confines of a ship.

1

OF MARINERS AND GENTLEMEN

IT is a seaman's right to grumble. It is a means by which he insulates his individuality against the intrusions of his relentlessly communal life. He signals discontent – in the sense of merely the lack of contentment – in order to keep at a distance those whom fate, the state or the system have placed above him. Grumbling makes his inferior status bearable, enabling him to cope with the petty irritations that the inconvenience of ship-board life constantly throws in his path. He is apt to growl at such things, but also to accept them as the natural outcome of the personal unfriendliness of the world in which he dwells.

In the past, a seafaring man ashore was a curiosity who dressed oddly and spoke an argot incomprehensible to his fellow countrymen. In Britain in particular he knew that he was set apart; he knew too that this separation ran deeper than the simple fact that he lived his life afloat, for he existed under a different set of rules from the rest of his nation. The very fact that he could be impressed for service in the Royal Navy left him in no doubt of his condition. When, during the eighteenth century, the notion of impressments was challenged at law as being an infringement of the liberties of a Briton, the court decided that it was a public necessity to curtail the liberties of a minority in order to preserve those of the far greater majority.

Grumbling was no prerogative of the British tar; seamen everywhere had always grumbled. Columbus was well aware of this trait and of how, under exceptional circumstances, it could provoke dissent, combination, and occasionally mutiny. For this reason he is said to have deceived his pilots by maintaining two logs, one secret, the other made public. In the latter he falsified the extent to which his little squadron, the *Santa Maria de Guia*, the *Niña* and the *Pinta*, were making westing, for he feared that if his crew knew how far west they had gone without sighting land, they would revolt. By this mild deception Columbus hoped to head off the rebellion he felt might otherwise brew, but on 10 October 1492, suspicious alike of his foreign nationality (he was born a Genoese) and his arguments, his men mutinied anyway, claiming they had sailed far enough west and discovered nothing. Columbus temporized; if they remained dutiful for three more days and by that time had still sighted no land, he would head for home. Almost miraculously, they made a landfall in the small hours of the 12th. Rodrigo de Triana aboard the *Pinta* saw ahead the moonlit sandhills of the Indies. A warning gun was fired, and the ships hove-to until daylight. Next morning Columbus and his men – not the ships . . . landed in the so-called New World, and a new epoch opened.

Columbus had avoided outright mutiny. At its simplest level, his men's disaffection had arisen out of fear for their lives: they were sailing into the unknown, and while only the ignorant still believed the world to be flat and there was no danger of tumbling over the edge into the abyss, their anxieties were extreme. Significantly, they had no confidence in their foreign leader.

A more serious and consequential lack of trust in their commander was the reason tendered for the mutiny against Ferdinand Magellan, and it threatened him directly and personally. Moreover it came from those who, in theory at least, he had most cause to trust: his own subordinate captains.

Magellan had been appointed captain general of the Armada de Molucca, a secret expedition sent by King Charles I of Spain, later the Holy Roman Emperor Charles V, to find a new way to the spice islands of the Moluccas in modern Indonesia. Competition between the two countries had led the Pope to settle the differences between Portugal and Spain by the Treaty of Tordesillas of 1494, which separated the globe into two by a line of demarcation corresponding to the meridian passing from north to south through a position 370 leagues west of the Cape Verde Islands. The Portuguese were to be free to exploit all to the east of this, the Spanish all to the west, thus confirming Spain's writ in the Caribbean claimed by Columbus, and Portugal's on the African coast and in India following Vasco de Gama's voyages. Contentious issues continued to arise between the two countries as Brazil was discovered by Europeans within the Portuguese area, and it was 1506 before anything like a final settlement was agreed upon.

What had still not been resolved was the problem of the opposite side of the world and Charles I, whose exchequer was empty, was eager to seize and monopolize the spice trade which by 1515 was spectacularly enriching Portugal. To this end he backed a proposed expedition to sail west, beyond the current limits of the known 'Spanish' hemisphere, by penetrating the American continent through a passage thought to exist somewhere upon its southern coast. The proponent of this scheme was another foreigner, one Ferdinand Magellan, a man born a subject of the King of Portugal but now prepared to swear fealty to the king of Spain. Spanish nationality was jealously guarded; Magellan could not therefore be naturalized, and although Charles granted him absolute powers over the four captains who commanded the other vessels in his Armada, or fleet, he was an unpopular choice. Understandably perhaps, Magellan's entourage included other Portuguese nationals, all of whom swore their allegiance to Magellan as Charles's viceroy, but this was not enough for the Spanish-born subordinate commanders. These men, being political appointees, were not all seamen, and while they had masters and pilots to handle the ships, they brought court intrigue aboard with them.

The five vessels, Magellan's *Trinidada*, Juan de Cartagena's *San Antonio*, Gaspar de Quesada's *Concepción*, Luis de Mendoza's *Vittoria* and Juan Rodrigo Serrano's *Santiago*, sailed from the Guadalquivir River on 20 September 1519. On arrival at the Canaries they watered and took aboard pitch, and while they were occupied with these tasks a caravel bearing despatches caught up with them. Among the letters was one from Magellan's father-in-law, Diego Barbosa. It contained a warning: 'Capitán-General, *mío*: keep a good watch. It has come to me that there are those among your captains, particularly Juan de Cartagena, who have told their friends that if there is doubt or trouble, they will kill you.'

Magellan also learned that ships from Portugal were in pursuit of him and that he was personally tainted with treason, and so he set a course south along the African shore, rather than sailing directly towards the coast of Brazil. His reasons for doing this are obscure, but not unreasonable. Perhaps he was attempting to throw the Portuguese off his expected track – though sailing south kept his ships well within the Portuguese hemisphere. More likely it was a seamanlike desire to avoid being set too far to the westward by the Equatorial Current, and to avoid the South East Trades heading him when he met them south of the Doldrums, for close to the South American coast these steady, fresh winds are more nearly from the SSE. Whatever his reasoning, he did not share it or consult with the other commanders as his instructions stated he should. In an enterprise already split by internal factions, Basque against Castilian, Spaniard against Portuguese, Magellan, vested with supreme authority and powers of 'knife and rope', demanded only obedience to himself.

On leaving the Canaries they ran into bad weather, strong gales which swept the ships with green seas, ruined some of their stores and compelled Magellan to shorten rations. These circumstances gave Cartagena the excuse he sought, and as soon as the weather moderated he began his attempt to undermine Magellan by calculated insolence. It was routine that every evening each ship in turn closed the *Trinidada*, respectfully greeted the Captain General, and received her night-orders. The greeting was to be made by the commander, but Juan de Cartagena left it to his Quartermaster, who in his turn omitted to give Magellan his correct title. Instead of referring to the Captain General, thus acknowledging Magellan's superior status, Cartagena's subordinate used plain *Capitán*. The calculated insult was not lost on Magellan: the *Trinidada* sheered alongside the *San Antonio* and there was a sharp and public exchange between Magellan and Cartagena. For three days thereafter Cartagena utterly declined to take any part in the quotidian ritual; Magellan bided his time until, when the sea was moderate and boat-work possible, he flung out the signal for the Armada to heave-to and all captains to repair on board his flagship. He had a pretext for this, for a gross offence had been committed aboard the *Vittoria*. As the main yards were braced aback and the Armada slowed to a standstill and the ships' boats were hoisted out, the *Trinidada*'s crew were quietly ordered under arms.

The commanders assembled in Magellan's cabin were hot to dispute the course, but it was the fate of the Sicilian master of the *Vittoria* that they had first to decide. Antonio Salamón had been caught sodomising one of his ship's boys, and Magellan pronounced the sentence of death upon him. He then confronted Cartagena with his insubordinate behaviour. In response Juan de Cartagena claimed King Charles had named him *persona conjunta* with Magellan, and thus of equal status with the Captain General. The Castilian claimed moreover that Magellan's action in conducting the fleet east of the line of demarcation and therefore within the Portuguese hemisphere was *prima facie* evidence that he was betraying King Charles. Magellan countered that he was in fact deceiving his own countrymen, and declared that his loyalty to Spain was, after his oath of loyalty made before God, unimpeachable. But this failed to placate Cartagena, the bastard son of the Bishop of Burgos and a man who considered himself superior to Magellan in every respect. Realizing the moment to be decisive and its outcome predictable, Magellan had prepared himself, and now gave a shout. Into the cabin burst armed men led by Gonzalo Gómez de Espinosa, *Trinidada*'s *alguacil*, or master-at-arms. Magellan stepped forward, clasped Cartagena by the shoulder and declared that he was a prisoner, and a mutineer against King Charles and the royal authority vested in Magellan himself. Cartagena now called upon Quesada and Mendoza to stab Magellan – clear evidence of the cabal that had been formed against the Captain General – but the captains of the *Concepción* and *Vittoria* quailed.

At this Espinosa dragged Cartagena out of the cabin and shackled him on deck, in full view of the hands. This was an extreme humiliation to a high-born Castilian, and Quesada and Mendoza subsequently pleaded with the Captain General to treat Cartagena with some sensitivity; Magellan demanded only their renewed allegiance. Depriving Cartagena of his command and handing the *San Antonio* over to Antonio de Coca, Magellan ordered Mendoza to take Cartagena and put him in irons aboard the *Vittoria*.

At the beginning of December the Armada made the coast of Brazil and ran down the coast to the Bahía Santa Lucía, near modern Rio de Janeiro, where they anchored on 13 December. On the 20th Salamón was executed in accordance with his sentence; his catamite was so ridiculed that he flung himself overboard in despair.

As the year turned Magellan's Armada stretched south by way the wide river estuary De Solis had thought fifteen years earlier looked like silver plate: the Rio de la Plata. They continued slowly south, enduring gales which buffeted the five ships as they probed every inlet in territory hitherto unseen by Europeans, seeking a passage to the west. At several places they remained at anchor, fraternizing with the native Pathagoni. As the Austral autumn drew on the weather worsened, and they were already discovering penguins and sea lions in the chilly climate of the higher latitudes. Concerned about the onset of winter Magellan sought shelter, and eventually led his ships into a bay where he ordered the Armada de Molucca to anchor in company. It was 31 March 1520, and their latitude was 49° 20' South. The Captain General named their haven Puerto San Julian. Here they were to replenish and refit the ships, careening them to scour their bottoms of weed and repay them to inhibit its further growth; but the lack of game so worried Magellan that he put them all on short commons.

At this point morale slumped. As the men worked to radoub their vessels, the intercourse between the ships gave conspirators every opportunity to combine, the urge to do so fuelled by the grumbling endemic among men uncertain of their future chances. The Castilian party considered Magellan an arrogant and incompetent Portuguese parvenu. He had with him a Portuguese coterie which included a relative and his own bastard son; these, the conspirators argued with subjective paranoia, would dispossess Spaniards of their rights and surrender the expedition to the Portuguese. For his part the Captain General showed no sign of giving up his quest, and it was argued that he could not, in any case, now return to Spain. The common sailors were aware of the tensions in their officers, and an air of desperation began to infect them, while aboard *Vittoria* Cartagena plotted with Mendoza.

The High Mass for Easter was celebrated ashore, but only Álvaro de Mesquita, Magellan's cousin, now appointed to command the *San Antonio*, accepted the Captain General's invitation to break his fast in the flagship. Magellan sensed what was brewing. Next day Mendoza struck off Cartagena's irons and, combining with Quesada and Sebastián Elcano, suborned the *Concepción*. Arming thirty men they boarded the *San Antonio* and captured de Mesquita, persuading her crew to desert the Captain General with the expectation of returning to Spain. Only her Basque master, Juan de Elorriaga, reminded them of their duty: 'In the name of God and King Charles, go back to your ships!' he roared, but Mendoza turned on him and stabbed him several times.

With three ships in the hands of the conspirators anchored between the *Trinidada* and the as yet neutral *Santiago*, Juan de

Cartagena demanded whether Magellan would follow King's orders and return to Spain, allowing the men better rations. There was no passage through the continent to the west, Cartagena argued, and if Magellan would agree, they would remain loyal; if, on the other hand, he intended to press on, they were resolved to interpret the discretion inherent in their orders according to their own rights and turn for home.

Magellan temporized; would they come aboard *Trinidada* and discuss the matter? That would be folly, they riposted, flinging insults. *He* must board the *San Antonio*, the largest, best-manned and heaviest armed ship in the Armada. Magellan returned to his cabin to consult his *alguacil*, Espinosa, and his brother-in-law, Duarte Barbosa. They resolved on a bold plan.

Entrusting a note for Mendoza to Espinosa, Magellan ordered the *alguacil*'s boat's crew to arm themselves but to conceal their weapons. Out of sight, on the side of the *Trinidada* opposite to the mutinous vessels, a second boat was loaded with a heavily armed party under Barbosa. Casting off, they were poised to strike the water with their oars the moment Espinosa boarded the *Vittoria*. When all was ready Magellan reappeared on deck, and called that a boat with a letter was coming to the *Vittoria*. Espinosa shoved off.

Mendoza suffered from over-confidence. He received the *alguacil* on the *Vittoria*'s poop and read the letter 'in a careless manner, unbefitting a man engaged in so serious an affair', scoffing at the presumption that he would surrender. When he refused to obey, Espinosa drew a dagger and thrust it into Mendoza's throat. At his shout his own boat's crew came up over the side and Barbosa's bent to their oars. In the space of a few confused moments the loyalists had seized the *Vittoria*'s upper deck, and shortly afterwards her company declared for Magellan. Triumphantly Barbosa hoisted Magellan's standard to her mainmasthead.

Serrano now affirmed his own loyalty and Magellan had all three ships go to quarters, ordering *Vittoria* to trip her anchor and drift closer to the *Trinidada*. Night drew on, a black night of gusty squalls. Coming from the south, they favoured the escape of the two mutinous ships, but the passage was not easy in the dark and the air was thick with uncertainty. Magellan had reached the point at which his leadership lay in the balance, and he was filled with resolution.

Quesada, aboard *Concepción*, was not: he was faltering, and consulted his officers. They promised only to obey his orders. Quesada ordered the anchor weighed, and as the cable shortened in scope the wind caused the *Concepción* to drag her anchor before it broke out of the sea-bed and they got sail on the ship. In the darkness the *Concepción* drifted down towards *Trinidada*, where Magellan's men were at their battle-stations. As the *Concepción* drew close, in imminent danger of running foul of the flagship, the cry went up '*El capitán general!*' Grappling irons were flung and the hapless *Concepción* was drawn alongside under the muzzles of Magellan's culverins, which promptly blasted the quiet of the night apart. On the *Concepción*'s far side Serrano veered his cable and set a foretopsail, ranging *Vittoria* alongside Quesada and boarding him in the stunned silence following the discharge of Magellan's guns. As the *Concepción* was boarded from both sides, the cry went up for quarter. 'To whom are you loyal?' Magellan demanded.

'To the King and the Captain General!' was the response, as the humiliated leaders of the mutiny were deserted by men whose only real interest was the preservation of their own lives. In the morning the *San Antonio* also capitulated: Juan de Cartagena was back in irons, and Magellan in undisputed command. In view of his ignominious end months later in a skirmish on a Philippine beach, this was Magellan's greatest moment. At the limits of the known world, with his voyage hardly begun, the Captain General had demonstrated enormous personal courage. He now consolidated his position; his justice was swift, and not without a terrible mercy. Under his extraordinary powers 'of rope and knife' and in the name of King Charles, Magellan ordered the body of Luis de Mendoza to be eviscerated and quartered. It was then hung upon a crude gibbet on what is, to this day, called Gallows Point.

Next he convened a court-martial in the *Trinidada*'s cabin, appointing his cousin Álvaro de Mesquita as President. Mesquita spent a fortnight gathering evidence and then arraigned the mutineers. Despite the frequently dubious evidence several were given minor penalties, while a number were severely punished, usually by the *strappado* or the wooden horse. Forty were sentenced to death, but in the event only confined in irons until the Armada proceeded on its voyage, whereupon Magellan pardoned and released them; he needed them to resume their duties. Gaspar Quesada was beheaded, then quartered and hung alongside Mendoza. His relationship to Juan Rodriguez de Fonseca, Bishop of Burgos, spared Juan de Cartagena, for a grimmer fate. Magellan avoided having the taint of Cartagena's blood upon his hands but not the duty of punishing mutiny and preserving his expedition by causing the bishop's bastard to be marooned with a priest some miles further south on the bleak coastline. Neither was heard of again.

Magellan had suppressed a mutiny among the commanders of the majority of his fleet. One of the forty men spared was the Basque pilot Juan Sebastián Elcano who was, in the words of the Venetian chronicler Antonio Pigafetta, 'to have greatness thrust upon him', for it was Elcano who on 6 September 1522 was to enter the Guadaquivir and head for San Lúcar de Barrameda in the Armada's remaining ship, the *Vittoria*. And it was Elcano who was to boast a coat of arms bearing a globe and the motto 'Thou hast encompassed me'.

Magellan, though left dead in the Philippines, had however discovered the strait which enabled him to pass from the Atlantic to the Pacific Ocean without doubling Cape Horn, and which to this day bears his name. And it is Magellan's name, rather than that of the mutineer Elcano, which is associated with this first troubled circumnavigation of the world.

It is clear that the fundamental reason for the mutiny in the Armada de Molucca was principally the ill-considered nature of its hierarchy. Such a politically fragile structure was almost bound to prove inadequate, particularly as the five ships of the squadron were bound for a voyage quite literally into the un– known. While the necessity of centralizing the command in the single person of a Captain General was understood, the mere empowerment of a single individual by regal authority was an insufficient guarantee to create a disciplined structure, particularly if doubts about his intention or competence intruded, or another officer was accorded near-equal status. In order to buttress his own standing and make his leadership enforceable, Magellan was driven to securing a personal band of loyal relatives and adherents. Far from achieving its objective, this merely made still worse a situation already exacerbated by the fact that these men were Portuguese. By coincidence, the world's second circumnavigation was to be beset by problems which came to a head, strangely enough, in the same location as the first.

On 13 December 1577, half a century after Magellan, the English sea officer Francis Drake sailed from Plymouth in the *Pelican*, flagship of a five-strong squadron manned by about a hundred and sixty men. Drake, who from a high position in the pantheon of English heroes has been reduced to little more than a pirate, occupied a station in life which, to be fair to him, requires some explanation. Although the crown owned a small 'Royal' navy, to supplement this fleet in times of national need, Tudor monarchs relied upon private citizens chartering their ships to the State. Although such vessels were built to carry cargo and engage in trade, they were well armed for self-defence. In addition to the risks run in wartime, merchant ships often encountered pirates, commonly in the Mediterranean, off the Iberian coast and even in the Channel, where the freebooting Barbary corsairs of North Africa ranged. It was not unusual for these predators to land on the south coast of England and abduct women and children, so all vessels in the sixteenth century were little different from purpose-built men-of-war and every seaman could serve a gun and fight hand-to-hand. Thus the division between merchant and naval ships and their crews was indistinguishable.

Drake was a mariner who grew up in this transitory period. In 1588 he was commissioned as vice-admiral in his own ship, and led a division of the English fleet against the Spanish Armada. But all this lay in the future. By 1577 Drake had established his reputation as a fiercely aggressive sea officer, as violently anti-Spanish as Nelson was a Francophobe and, like Nelson, the son of a Protestant minister. Drake not only hated the Roman church, which had reasserted itself during the reign of Mary Tudor and deprived Edmund Drake of his living, but bore the Catholic Spanish a grudge for the failure of an expedition led ten years earlier by his cousin John Hawkins in which he himself had participated. Hawkins and Drake had been attacked by the Spanish at San Juan de Ulloa on the Mexican coast in what Drake always maintained was a treacherous manner, and the incident kindled an intense antipathy towards the nation which considered its mariners lords of the Caribbean. Like Hawkins, Drake deeply resented the global ascendancy the Papacy had conferred upon the two Iberian states by the Treaty of Tordesillas, and as hostile acts flared intermittently between the English and Spanish he acquired a letter of marque and reprisal, enabling him to raid Spanish possessions on the Isthmus of Panama and following these raids, to enjoy a growing reputation in court circles in London.

While ashore attacking the Spanish mule train bearing silver from the Pacific to the Caribbean coast for shipment to Spain, Drake is said to have seen the 'Great South Sea' and to have vowed 'to sail an English ship in those seas'. Five years later he was to have his desire fulfilled, for as the nation's most prominent and daring sea captain he was summoned to London for secret negotiations.

Bigoted, self-sufficient and largely self-made (though his connection with Hawkins and having Lord Russell's heir as his godfather helped) as he was, Drake's attitude towards his new benefactors was ambivalent. He was the embodiment of that distance that separated the seaman from his brethren ashore. While he craved respectability and displayed his personal wealth in his apparel and the way he lived, he was contemptuous of the soft and purring ways of the Court; intrigue moreover was utterly inimical to him as it had been to Magellan.

Under Queen Elizabeth I English foreign policy vacillated, one party under the Earl of Leicester seeking to break the Spanish hegemony and allow English trade and ambition a free rein, the other under Lord Burghley, the Lord Treasurer, favouring a softer, more conciliatory approach by means of which inroads into Spanish spheres of influence could be the more subtly gained without matters coming to a head. Among these intriguers was Thomas Doughty, a courtier, a lawyer, a charmer, and an intriguer. In the shadowy dealings that preceded Drake's commission, Doughty appears to have acted as go-between. In due course Drake was summoned to an audience with Elizabeth, in which she complained of receiving 'divers injuries of the King of Spain, for which she desired to have some revenge.' Drake was sworn to secrecy as he undertook a mission to strike at the Spanish empire in the Pacific, where the shipment of silver and other riches in Spanish *nãos* and galleons went on unimpeded. Elizabeth 'did swear by her Crown that if any within her realm did give the King of Spain to understand hereof, as she suspected to well, they should lose their heads therefore,' and to this end particularly enjoined Drake by 'special commandment that of all men my Lord Treasurer should not know of it'.

Despite its clandestine nature, Drake's mission was backed by a secret syndicate in which Elizabeth was embroiled to the tune of one thousand pounds. As far as the public and the seamen in his ships were concerned, Drake's little fleet was on its way to Alexandria. It left the Thames in mid-November and Plymouth a month later, and it headed south. Almost immediately it was troubled by a cabal as determined to undermine Drake as Cartagena had been to undermine Magellan. Representing the syndicate and heading a number of gentlemen-at-arms was Thomas Doughty himself, ably seconded by his brother John. Once they had recovered from their sea-sickness, these gentlemen-volunteers were pleased to find the rude mariners amusing and Drake nothing more than a common fellow unworthy of their respect. They had no proper duty to attend to and their idleness fomented discontent and fault-finding, while they were too ignorant to be impressed by Drake's skill at the cunning and the astrolabe. The mariner's craft, they argued, could not amount to much if such a pretentious knave could master it.

Taking supplies out of captured Spanish and Portuguese ships, Drake also plundered a Portuguese pilot, Nuño de Silva, whose services proved invaluable in the absence of charts. In putting a prize crew aboard de Silva's ship Drake chose Thomas Doughty to command her, putting his own younger brother Thomas aboard as sailing master to provide the required expertise. Unknown to Drake, Doughty had informed Burghley of the purpose of the voyage, and in alarm Burghley had persuaded Doughty that his duty lay in wrecking the expedition, underlining the patriotic gloss with hints of forthcoming gratitude and beneficial influence. The first intimation of trouble came when Drake learned that the prize's valuable cargo of silks and wines had been pilfered, and that the division of this spoil was being disputed. Doughty accused Thomas Drake of the perfidy, but Drake was not deceived. Doughty was ordered to return to the *Pelican* and Tom Drake was elevated to the command of the prize; Drake was having no further truck with the conventions of a courtier 'captain', as distinct from a 'master'.

As Drake's squadron made its way down the South American coast it was beset by fogs and strong winds in alternate measure: Drake began to suspect sorcery. This was a common prejudice of the time, and it did not help when John Doughty boasted to the ignorant and credulous 'that he and his brother could conjure as well as any man . . . raise the devil and make him . . . in the likeness of a bear, a lion or a man in harness' – by which they meant armour. Taken together with the reports extant since Magellan's day of Patagonian giants, ostriches, and leaves so toxic that the juices squeezed from them onto an arrow-tip made it instantly fatal to any man struck, such a claim unsettled Doughty's anxious, biddable audience. Finding the presence of the two Doughty brothers increasingly irksome, Drake had them transferred to the *Elizabeth*, under the command of John Winter. First boarding her himself Drake, a popular commander, addressed the *Elizabeth*'s mustered crew and told them he was sending among them Thomas Doughty 'who is a seditious fellow', and his brother who was 'a witch and a poisoner, and such a one as the world can judge of.' By way of compensation he then promised his true-hearted and stout seamen that the ships would eventually be filled 'with gold and make the meanest boy in the fleet a gentleman'. Having thus played upon the deep insecurities of the class-conscious, he left the Doughtys – fine specimens of that desirable status – in their rough hands.

Drake now found himself in the same plight as Magellan, with the southern winter fast approaching and the weather ever worsening. He also found himself in the same place, seeking shelter in Puerto San Julian, where the remains of Mendoza and Quesada lay heaped at the foot of the remains of the gibbet on Gallows Point. The grisly spectacle reflected the prevalent mood of gloom, which was increased when they were attacked by Patagonians. Drake himself secured the outcome of the skirmish when he loosed a fouling piece and hit the leader 'in the paunch . . . and sent his guts abroad.'

But their continuing tribulations seemed not so much trials sent to test them by Almighty God as further evil manifestations conjured by sorcery. Drake knew that the voyage could not continue under its present cloud. Although there was no legality on his proceedings, for he bore no powers of knife and rope, such was his boundless confidence in both himself and the loyalty of his men that he acted to preserve the greater objective: the successful prosecution of the expedition. He was in no doubt that Thomas Doughty had been fomenting trouble, and that it was Doughty who obstructed that purpose. Drake had him arrested on charges of witchcraft and set up a tent on a bleak isle in which to try his victim, under the foremanship of the *Elizabeth*'s commander Captain John Winter, cleverly convening a jury which included some of Doughty's own faction. Alongside himself as president of the court he set Captain John Thomas of the *Marigold* as assessor. In his own defence Doughty challenged Drake's powers, and insisted upon being tried in England 'under Her Majesty's laws', but Drake was having none of it and roundly abused Doughty, charging him with the core crime, that of trying to 'overthrow the voyage'. John Thomas read out the formal charge and Doughty knew he was doomed. Whatever formalities might lie between the two men, he was Drake's enemy – and here, at the very edge of the world known to Europeans, Drake's law prevailed. As for Drake, it seems that now, faced with the enormity of his intentions, he faltered. Doughty was an obstruction, but he was also a man of influence, as much a Court favourite as Cartagena had been. Then Edward Bright, master of the *Marigold*, gave evidence: at Plymouth, in his hearing, Doughty had said that Drake had offered a bribe to have the command of the expedition given him, and that the Queen's Majesty would be corrupted by this association. Doughty denied this, but admitted that Burghley knew of the voyage and had counselled against it.

Aware of the secrecy under which the expedition had been formed Drake said this was not true, but Doughty, wreaking his last mischief, told Drake it was so, and that the Lord Treasurer had been informed by none other than himself. At this revelation Drake exploded. Recalling the Queen's remarks, he pointed at Doughty: 'His own mouth has betrayed him!' Doughty's admission removed all trace of ambiguity from the proceedings; above the fomentations and the snobbish one-upmanship, by his own admission Doughty had betrayed the Queen, and was thus guilty of treason. Speaking for the jury, which now hedged its own bets, John Winter gave the verdict: that Doughty was guilty, not of treason, but of mutiny.

In a remarkable example of seizing the moment Drake summoned all the crews. About to condemn a fellow human to death, he now sought to use Doughty's downfall to raise morale by making the 'seditious fellow' a scapegoat for all their miseries. They had sailed on the promise of riches from the Mediterranean;

instead, months later, they found themselves shivering in a remote spot visited only once before by Europeans and marked not once but now twice as a place of execution. All hands were cognisant of the trials that lay ahead of them. Whatever the true causes of their tribulations, much might be laid at Doughty's feet, and his 'confession' was interpreted as evidence of the power and mercy of God. Thus Drake played a high and a clever hand, involving them all. Reminding them of the opportunities for riches the voyage still held, he stated: 'You may see whether this fellow has sought me discredit or no, and what should hereby be meant but the very overthrow of the voyage, as first by taking away my good name . . . and then my life. So then what would you have done? . . . And if this voyage does not go forward, which I cannot see as possible while this man still lives, what reproach it would be, not only to your country, but especially to us all . . . Therefore, my masters,' he concluded, 'they that think this man worthy to die let them with me hold up their hands, and they that think him not worthy hold down their hands.'

According to the record there was neither opposition nor abstention. Finally Drake showed magnanimity, saying that if any man could 'devise a way that might save Doughty's life' he 'would gladly listen to it.' Only one was forthcoming and that from Doughty himself, who asked to be set ashore once they reached Peru. Drake was bound to ask if any vessel would take the prisoner, and Winter said that he might be confined aboard the *Elizabeth*. To this Drake agreed, under pain of close confinement, but now the men objected: Doughty should be allowed no further rope. Drake shook off the yoke of guilt. He had achieved his objective: in the end it was a matter of consensus for the good of them all.

Doughty was given two days to make his peace and choose the manner of his execution. He would, as befitted a gentleman, have his head struck off. His last days on this earth earned him praise from all and 'fully blotted out whatever stain his fault might seem to bring upon him'. In his last hours he received the holy sacrament alongside Drake. They then took a meal together, sitting at a table set up ashore near to the appointed place of execution in full view of the curious, 'as cheerfully in sobriety as ever in their lives they had done aforetime, each cheering up the other and taking their leave by drinking to each other, as if some journey only had been in hand.' At last Doughty told Drake that he was ready, but that he first wanted a few private words with 'my good captain'. Withdrawing, they spoke quietly for 'seven or eight minutes', then Doughty was led away. He asked permission to speak to the assembled company, which being granted he asked their forgiveness and their prayers for his soul. He stated that no others had wished harm to Drake, naming several of his circle and asking forgiveness if any of them had caused the captain displeasure. Then he bade Drake farewell and laid his head upon the block. Drake, who never revealed the substance of that last conversation, stepped forward the instant the axe had fallen and held the head aloft: 'Lo!' he cried, 'this is the end of all traitors!' Afterwards Doughty was decently buried.

As his men resumed the refitting of the fleet, burning the Portuguese prize and condemning the two other smaller ships as unseaworthy, Drake became a changed man. He was no longer the opportunistic, extemporized leader of a band of adventurers, but a commander-in-chief with vice-regal powers. These he had assumed himself, for his principals had lacked foresight and failed him in this respect. As for his squadron, it consisted now of only the *Pelican*, *Elizabeth* and *Marigold*, but the labour of preparing these three ships once again threw up contentious differences between the occupied mariners and the indolent gentry. On 17 August 1578 they left the bleak shores of the Puerto San Julian, but before they did so Drake again mustered his company. His harangue has become famous: 'Here is such controversy between the mariners and the gentlemen, and such stomaching between the gentlemen and the mariners, it doth make me mad to hear it. But, my masters, I must have it left. For I must have the gentleman to haul and draw with the mariner, and the mariner with the gentleman. Come, let us show ourselves all to be of one company and let us not give occasion to the enemy to rejoice at our decay and overthrow. I would know him that would refuse to set his hand to a rope, but I know that there is not any such a one here . . .'

Once in Magellan's strait they gave thanks to God and made formal obeisance to the distant authority of Queen Elizabeth. Then Drake, in a further act of appeasement, renamed the *Pelican* the *Golden Hinde* as a token of respect to Sir Christopher Hatton. Hatton, the Queen's current favourite, had been Doughty's patron, and his arms bore a 'hinde trippant or'.

They cleared the strait and entered the Great Southern Sea on 7 September, fulfilling Drake's prophecy. Hours later they were struck by a vicious gale which drove them south-west under bare poles until the 30th, when in 'an extreme tempest' the *Marigold*, a small vessel of only 30 tons burthen, foundered in heavy seas. The terrified cries of her helpless crew could be heard above the howl of the gale, and the superstitious among those in the *Golden Hinde* and *Elizabeth* remembered Doughty's reputed sorcery and the fact that Ned Bright, the *Marigold's* master, had made the crucial allegation against him. That night the wind backed and drove the two remaining ships north again, and on 7 October they anchored in the shelter of the western entrance to the Strait of Magellan, which they had quitted a month earlier. But even here, under the frozen shoulders of the mighty Cordilleras, they were still not safe. Sheering at their cables in the violent gusts, they broke adrift from their anchors and separated.

John Winter struggled back through the strait to the Atlantic and so, in time, safely home to England. Drake drifted south again until he saw 'the uttermost cape or headland of all these islands' and found where 'the Atlantic Ocean and the South Sea meet in a large and free scope'.

Drake had suppressed mutiny and, like Magellan before him, established his own authority as supreme. Unlike Magellan, he returned home to honour and a knighthood, being dubbed upon the deck of the *Golden Hinde* off Deptford by the Queen. In the course of his voyage he raided Spanish towns on the coasts of modern Chile and Peru, plundering the plate of every Catholic church and cathedral. He also seized several Spanish galleons. One, under the command of Pedro Sarmiento de Gamboa, yielded a vast quantity of gold to the value of 37,000 ducats; others were laden with silver from the mines of Potosí. Drake's cruise culminated with the bloodless capture of the *Cacafuego* off Lima. The great *não* was laden with bullion, jewellery, ivories and jade loaded in Manila.

Drake went on to land near today's San Francisco and claim the coast as 'New Albion', then he crossed the Pacific to load six tons of cloves in the Moluccas. Thereafter he headed for home. The expedition yielded £47 for every £1 invested by the syndicate. When Drake discharged his booty at Plymouth on 26 September 1580 it was said to amount to half a million pounds, a sum so immense that it was also said to have underwritten the costs to the State of the fleet raised to defend the realm against the Armada sent against England eight years later.

Threatened by faction, both Magellan and Drake were bound to take action which in the absence of a proper command structure appeared highly dubious. Both men risked, at the least, the severe disapprobation of their royal principals; but their hands were forced by the conduct of those with entirely specious pretensions to equality with the two captains-general – for so Drake too was styled. Both Magellan and Drake were mariners who knew their own dynamism, leadership and skill as seamen were essential to the outcome of their respective voyages. Yet despite the opprobrium that lingered over the reputations of both men for the perceived injustices they had inflicted, governments were slow to learn from the predicaments of these isolated pioneers. And while men pursued voyages to the edges of the known world, disquiet among the mariners would prove a constant threat to their lives as much as the success of their commanders.

2

'SO FOULE A THING'

THE supposed prerogatives of the two Iberian kingdoms had persuaded the newly aspiring maritime state of England to pursue her own explorations for a secret route to Cathay through sub-polar waters. Early ventures had failed to find the great Chan but had established trade with Muscovy; others had sought an alternative route not east but west, among the ice floes between Greenland and Newfoundland. This had seemed more promising, and in both England and the Netherlands, companies determined to trade with the East Indies had been established. Both sought a quicker route to the 'Spice Islands' than the long haul round Africa. In May 1602 the English East India Company sent Captain George Waymouth in the *Discovery* and the *Godspeed* to follow up the discoveries of Martin Frobisher and John Davis. Waymouth's voyage was terminated by a rebellion, but he preserved his life by acquiescing to the demands of the mutineers. Turning for home, he arrived to report an inlet through which he had sailed 'one hundred leagues west and by south'.

Fascinated by Davis's and Waymouth's claims and experienced in the Arctic waters around Spitsbergen, a sea captain named

Henry Hudson, having served the Muscovy Company, entered the service of the Dutch East India Company. Leaving the Texel in April 1609 Hudson's small 80-ton *Half Moon* headed north and on 5 May passed the North Cape of Norway. Manned by an Anglo–Dutch crew of some twenty men, the *Half Moon* now ran into foul weather with heavy icing on her rigging and an apparently impenetrable barrier of floes. Here the crew, led by the mate, one Robert Ivet (sometimes called Juet), came aft in a body and demanded that Hudson turn back. Hudson made a virtue of necessity. His studies of the alternative route by way of the putative 'North West Passage' led him to propose to his crew that they lay their course south-west, double Cape Farewell and head either into the Strait named after John Davis or to make a landfall south of the St Lawrence and north of the English colony of Virginia. The mutineers favoured the latter, and agreed. By July the *Half Moon* lay at anchor off the Maine coast, taking in wood and water. Ivet and his fellows cheated the natives and ransacked their village, a treacherous act that Hudson apparently ignored. The *Half Moon* then ran south, penetrating every major estuary in expectation of another strait that would lead them to the Pacific. Hudson made his deepest inroad into the river that now bears his name, and to placate his employers, whose orders he had broken, identified the site of what later became New Amsterdam and, later still, New York.

On his way back to old Amsterdam Hudson put in to Dartmouth in Devon on 7 November. From here he was able to inform the Dutch East India Company of his discoveries, which they were quick to capitalize upon, but he and his English seamen were proscribed from further service under the flag of the Amsterdam Admiralty. Instead Hudson was commissioned by a syndicate of London investors led by Henry, Prince of Wales, to command a voyage of exploration in search of the North West Passage. The extent to which Hudson had solicited this commission is uncertain, but his experience of navigating in high latitudes was considerable, and clearly commended him to his backers.

Henry Hudson was a man of uncertain character and, while professionally able, seems to have lacked the firmness desirable in a leader. He had acquiesced in his crew's treatment of the native Americans, and his own conduct was inconsistent. Worst of all was his incomprehensible adherence to Robert Ivet, a man 'filled with mean tempers' who served with him on several voyages and was, inexplicably and fatally, again appointed mate.

Hudson's ship was Waymouth's *Discovery*, at 55 tons even smaller than the *Half Moon*, and she was manned by twenty-two men and boys, including Hudson's son John. The voyage's sponsors put an agent aboard, a former haberdasher named Abacuk Prickett, and three other former shipmates of Hudson also joined, in addition to Ivet. These were the carpenter Philip Staffe and two seamen, Arnold Lollo and Michael Perse. The other seamen were Michael Butt, Robert Bylot, Syrake Fanning, Adam Moore, Adrian Motter, Nicholas Syms, John Thomas and William Wilson; Francis Clemens signed on as boatswain, John King as quartermaster, John Williams as gunner, Sylvanus Bond as cooper, and Bennett Mathues as cook. One Edward Wilson was appointed surgeon, and also aboard were an odd, shady protégé of Hudson named Henry Greene and an Oxford undergraduate mathematician named Thomas Woodhouse. They were a curious lot, and since Hudson's patronage and reputation would have assured him the choice of London's finest seamen, the composition of the *Discovery*'s crew is suspect. Whatever Hudson's skills as a seaman and navigator, in his failure to select a suitable crew he sowed the seeds of his own destruction. Why did he persist in appointing Robert Ivet as mate? Did Ivet have a hold over him? And who was the cocky young Greene? Hudson had taken him into his household, and provided him with 'meat, and drink and lodging'. He 'would have [Greene] to sea with him because he could write so well', so Greene was ostensibly the master's clerk, but he was not entered in the *Discovery*'s books, nor did he join the ship as she lay in St Katherine's Pool, off the Tower of London. Instead he boarded downstream, by boat, at Gravesend. Prickett wrote of Greene that 'by his lewd life and conversation he had lost the goodwill of all his friends.' Greene himself boasted that he was free of moral restraint, 'for religion, he would say, he was cleane paper, whereon he would write what he would.' Although he had fathered three sons, there are dark and ambiguous hints about Hudson's sexual orientation, and perhaps therein lies the mystery of Greene, of Ivet's malign presence, and of the flaw in Hudson: he chose his ship's company for reasons contrary to good sense.

The *Discovery* sailed on 17 April 1610. She was off the Orkneys by 5 May and the Faeroes three days later. Beset by typical spring weather in the North Atlantic, fog and westerly gales, by 11 May the *Discovery* lay at anchor off the Icelandic coast. Landing, they fished and went wild-fowling, and while they were ashore Greene and Surgeon Wilson fell out. Prickett took the surgeon's part, Hudson favoured Greene. Later, after the *Discovery* had passed south of Cape Farewell and approached the coast of Labrador to enter the passage that today bears Hudson's name, Ivet began to complain of Greene.

By early July the *Discovery* was icebound in Ungava Bay and they 'could go no further. Here,' recorded Prickett, 'our master was in despaire, and, as he told me after, he thought he should never have got out of the ice, but there have perished . . . ' While they languished for three weeks surrounded by impenetrable ice, quarrelling and disputes again broke out. Hudson sought to temporize by again offering to turn back, which brought a measure of unanimity as they were compelled to join forces to save the ship from being beset but, once they were clear, Hudson thought better of his offer and pressed on to the westward. This vacillating conduct only served to provoke further discontent and erode what trust the crew had in him.

Now Hudson's decision to head west seemed vindicated: having passed between two headlands – on 2 August Hudson named them after two of his sponsors, Sir Dudley Digges and John Wolstenholme – they found before them an open sea stretching away to the south and west. So eager was Hudson to proceed that he refused to let the men hunt and salt down the caribou and birds that proliferated. The water ahead of them was ice-free, and Hudson was convinced they were heading for the Pacific, Cathay and the Spice Islands. The *Discovery* turned south in expectation of warmer waters. Alas, what they had discovered was the vast enclosed sea now known as Hudson Bay, and in following the eastern shore they found themselves enclosed in a large southern inlet, James Bay. Here, in a clear demonstration of indecision and possible derangement, they stood 'up to the north . . . till we raised the land, then down to the south, and up to the north, then down again to the south.'

It was now September, and as their further progress began to seem purposeless matters came to a head: 'There were some who then spake words which were to be remembered a great while after.' Ivet and the boatswain began to criticize Hudson's conduct, and Hudson accused the mate of treachery. Ivet insisted on a public trial. Lodlo and Staffe gave evidence that Ivet had told them to keep their weapons handy, for assuredly their firelocks would be 'charged with shot ere the voyage was over'. Another seaman testified that Ivet had openly boasted that he would 'turn the ship's head homeward'. Ivet was condemned 'for words spoken when in the ice', but once again Hudson was inexplicably lenient, sending Ivet forward and promoting Robert Bylot, who was able to navigate, in his place. Hudson also demoted Clemens, replacing him as boatswain with William Wilson, one of the most persistent grumblers and worst trouble-makers.

It seems that a catalepsy now fell upon Hudson; he was losing his grip on reality and, quite contrary to common practice, had ceased to maintain a journal after 3 August, when off Capes Digges and Wolstenholme. Now he persisted in aimlessly standing off and on in James Bay 'in a labyrinth without end' until, on 1 November, he finally anchored in Rupert Bay, an inlet at its head. Nine days later they were frozen in. Hudson now bitterly regretted not having reprovisioned at 'the capes where the fowles bred', but they estimated that they could survive on their salt provisions, which 'was all the hope we had to bring us home'.

John Williams, the gunner, died in mid-November. The cause of his death is unknown, but Prickett records a plea that 'God pardon the master's [Hudson's] uncharitable dealing with this man.' The crew held the customary auction of the dead man's kit to raise money for his dependants. Against convention Hudson removed a jacket and let Greene have it, an action towards a favourite that speaks for itself and may well have been intended to worm his way back into Greene's good opinion, for the young man had taken a shine to Staffe, whose suggestion to build a hut for shelter had been rejected by Hudson. Greene and Staffe went hunting the small willow ptarmigan together, an association that seems to have excited Hudson's jealousy. In a fit of pique he repossessed the jacket and passed it to Robert Bylot; Greene protested, whereupon Hudson rounded on him and subjected him to a torrent of invective. Greene, he raved, was a vicious, dishonest ingrate, and he [Hudson] would deny him all his pay when they returned home.

It is clear that by now Hudson's reason was impaired, for having ridiculed Staffe's hut he then recognized the need for such a refuge – too late. 'The snowe and the frost were such that he neither could nor would go on with the worke,' whereupon a demented Hudson 'ferreted him out of his cabin to strike him, and calling him by many foule names, and threatened to hang him.' The loyal Staffe was aghast, and as the Boreal winter closed its frozen grip upon them, Hudson lost all control of the ship; frozen in the ice the *Discovery* was no longer a sea-going entity, and such authority as Hudson still possessed waned accordingly. She spent seven months fast in the ice, during which time Hudson attempted to patch up previous quarrels, particularly that with Staffe.

Now they were visited by scurvy and frostbite, and their provisions dwindled as the supply of ptarmigan dried up. For a time, as the ice froze, they obtained some fresh fish, 'but this supply soon failed them', though the visit of a solitary 'Indian', appearing with some skins, raised their spirits as to a possible source of food. These hopes were dashed when the man failed to return a second time, though Hudson bestirred himself and went off in the shallop, the ship's boat, 'to see if he could meet with the people.' This too failed, for the nomads eluded him. When spring came, the migrating duck and geese were 'so difficult to procure . . . that they were reduced to eat[ing] the moss and frogs.'

However, the ice was now breaking up as the solstice approached and Hudson, reasserting himself, ordered the *Discovery* prepared for sea. Once more he compounded his previous follies: in place of the competent Bylot as mate, he elevated a new favourite, Philip Staffe, and at the same time secured the traverse board and the backstaff in his own cabin. His purpose in this was clear: since Staffe could neither write nor work the ship's reckoning, no one but Hudson would know where the *Discovery* was. It was an old trick, but unsubtly done. To a suspicious crew it meant that Hudson intended penetrating the unknown seas further.

Despite this, Hudson now issued the last of the bread and cheese, weeping 'when he gave it unto them'. There was enough for about a fortnight if it was eked out, but many ate it up almost immediately. Some, probably Ivet, Greene and Wilson, fomented trouble by suggesting Hudson had done this as a further deception, and had retained a stock of food for himself and his son, whom he had kept in his cabin; Hudson, meanwhile, ordered a search of the ship for caches of foodstuffs hidden by the seamen. It was bruited abroad that some men had been issued with more than others, and Wilson asked Staffe 'why the master should so favour to give meate to some of the companie and not the rest?' 'It was necessary,' Staffe replied, 'that some of them should be kepte up,' meaning their strength should be maintained. This remark was all that was needed to activate the mutiny that had been simmering for months. Wilson reported the news to Greene, to whom it was clear evidence of how far he had himself fallen from Hudson's favour.

The *Discovery* made her way north, but on 18 June again encountered ice. On the 23rd they broke free, and it was thought from their course that Hudson had no intention of heading for home. Late that night Wilson and Greene woke and confronted Prickett in his cabin. Abacuk Prickett was afflicted by scurvy. His teeth were loose, he was weak to the point of immobility and his breath stank, but he was the owning syndicate's agent, and was maintaining an account of the voyage. It was necessary that the mutineers should suborn Prickett and detach him from Hudson, so that Prickett would represent their proposed action in a favourable light when reporting to Digges, Wolstenholme and their partners. In this they were both crafty and careful, but if Prickett did not comply, he might suffer the same fate as was mooted for Hudson: abandonment in the shallop.

Prickett professed himself horrified. 'I told them I marvelled to hear so much from them, considering that they were married men, and had wives and children, and that for their sakes they should not commit so foul a thing in the sight of God.' Greene responded that there was insufficient food on board to sustain them for more than a little while, that they themselves had eaten nothing for three days. They would 'either mend or end and what they had begun they would go through with it or die.' Greene affirmed that 'he would rather be hanged at home than starved abroad.' Prickett sounded the extent of the mutinous party: there were seven of them, and they included Ivet. Prickett acquiesced under protest. Greene then summoned the other conspirators, and in Prickett's cabin they all swore an oath 'to God, your prince, and country; you shall do nothing but to the glory of God and the good of the action in hand, and harm to no man.'

Having secured this cloak of respectability for their conspiracy, Greene and Wilson put their plan into action. At dawn Staffe, who had the deck, was distracted, and as Hudson came out of his cabin he was seized, bound and bundled into the shallop, which had been towing astern and was brought alongside. John Hudson followed his father, as did two loyalists, King and Woodhouse. Then 'the poore sick and lame men were called upon to get them out of their cabins into the shallop.' These were Butt, Lollo, Moore and Fanning, all of whom were suffering seriously from scurvy. Seeing what was happening, Staffe protested, and had to be secured. The mutineers valued Staffe for his skills, but he would have none of them. He and Hudson had had their differences, but Staffe was a steadfast loyalist and probably hated Greene and Wilson. Demanding that they had no right to restrain him, he insisted on joining his legitimate commander. He then asserted that the mutineers had no right to separate a craftsman from his tools, and had his chest passed down into the boat. The mutineers also allowed Hudson a fowling gun, powder and shot, a few pikes, an iron cooking pot and a small bag of meal. After this brief flurry the shallop's painter was cast off.

Prickett's account was self-exculpatory, but nevertheless there seems little doubt that Hudson, whatever his skills as a seaman and his experience as an explorer, was a feeble commander. Setting aside the suggested ambiguities in his sexuality, his vacillations and his biddable character are enough to condemn him. He was certainly not the blameless victim of later myth, though he and the others were undoubtedly subjected to an act of extreme cruelty. However, odious as Greene and his associates probably were, and inhuman the method they chose to employ, there was some justification for them contesting Hudson's right to command the expedition. Unlike Magellan and Drake, Hudson had utterly failed to assert his authority or to conduct his affairs with the necessary decisiveness. For all his faults, it was a heavy price to pay – turned out of his ship and left with his handful of sick and loyal adherents to drift to his death in the great bay that bears his name.

The aftermath of this mutiny is of particular interest. The *Discovery* was no *Bounty*, destroyed to unite the mutineers; on the contrary, she went on to further voyages of exploration, and afterwards her name was borne proudly by successive ships bound on similar quests. As for Greene, his success was short-lived. As soon as Hudson had been cast off he took command and, according to the now detached Prickett, 'Then out with their topsayles and towards the east they stood in a cleere sea.' Once they had dropped the shallop over the horizon they hove-to to dispute their course of action. First they searched the hold, finding some meal, a quantity of pork, two small casks of butter and half a bushel of peas. Prickett was directed to Hudson's quarters, where 'in the master's cabin we found two hundred of bisket cakes, a pecke of meal, of beere to the quantitie of a butt.' As this search was in process the shallop was seen approaching, whereupon the *Discovery* made sail 'as from an enemy'. Hudson and his party were never seen or heard of again.

A day or two later those on the *Discovery* found themselves again beset by ice, and so the ship remained for a fortnight, at the end of which they managed to land on some islands and found some scurvy grass to eat. This had a remarkably restorative effect, and they began to consider their future. Greene had assumed command but was incapable of navigating the ship. Ivet favoured a course to the north-west by which means he thought they could escape the bay, but Robert Bylot knew better: they must head north-east in order to extricate themselves – though what they should next do remained debatable. Greene, perhaps only now aware of what he had initiated, 'swore the shippe should not come into any place, but keep the sea . . . till he had the king's majestie's hand and seale to shew for his safety.' How he thought this might be achieved is uncertain but it is clear that Greene's hold over his shipmates was weak, and that a struggle for power was bound to ensue.

First, however, was the pressing question of provisions. Thanks to Bylot they managed to return to Digges Island, where they knew birds were plentiful, reaching it on 27 July. Hoisting out their second boat, Greene, Wilson and Prickett made a landing and encountered some Inuit, with whom they attempted to trade. Prickett thought them 'simple and kind' and an offer of caribou meat was accepted, which it was thought the Inuit would bring the following day. Next day, however, as the boat approached the shore, a group of the nomads were seen 'dancing and leaping'. When Greene, armed with a pike, stepped ashore he discovered there was no meat, only a gathering of the curious. He refused to trade, and 'swore they should have nothing till he had venison'. This denial clinched the matter: as others in the party gathered sorrel and scurvy grass they were all suddenly attacked, the Inuit stabbing them in their bellies. One man fell dead; Greene swung his pike and fell back towards the boat, as did Wilson. Perse buried the hatchet he was wielding in his attacker's body, while Motter ran and tried to swim back to the ship. Prickett, who had been left in the boat because of his continuing weakness from scurvy, was set upon and slashed across the chest and wounded in his thigh, right arm and left hand before he could stab his assailant. William Wilson, Michael Perse and Henry Greene, all wounded, fought their way back to the boat and shoved off. The Inuit fired arrows after them, again wounding Prickett and Perse but killing Greene, whose body was tumbled unceremoniously overboard as they dragged Motter out of the water. Then, plying their oars, they pulled off to the *Discovery*, which lay just beyond a headland and therefore out of sight.

Once they were on board, the surgeon, Edward Wilson, did what he could for them. Miraculously he saved Prickett, but his namesake, the obstreperous William Wilson, died 'swearing and cursing in the most fearful manner', to be followed two days later by Perse.

The deaths of Greene and Wilson cleared the air, and it was the highly competent Bylot who now emerged as leader. A second landing in the area of Cape Wolstenholme under the noisy cover of the *Discovery*'s guns secured 'a supply of sea fowles' and some scurvy grass, sufficient to see at least some of them out of immediate danger of starvation. 'We had flayed our fowle, for they [the feathers] will not pull and Robert Ivet was the first to make use of the skins by burning off the feathers; so they became a great dish of meate, and as for the garbidge, it was not thrown away . . . [but] at length was all our meat spent, and our fowle restie [rancid] and dry; but [there] being no remedy, we were content with the salt broth for dinner, and the half fowle for supper.' This was eked out until at last they fried the 'garbidge' with a little vinegar in candle grease, making 'a good dish of meate'. But by the time they were approaching the west coast of Ireland 'all our men were in despaire', and at this point Ivet, 'next to Greene the chief mutineer, died for sheer want.'

The *Discovery*'s company now stood at a third of its original strength, and all were weak. Only Bylot seems to have been capable of real effort as they passed Inishmore and entered Galway Bay. It was 6 September; in the bay lay a fishing-smack from Fowey in Cornwall, and her crew helped them. Prickett negotiated a passage home, leaving Bylot and his handful of companions to bring the ship up the Thames, anchoring finally off Deptford on 20 October 1611.

Both Prickett and Bylot were questioned first by Sir Thomas Smith and then by other members of the syndicate. The opinion that they should all hang was aired, but it was clear from their physical condition that the survivors had endured a singular ordeal. The submission of Abacuck Prickett's journal, together with his testimony and that of Bylot, suggested that the mutineers had all died, and that the survivors had only acted to save their own lives. Besides, there was a slight chance that Hudson too would survive, and no evidence of his actual death. More important to their interrogators was the affirmation, supported by documentary evidence in the form of a rough chart, that Hudson had in fact discovered in the great bay a passage to the Indies. Bylot's skills and experience, moreover, inclined their principals to ensure his survival. Wild stories circulated along the waterfront and the Establishment deliberated, but nothing was done.

When in 1618 it was finally discovered that Hudson Bay was not in fact the elusive North West Passage, five of the *Discovery*'s surviving men were arraigned in the High Court of Admiralty on charges of mutiny and murder. Nicholas Syms was excused as he had been a minor at the time; as for the others – Prickett, Clemens, Mathues and Edward Wilson the surgeon – they all pleaded their innocence, blaming Greene, Ivet and William Wilson for the mutiny. In the absence of any real evidence, all were acquitted of the alleged crime.

Bylot was not charged, for he had assisted in refuting the notion that the sought-for passage had been found. Both he and Prickett had returned to the region with Sir Thomas Button the following year and Bylot distinguished himself on this and on subsequent voyages, making a formidable team with the admirable William Baffin. Their last voyage together was made in 1616, with Bylot in command and Baffin pilot of, once again, the 55-ton bark *Discovery*. It is Bylot rather than Hudson who emerges with credit from that tragic and mismanaged voyage, but although an island bears his name, it is Hudson's which is better remembered by posterity.

Button's expedition was also sent under the patronage of Prince Henry, who had insisted that for mutual support two ships must go, namely the *Resolution* and *Discovery*. The prince had also drawn up explicit instructions that Button was to observe Sunday worship 'with godlie meditation', and that all forms of excess, profanity, blasphemy, drunkenness and lewdness were to be severely punished. Was there in this a hint of the reasons for Hudson's failure? The commanders of both vessels were to guard against and 'prevent all Mutynie amongst your people ... ' Although not 'royal' ships, the *Resolution* and *Discovery* were to be governed by royal regulation.

The English had sought to regulate shipping and codify maritime law as early as 1190 when Richard I introduced the Laws of Oléron, enacted by his mother Eleanor of Aquitaine when she was in the island of that name, prior to her marriage to Henry II of England. The Code bore particularly upon the thriving wine trade with Bordeaux, then part of Richard's French possessions, and their chief effect was to establish the authority of the master of a ship, particularly in respect of duty and discipline, cargo, pilotage and mutiny. The powers they conferred upon a master were near-absolute, and they provided for masters who were not themselves owners of a ship but empowered to act as the owner's agent. The laws were further embedded in English civil law in 1336 in The Black Book of the Admiralty, where 'admiralty' refers to shipping in general. Also included in The

Black Book were the ancient customs and usages of the sea which dignified certain practices with precedent.

Specific regulations for 'naval' expeditions, which nevertheless included chartered private ships, were drawn up on an *ad hoc* basis. Thus when Lord Howard of Effingham and the Earl of Essex made a punitive attack on Cadiz in 1598 their mixed fleet was governed by some thirty Articles of War which included ordinances against gambling, theft and blasphemy, and sought to encourage a high moral tone by making the worship of God compulsory and the striking of an officer or other mutinous conduct capital offences. Unfortunately, discipline broke down when the fleet's members fell upon the enormous booty captured at Cadiz, more evidence, if it were needed, that regulation alone was insufficient to check the worst excesses of human behaviour.

Prince Henry had hardly approved the regulations by which Button's ships were to be governed when he died of typhoid fever, aged eighteen. His father, James I, was thus in due course succeeded by the equally ill-fated Charles I, destined to lose his head after first losing a civil war caused in part by his desire to establish an effective Royal Navy which would forever remove the need for the crown to rely upon a levy of private men-of-war. The levy of ship money in lieu of ships was unpopular as much because it denied those their gains who had hitherto supplied, manned, and profited from such maritime war as because it required those taxed to dig into their own pockets. The separation of the state's own ships from those of its citizens denied those same citizen shipowners the access to the rungs of the social ladder they had previously enjoyed, and marks the first manifestation of the divergence of the royal and the mercantile sea officer – though it never prevented the navy from pressing or conscripting the common sailor.

But Charles's attempts to form a Royal Navy loyal to the Crown were inept. At the instigation of his chief adviser George Villiers, Duke of Buckingham, a man much fondled by the late and bi-sexual King James, Charles sent the royal fleet to support

King Louis XIII against rebellious French Protestants, a fact which combined with the ill-found state of the ships to incite mutiny among both officers and men as English society fractured along politico-religious faults and England descended into civil strife. Court favourites were appointed as captains, relying upon their tarpaulin 'masters' to manoeuvre and fight their ships, while a lack of resources and poor supply arrangements made conditions on board, even in port, a subject of constant contention. To hold this increasingly unruly state of affairs in check, discipline was severe: *this* was the age of keel-hauling, among other vicious and sadistic forms of punishment. Lack of pay, a want of the necessaries of life on board, poor food and the rapid onset of scurvy caused seamen to riot even on shore, while corruption was rampant among many officers and dockyard officials and went unchecked. Between them, and despite advances in shipbuilding, James I and Charles I 'allowed the seamanship of *Elizabeth* to die out in a generation'.

When civil war finally broke out the so-called 'Royal' Navy largely sided with the rebellious Parliament, and conditions improved significantly. Under the Commonwealth it was called upon to fight the first of three short but bloody wars against the Dutch, and although at the Restoration of the monarchy in 1660 many of the Parliamentary officers remained in the service, many royalists who had served at sea in the exiled and hostile squadrons rejoined the reconstituted Royal Navy. Charles II, a better pragmatist than his father, refused to countenance faction, provided the former Parliamentarian officers had not been regicides. He appointed his brother James, Duke of York, Lord High Admiral. York was himself a practical seaman and appointed one of his protégés, Samuel Pepys, as Clerk of the Acts of the Navy. In 1673 Pepys took over as secretary for naval affairs and began to force through a number of necessary administrative reforms. He also advocated the promotion to captain only of men with proper sea-faring skills and experience, determined if he could to break the Court and petticoat influence that had created two classes of naval officer; the gentlemen and the tarpaulins – the 'worst' of the latter were men who had climbed to the quarter-deck by way of the lower-deck.

Sadly, Pepys's reforms were almost lost when he fell from favour as a consequence of his attachment to James, whose Catholicism condemned him as king and led to the Glorious Revolution of 1688. Matters maritime rapidly reverted to what they had been in the worst days of Charles I – but while the Royal Navy again threatened to fall apart, the administration put in place by Pepys did not.

3

'NOT FITT TO ENGAGE THE ENEMY'

THE seething discontent in the Royal Navy during the seventeenth century, seems but one more manifestation of the breakdown in society produced by religious dissent and constitutional up-heaval. Mutiny among seamen at sea was in effect unremarkable during such a period of momentous change, and where it did have impact, it remained a rebellion not of sailors but of their officers. In one of the most shameful, not to say curious, events in the annals of the Royal Navy the focus of one mutiny emerges, mysteriously, as the hero.

Among the tarpaulins enabled by Pepys's reforms to rise in the King's service was John Benbow. Benbow, the son of a tanner, ran away to sea and after some time in merchant ships joined the navy. Here he distinguished himself and rose to warrant rank under the future Lord Torrington, but was later court-martialled for alleged disparagement of a senior officer. His plea was accepted and he was acquitted, but he soon afterwards left the navy and acquired his own merchant ship. In this he fought an engagement with an Algerine corsair from which he is supposed to have brought back the heads of thirteen of the pirates, in order to claim the 'head-money' paid on them. The truth of this is uncertain, but on the renewal of war with France he rejoined Torrington, now an admiral and noted for his blunt coarseness. Benbow distinguished himself in several actions, and in 1693 court-martialled a commander he did not consider had done his utmost against the enemy. After a period as Master-Attendant at Deptford Dockyard he hoisted his flag and as a rear admiral was appointed Commander-in-Chief in the West Indies. Here he took a high-handed attitude in his attempts to maintain the effectiveness of his squadron, a circumstance that did not endear him to either the local merchants, from whose ships he pressed seamen, or the Governor of Jamaica. Able and efficient though he was, it is clear that Benbow cared little for the opinions of others, while it is probable that his unpolished nature made him an object of private contempt among the better-born of his squadron's captains.

Benbow, now a vice admiral, was serving a second term in the West Indies when the War of the Spanish Succession broke out in 1702. Learning of the approach of a French squadron he took measures to intercept it. The French commander, Admiral Ducasse, was bound for Cartagena on the coast of modern Colombia with troops escorted by his 68-gun flagship *Heureux*, the *Phénix* of 60 guns, *Apollon* and *Agréable* each of 50 guns, and the smaller 30-gun *Prince de Frise*. Off Santa Marta on 19 August Benbow sighted Ducasse from the quarterdeck of his own flagship, the 70-gun *Breda*. With Benbow's flag were the 64-gun *Defiance*, the 54-gun *Greenwich*, the *Windsor*, 60, and three 48-gun ships, *Pendennis*, *Ruby* and *Falmouth*, an altogether superior force to that of Ducasse.

Prior to their departure from Port Royal in Jamaica Benbow is said to have spoken 'a little briskly' to Captain Kirkby 'and the rest of the gentlemen [the captains] . . . when he found them not quite so ready to obey his orders as he thought was their duty.' This briskness probably (but it is only conjecture) consisted of that coarseness of expression common to tarpaulin officers and given a certain cachet by the Earl of Torrington. It was something in which men of Benbow's stamp might be said to have taken a conscious pride, a snub to the 'gentlemen' who were court appointees and not only lacked the skills of men bred to the sea, but had a mild contempt for them. In view of the consequences of this dressing down, it has to be assumed that before Kirkby and the others sailed from Port Royal, they had come to some plan to discredit their admiral. Little is known of Kirkby (sometimes spelled Kirby), who commanded the *Defiance,* other than hints of his superior social standing and that he had acquired a reputation for meting out excessive punishments. He seems to have possessed sufficient personality to ingratiate himself with the colonial authorities, who themselves disliked Benbow, and to subvert Captains Wade of the *Greenwich*, Hudson of the *Pendennis* and Constable of the *Windsor*. Their meditated disloyalty was unlikely to have been as serious as it turned out to be; that it did so illustrates the dangers – personal, political and naval – of allowing any crack whatsoever in the structure of command.

Unaware of the cabal against him, in sighting Ducasse, Benbow was confident of his superiority. Shortly after noon on the 19th he hoisted the signal for action, clewing up his courses and slowing the *Breda* so that his ships could form a line of battle with Kirkby's *Defiance* in the van, followed by Hudson's *Pendennis* and Constable's *Windsor*. The *Breda* was to occupy the centre of the line, the traditional position for the flag-officer commanding, with Wade's *Greenwich* just astern, Walton's *Ruby* following and Vincent's *Falmouth* bringing up the rear. Thus Benbow's most powerful ships were to be concentrated in the van and centre – but Kirkby was so dilatory in taking his station that Benbow was driven to send a lieutenant in a pulling-boat to chivvy him. Kirkby eventually obeyed, but his actions had signalled his intentions to his co-conspirators. Although *Pendennis* was not yet in station, by four o'clock the two squadrons were in range and an engagement began. The *Breda* and *Falmouth* opened a spirited fire and Kirkby fired three broadsides, then bore away out of line and was soon out of range. The others exchanged shots with the enemy and then, as often happened in that locality, the wind died with the day, hastened by the concussion of the guns. By nightfall most of the British ships had fallen out of line, leaving Benbow's *Breda*, commanded by Captain Christopher Fogg, supported only by *Ruby* and *Falmouth*, which threw far less weight of metal than *Defiance*, *Windsor* or *Greenwich*. Whether or not Captain Walton of the *Ruby* had originally sided with Kirkby, he had little doubt of his duty, and followed the flagship's battle lanterns throughout the night.

At daybreak on the 20th only *Ruby* was in support of Benbow's flag and in a position to resume the action; the remainder of the squadron was three or four miles away. Exasperated, Benbow dispatched another officer by boat with orders to redeploy his ships and explicitly informing each captain, especially Kirkby, of his new position in the line of battle. *Breda* would now lead the squadron, followed by *Defiance*, *Windsor*, *Greenwich*, *Ruby*, *Pendennis* and *Falmouth*. This quite clearly placed the ships in descending order of force, and would have recalled all but the most recalcitrant commanders to their duty. It was to little effect; again only Walton in *Ruby* supported Benbow during the long forenoon as *Breda* kept up pressure on Ducasse. He threw away his own opportunity to destroy the British squadron in detail through being 'so civil as not to fire'. To Benbow's disgust his other ships followed like spectators in the offing. A fresh breeze sprang up in the afternoon and Benbow clung onto the enemy as Ducasse's ships, in perfect order, made sail offshore to the westward.

Next morning *Ruby* was abeam of the rearmost French man-of-war with *Breda* lying on her starboard quarter; both were firing their bow-chasers. Benbow ordered Fogg to close, luff up and rake their quarry – something Ducasse, with troops to look after, was unlikely to withstand. But the French ship edged away and closed with the *Ruby*, so concentrating her gun-fire that Walton's ship was soon disabled and Benbow sent his boats to tow her out of trouble while engaging the Frenchman himself. All the other ships were within range of the enemy, but made no attempt to join the action. It was now about eight o'clock in the morning and again a breeze enabled Ducasse to make sail to the westward. Benbow followed, and so did his squadron, with the exception of the shattered *Ruby* which he soon afterwards ordered to make for Jamaica. Only *Breda* engaged, having her rigging cut up and losing her main topsail yard. Kirkby lay less than a quarter of a mile astern of the flagship, but he took no part in the action, despite the admiral's signals.

At daylight on the 22nd *Breda* was a mile astern of the rearmost French ship, and with one exception Benbow's squadron straggled out astern with Hudson's *Pendennis* nine miles away. Kirkby still lay in *Breda*'s wake but Captain Vincent, appalled at what he knew the world would judge to be rank cowardice and no mere nettling of their admiral, brought *Falmouth* up with the flagship and sought permission to relinquish the rear station and assume one more consonant with his honour. Benbow rapidly welcomed this assistance, but the wind fell light and although the two ships closed the enemy's rear, there was only a brief exchange of fire in the twilight. During the day Ducasse seems to have detached the frigate *Prince de Frise*, further reducing the odds confronting the British.

By the morning of the 23rd Kirkby and all, except Vincent, were some four miles astern despite Benbow's signals for close order. But *Breda* and *Falmouth* pressed on and for a short period fought a lively close action, in the course of which they separated a French prize, recapturing the *Anne*, a British merchantman seized off Lisbon. During the day the other vessels shortened the distance between them and Benbow, but their guns again remained silent. The chase ran on into the darkness and at about half-past two in the morning *Breda* and *Falmouth* ranged up on the rear Frenchman and a furious action ensued. At three a chain shot swept across the quarterdeck and struck Benbow's right leg. He was taken below for a few moments; after the application of a tourniquet he ordered himself carried back on deck where, in great pain, he continued the running fight. Dawn revealed their quarry disabled: her mizzen had gone, her mainyard sagged in the slings, her rigging was cut up and her upperworks were battered by shot. Benbow ordered Fogg to board but, now convinced that his captains would not come to their admiral's support, Ducasse hauled his wind and doubled round to come to the assistance of the rearmost French vessel in a breeze that was falling light and fickle.

Although Constable, Hudson and Wade brought their ships up, they fired only token broadsides before hauling away to the southward. As for Kirkby, he brought the *Defiance* into range, fired a handful of guns and turned away as soon as the disabled enemy returned fire. It must by now have fallen almost calm, for boats were hoisted out and Ducasse was arriving to assist his wounded consort. The *Breda* was forced to edge away under fire. Withdrawing again with his squadron intact, Ducasse resumed his progress to the west. At this point Wade seems to have been summoned aboard the *Breda* for a dressing down. Benbow remonstrated with him, sending him back to his ship with instructions to the others to 'keep in better order'. Passing *Defiance* in his boat, Wade communicated this state of affairs to Kirkby who in turn lowered his gig and boarded the flagship.

By now a wind shift had placed the disorderly gaggle of British men-of-war directly to windward of the French. Acutely aware that, holding what was called 'the weather-gauge', he would have no finer opportunity, Benbow admonished Kirkby, who quite spuriously pleaded their own weakness in comparison with the French. In this curious hiatus Benbow, by now aware that his captains were in open defiance of him, ordered Fogg to signal for 'all captains'. When he arrived on *Breda*'s quarterdeck, Kirkby employed his persuasive talents and drew up for them all to sign a document giving their reasons for refusing action. Confronted with this, Benbow snarled 'that paper would ruin them all', while Kirkby added that they would 'defer fighting until a better opportunity'. Benbow, his face contorted with rage and pain, gestured aloft to the now freshening wind, pointing out through clenched teeth that with only four enemy vessels dead to leeward opposed to their six, and with their own ships untouched by action, there would never be a better opportunity.

Any deferment 'seemed a perfect denial [to Benbow] who having seen the cowardly behaviour of some of them before had reason to believe that either they had a design against him, or [they were] traitors to their country . . . '

Incredibly, pleading a want of fit men, a lack of ammunition, a 'measure' of disablement in the rig of each ship, the lack of a steady wind, and an opposition exaggerated in force and 'having a great Number of Seamen and Soldiers on board for the service of Spaine', *all* the captains concluded that 'we think it not fitt [sic] to Engage the Enemy at this time.' However, to avoid any suggestion of cowardice, they agreed 'to keep [the enemy] Company this night and observe their motion, and if a fair oppertunity [sic] shall happen (of Wind and Weather) once more to trye our Stength with them.'

How Kirkby and the others coerced Fogg and Vincent to join them in signing (Walton having of course long since departed) is a matter for conjecture. The only explanation is to assume that it was clear to them that Benbow would probably not survive his wound, and that Kirkby, as the senior captain, would subsequently assume command of the squadron. How this must have further infuriated Benbow is not difficult to imagine and Kirkby's effrontery in acting thus in the face of the enemy and upon his admiral's own quarterdeck is powerful evidence that he was confident of his position and the influence he commanded in high places. Apart from all this, with the exception of *Ruby* and *Breda,* which were indeed less than fighting fit from having been in action, Kirkby's assertions were entirely false. Some play may be made of the fickleness of the wind, but it had hampered neither *Breda* nor *Falmouth,* and was no excuse. Nevertheless, Kirkby achieved his objective; wounded as he was, Benbow could do nothing with both his flag-captain and Vincent party to the plot. Ducasse escaped as the British squadron hauled its wind for Jamaica.

At Port Royal Benbow's leg was amputated and he succumbed to a high fever, but not before he had ordered his second-in-command on the station, Rear Admiral Whetstone whose ships had been elsewhere, to convene a court martial from among the captains of his own squadron, with a lawyer named Arnold Browne sitting as Judge Advocate. All Benbow's captains were accused except Walton, who was sworn in as a member of the court, though Fogg and Vincent were charged only with signing the infamous letter, not of any dereliction of duty. Hudson too avoided any charge, for shortly after *Pendennis* anchored off Port Royal he inexplicably died. On 8 October Whetstone presided over the court assembled in *Breda*'s cabin. The indictments were read out. Kirkby was accused of cowardice, neglect of duty and breach of orders, and Benbow and Fogg led the witnesses sworn to testify for the Queen. What emerged was even more extraordinary than the conduct of the *Defiance* had suggested, for Kirkby seems to have been subject to a mental breakdown, refusing his men powder and shot, dodging behind the mizzen mast and falling down at the sound of a shot. It was not his first action, but he had ordered the master's log to be falsified. He denied all charges, but could produce no evidence to counter them. Asked why he had failed to fire at the enemy, he said 'because they did not fire at him, but that they had a respect for him.' Kirkby was sentenced to death.

Constable was similarly arraigned; witnesses said he had ignored Benbow's signals even when reinforced by guns or sent by the hand of Lieutenant Langridge, that he was drunk during part of the action, and took his orders from Kirkby. Constable pleaded that he thought Langridge meant him to keep close astern of his next ahead – Kirkby's *Defiance*. He was sentenced to be cashiered and declared unfit to serve Her Majesty in any capacity whatsoever.

Wade defended his supine conduct ineffectually but paid tribute to Benbow's 'courage and conduct . . . during the whole six days engagement, declaring the bravery of the Admiral in this time of action and that no man living could do more or better for the Honour of the Queen and Nation.' That was not quite the point, and it failed to impress the court; he too was sentenced to death.

Finally Fogg and Vincent were called to answer for 'high crimes, misdemeanours and ill practices', which actually meant the signing of Kirkby's document. Both attested they had been compelled to do so to save their own ships from capture if the enemy turned upon them and Benbow, despite his fever, testified to their manly conduct during the action. The court found them guilty but sentenced them only to be suspended pending the pleasure of the Lord High Admiral becoming known. The proceedings were wound up on 12 October and Whetstone's dispatch was sent home as Benbow approached his end, consumed by fever and rage. Almost his last act was to write to Prince George of Denmark, consort to Queen Anne and Lord High Admiral, to ask that Fogg and Vincent should not be suspended from their posts. Benbow died of his wound on 4 November.

As he waited to be sent home Kirkby wrote to the Secretary of the Admiralty, Josiah Burchett, justifying his conduct and complaining of Benbow having proceeded against him in a court martial after 'shamefully parting with Monsieur Du Cost [sic] on the coast of Carthagena.' It is a curious attempt at self-exculpation which serves only to increase the suspicion that Kirkby relied upon getting away with his scandalous conduct with the aid of his connections. Benbow has been criticized for not, at the first sign of disaffection, having replaced his captains by their first lieutenants, who 'would have fought well, were it for no other reason than the Hopes of being continued in those Commands had they survived'. Perhaps; but what would it have looked like in London had a Commander-in-Chief replaced so great a number of captains at a blow? Benbow could not risk the workings of political faction upon which Kirkby so unwisely relied, as this letter to Burchett makes clear. In it he admits that 'several accidents have discovered [i.e., made clear to Kirkby] he [Benbow] did not think himself safe from the question at home while I lived, and 'tis thought the trouble of his apprehension hastened his death (the wound in his leg being only a common fracture) which has since happened for which reason I shall urge no further concerning him than is necessary to maintain my own innocence of what is laid to my charge with all the scandal he could invent.'

Kirkby's belittlement of Benbow's injury appears to have been a calumny: naval medicine in 1702 was not as primitive as popular imagination has it, and a common fracture would not have necessitated amputation. Kirby also tried to mount a belated defence under Admiral Russell's Fighting Instructions, which held that two opposing squadrons must not engage unless their lines be conterminous, ship-to-ship. But Benbow was in chase, and although one might invoke the letter of the Instructions as a pettifogging technique, it was the failure from the start of the action of Kirkby and his cabal not to form line that had placed Benbow in so difficult a position. Kirkby, his aim being to discredit his admiral, would have preferred Benbow to have declined to engage on the grounds that he [Kirkby] had failed to form line, a circumstance which would have played exactly into Kirkby's hands and laid Benbow himself open to charges of cowardice. The notion that Kirkby and his fellows were being forced into positions with no enemy against whom they could fire 'upon a point blank', as Article No. 19 of the Fighting Instructions has it, was not only disingenuous, it was dishonourable.

On 13 January 1703 Queen Anne wrote to her husband in his capacity as Lord High Admiral to declare that she found 'no reason to shew favour to captains Richard Kirkby and Cooper Wade who have been condemned to be shot, or to Captain John Constable, who has been condemned to be cashiered, to be unfit for the Queen's Service . . . ' Warrants for the immediate execution of Kirkby and Wade were issued to all the western ports in anticipation of the arrival of the miscreants, and on 16 April the *Bristol* arrived at Plymouth from Jamaica. Both men were shot on the *Bristol*'s quarterdeck before the sun went down.

Constable was imprisoned, and the date of his death is unknown; Fogg died in 1708 and Vincent in 1729, neither achieving anything beyond this notoriety. George Walton was knighted in 1722 and died an admiral seventeen years later. Much more about the poor state of morale in Benbow's squadron must have been known by the officers in his ships, yet no one divulged a single tantalizing fact and Benbow has become a hero, described upon the monument erected to him over a century later as 'the Nelson of his times'. The extent to which Benbow had provoked the calculating disloyalty of his captains must have been a factor in their unity in combining against him and stands to disprove the encomium a later generation granted him; his son-in-law worked hard at creating a myth and is largely responsible for our uncritical picture of him. That Benbow was a fierce and courageous sea officer, an able navigator and a prime seaman is beyond dispute, but his style and manner of leadership remain questionable.

However, Richard Kirkby and Cooper Wade were foolish and conceited men, intriguers of the worst sort, who took calumny too far and, whatever their private justifications, were the cowards they were accused of having been when in the presence of the enemy. There is some evidence to suggest that Kirkby had become unhinged; the climate, the drink and over-weening pride may all have played their part, while seniority and a dominating personality backed up by faction allowed him to lead the others on, weaker pawns in his infamous game. That curious suggestion that he did not engage because Ducasse had 'a respect for him' hints at something far worse, treason of a greater sort than cowardice – but we shall never know. Much was lost as other men went to their graves tight-lipped, more when a fire consumed part of the Admiralty office in Spring Gardens on 2 December 1716 – for in the flames was most of Admiral Benbow's official correspondence.

4

'AN ILLEGAL MUTINOUS PROCEDURE'

IT is not in the collective interest of a ship's company to overthrow authority. It is therefore a paradox that rebellion aboard ship most notoriously occurs when the vessel is far distant from the constitutional authority from which a commander draws his power, yet at the same time a crew must act in concert or perish, whether from the malice of the enemy or from the natural hostility of the elements compounded by distance from home. Such a case occurred in 1720 when the crew of the British privateer *Speedwell* mutinied after the loss of their ship on the Island of Juan Fernandez, blaming the wreck on the carelessness of her commander, a former naval lieutenant named George Shelvocke, and on the shooting of a black albatross by the *Speedwell*'s first lieutenant, Simon Hatley, while she was in the Straits of le Maire earlier in the voyage. The mutineers divided up their spoils according to rank but included Shelvocke in the deal. He escaped in one of his prizes, the Spanish vessel *Sacra Familia*, and is said to have acquired gold on the coast of California, though he lost it before returning home. He was arrested on a charge of piracy but this was unproved, and

Shelvocke escaped from prison while being detained on a lesser charge. He lived for a while in France before returning to die in London. He is chiefly interesting not so much because his crew mutinied, or because Hatley's action inspired Coleridge's poem *The Ancient Mariner*, or because his authority was derived from a letter of marque and reprisal (the purpose of which he had corrupted), but because the *Speedwell* incident was long remembered among seamen.

During the first half of the eighteenth century the Royal Navy was very far from the efficient fighting force it had become by the end of it. While its directors of policy had begun to think in terms of global strategy, the ability of the navy to cope with the demands of implementing such policies was poor. It learned fast, however, and as is the manner of such things, tragedy was the spring from which reform came.

The Peace of Utrecht which ended the War of Spanish Succession in 1713 granted to Britain the *Asiento des negros*, a contract permitting British ships to carry slaves across the Atlantic to Spanish colonies in Central and South America, though only one British ship per annum was allowed the carriage of commercial trade goods. This restriction ran contrary to the spirit of British mercantilism and was frequently broken, British shipowners finding ready and eager markets in the Caribbean but equally enthusiastic opposition in the Spanish authorities. There were a number of incidents involving excise officers, then in 1739 Captain Jenkins of the *Rebecca* claimed to have had his ear sliced off by a *guarda-costa* who threatened to do the same to King George II. It was afterwards observed that an inspection under his wig would reveal both Jenkins' ears in place; nevertheless the outrage was a sufficient cause for war. The so-called War of Jenkins' Ear rapidly escalated into the War of the Austrian Succession, and among the naval expeditions mounted by the government of Sir Robert Walpole was one to attack Spanish possessions on the Pacific Coast of South America.

A squadron was accordingly placed under the command of Commodore George Anson consisting of the *Centurion* of 60 guns, the *Gloucester* and *Severn*, each of 50 guns, the 40-gun

Pearl, the small 28-gun frigate *Wager*, the sloop *Tryal* and two store ships, *Anna* and *Industry*. Anson's squadron left St Helen's Roads off the Isle of Wight on 18 September 1740, making a brave sight but flawed from the beginning. Owing to general neglect and corruption in the Royal Dockyards, where a system of low salaries and permissible perquisites encouraged license and greed, none of the ships was well-found. To add to this woeful situation problems had been experienced in manning them and the Admiralty had been driven to the expedient of drafting pensioners from Greenwich Hospital.

An able and experienced officer, Anson wrought havoc on the coast of Chile and in June 1743 captured the *Nuestra Señora de Covadonga,* the annual Manila galleon, which yielded treasure valued at over half a million pounds, an enormous sum which made him immensely rich. But by the time Anson returned home in triumph his squadron had been reduced to his own ship, the *Centurion*; and while he had lost 4 four men to enemy action, out of the 6 men-of-war's crews about 1,350 had died of scurvy. Like Magellan and Drake before him Anson had ordered a rendezvous at St Julian's Bay, where he learned that a Spanish squadron was in chase. Leaving St Julian's, Anson's ships headed for Cape Horn and a new rendezvous off Juan Fernandez Island in the Pacific. The British ships had already endured a considerable amount of bad weather, their provisions had been found inadequate, and scurvy was rampant. As a consequence of the mounting number of deaths, several reappointments had been required. On 19 February 1741, shortly before leaving St Julian's Bay, Anson had summoned Lieutenant David Cheap, first lieutenant of the *Tryal*, and made out an acting commission for him to command the *Wager*, an elevation that appears to have had a bad effect upon Cheap.

Although rated as a frigate the *Wager* was in fact a converted East Indiaman, purchased into the naval service the previous year. Dandy Kidd was her captain when she left England, and when he died his last words were of the *Wager* being cursed. Her company, he said, should 'know poverty, vermin, famine and absolute ruin'. The *Wager* was in no worse condition than the other vessels and had suffered no more grievously from losses due to scurvy, but Kidd's dying words clung to the frigate like a bad smell. By the end of March, as the squadron stretched down to high southern latitudes in order to keep well clear of Cape Horn, she had most of her crew on the sick-list and only about twenty seamen fit to stand a watch on deck.

Cheap had only one other commissioned sea officer to support him, a Lieutenant Robert Baynes, or Beans, who proved ineffectual, plus a Lieutenant Hamilton commanding a detachment of marines. There were also a number of midshipmen on board, including The Honourable John Byron (the poet's grandfather), Henry Cozens, Isaac Morris and Alexander Campbell, plus an infantry captain and two lieutenants commanding 'the land forces assigned to *Wager*'. Among the ship's standing warrant officers the senior, Thomas Clark the sailing master, was like Baynes a weak character, while John Bulkeley and John King, the warrant gunner and boatswain, next in the ship's hierarchy, were both men of forceful personality. Bulkeley was a man of considerable ability and knew at least the rudiments of navigation – he could find his latitude and work a traverse. With Baynes and Clark he stood and watched as officer of the deck.

The first sign of trouble came after the ships had passed the Strait of le Maire and opened the fetch of the Southern Ocean, encountering strong westerly gales and with them a current to the eastwards. On 31 March the *Gloucester*'s mainyard broke in the slings, and with a brief moderation in the weather all carpenters were put aboard her to speed the repair work; but far worse was to come. At three o'clock in the morning of 8 April, as the squadron tried but failed to gain ground to windward, the wind rose to storm force. Several of the vessels fired guns indicating to Anson that they were in distress: one of these was *Wager*, which had lost her mizen mast. Next day the *Anna* was in trouble, and on the night of the 10th *Pearl* and *Severn* dropped away to leeward and Anson never again saw them during his voyage. At this time 102 men were sick in *Pearl* and the ship was being worked by eight men in one watch and seven in the other.

Things were no better aboard *Wager*. By the 12th the wind had increased to hurricane strength and at seven in the morning, with Cheap sick in his cot and Bulkeley on watch, the *Wager* was swept by a green sea which holed the ship's cutter and filled the longboat. Next morning *Centurion*, the best sailer in the squadron, bore down upon the *Wager*. According to the reckoning they had beaten far enough to the west, and Anson wished to alter course to the north west and head for the Pacific, as the weather was moderating, he was therefore concerned about the *Wager*'s loss of her mizen and her inability to work to windward. He hailed her and enquired about the likelihood of fitting a jury rig, and in due course the squadron hauled their yards and began to edge towards balmier climes.

In the early hours of the 14th, however, 'the weather, which till then had been hazy, accidentally cleared up, the pink [the *Anna*] made a signal for seeing land right ahead and it being but two miles distant, we were all under the most dreadful apprehensions of running on shore, which, had either the wind blown from its usual quarter with its wonted vigour, or had not the moon suddenly shone out, not a ship amongst us could possibly have avoided: but the wind, which some few hours before blew from the SW, having fortunately shifted to WNW, we were enabled to stand to the southward, and to clear ourselves of this unexpected danger.' Later that morning, with a dramatic moderation in the weather, John Cummins the carpenter returned from the *Gloucester*. The task of raising a jury mizzen mast worried Cheap, and when Cummins blamed the failure of the chain-plates which secured the shrouds which in turn supported the mizen, Cheap railed against the master, Clark, who had been on deck when the mast was torn out of the ship.

On the 19th the weather was kinder still; *Centurion* was still in sight of *Wager*, *Gloucester*, *Anna* and *Tryal*, but all except the last were lagging astern effecting repairs. Demoralization was now rife, both a cause and a symptom of scurvy, depressing the immune system and feeding the progress of the disease. Despite this a jury spar was fished to the stump of *Wager's* mizen and a scrap of sail was set. When Clark relieved Bulkeley after dark that evening the light on *Centurion*'s poop could be seen, but the wind got up again in Baynes's watch and it was lost. Then in furling the fore course a man was lost off the yard; in falling overboard the topman struck Midshipman Campbell, who in turn crashed to the deck, bruised but sensible. That day, with *Centurion* and *Tryal* already out of sight, *Gloucester* and *Anna* drew ahead: finally the *Wager* was alone.

On 1st May Cheap decided the *Wager* had made sufficient westing to tack to the northward. Bulkeley debated with Baynes the wisdom of heading NNW again so soon, arguing that the rendezvous was well offshore and there was no need to close the land. Baynes agreed with him about the dangers the ship ran, but explained that Cheap had received orders to rendezvous off Socorro Island prior to mounting an attack on the Spanish port of Valdivia. Shortly afterwards Byron reported rockweed on the sea, a sure indication of land; later Cheap sent for Bulkeley and sought his reckoning as to their longitude – at best an estimate. Bulkeley took the opportunity of warning Cheap of the dangers of falling in with a lee shore, particularly as the mizen mast was ineffective should they have to beat to windward and there were only twelve seamen fit for duty.

In the forenoon of 13th May, with the wind veering from the south to the south-west and strengthening, gear carried away on the foremast, the foreyard came down on deck and the ship was hove-to: she continued to drift slowly east. A little later in the morning Carpenter Cummins reported land to the NNW, Baynes thought this impossible. According to the chart, which was out of date and inaccurate, no land should have been visible in that quarter: it was in fact the Peninsula de Tres Montes, which encloses the northern side of the Golfo de Penas. No one appreciated the fact at the time, but the *Wager* was already embayed and the wind was now due west.

That afternoon those fit enough, who included Bulkeley, then officer of the watch, were aloft resecuring the foreyard when the gunner saw the land himself. Quickly realizing the vessel was compromised he called Cheap, and it took the dozen fit men three hours to wear the ship round onto the starboard tack. But although their head now lay to the south-west they had lost ground to leeward in wearing, and were still making leeway. At this point Cheap was washed down the deck by a green sea and dislocated his shoulder 'soe that the head of the Bone came down below his Armpit'. He was carried below to the surgeon. Mortified at his injury and ignoring Clark, whom he considered quite incompetent, he gave instructions to Baynes and Bulkeley: they must make an offing and should set the maintopsail.

The darkness of night and the extremity of their predicament were made more fearful by torrential rain out of a heavy overcast. The *Wager* was carrying her foresail, mainsail and a mizen staysail, but Bulkeley found it impossible to set the main topsail and let Cheap know as the ship made good a course of roughly due south. Bulkeley relieved Baynes again at four in the morning and found the ship's head at west; perhaps they had a chance, though the howling wind and the very darkness seemed to conspire against them. Half an hour later, the *Wager*'s stern struck a rock with a jarring of the hull. She lifted to an incoming sea and, when the lead was cast, appeared to be in fourteen fathoms. Cheap told them to anchor, but a moment later the ship struck again, the tiller carried away and the ship was driven over on her side and swept by heavy seas. As she pounded, the fluke of a heavy bower anchor being carried in her hold for the *Centurion* was driven through her bottom; then she lifted to another sea and was carried clear. With considerable presence of mind Bulkeley ordered the mainsail clewed up and let the ship run off under her foresail. With Cummins reporting water rising in the hold and the *Wager*'s rudder uncontrollable, Bulkeley had only the forebraces and sheets with which to attempt to steer and decided they must drive the vessel ashore.

All hands capable of doing so had now dragged themselves on deck; those incapacitated by scurvy were destined to drown in their hammocks. One of the former, John Jones, a master's mate, exhorted the men as the dawn revealed them to be tearing downwind amid a chaos of rocks and foaming breakers where the Southern Ocean drove itself against the Patagonian coast. Some were stupefied with terror, others helped Jones and Bulkeley; one man ran amok with a cutlass and had to be knocked down. For a while they ran unscathed, and then with a monstrous shudder the *Wager* drove ashore in a cleft between two rocks. She lifted once and then, her sides bilged, she settled; the rock to windward of them broke the worst of the seas, but water poured into her hold and lower deck.

Daylight revealed the mainland not far off: 'Some expressions [of gratitude] were uttered; but oaths and execrations greatly prevailed,' wrote the cooper afterwards. Under Bulkeley, who had taken charge, they managed to launch the cutter, the yawl and the barge, many of the indisposed finding a new lease of life now that death confronted them. The first boat party under Master's Mate John Snow landed and refused to return to the ship. Baynes commanded the second in the yawl, and although the yawl returned, Baynes, in direct defiance of Cheap's orders, did not. With Lieutenant Baynes absent from his duty and Cheap confined by the surgeon and his injury, active command fell upon Bulkeley, who was at least competent to exercise it. Once the majority of the hands had been got ashore, Cheap and the army officers left the ship. Others attempted to save what they could; a few, under the boatswain King, remained and raided the spirit store. Discipline disintegrated with the *Wager* herself.

As these things will in a tight-knit community like a ship, it had quickly become common knowledge that Cheap was endangering the ship by tacking too soon to the northwards. Bulkeley made this known and now, notwithstanding Cheap's sad and painful condition, word ran through the nervous and frightened men that his intransigence had directly caused the disaster. It was a fact not lost on the men that Bulkeley had counselled against the captain's proposed action, while the un-reliability of Baynes and Clark were condemned throughout the ship. To this the jeremiahs among them would have added two more doom-laden considerations. First, they were cast away in a remote and desolate area which, if it was capable of offering them anything, was likely to produce either hostile 'Indians' or equally hostile Spanish. And secondly, their pay stopped with the loss of their ship, a matter of great significance to men frightened for their lives and already weakened by scurvy. Under such conditions discipline was too fragile to be maintained for long and as Midshipman Campbell reported when attempting to persuade those left aboard to leave the wreck, 'I . . . found them all in such Confusion as cannot be imagined . . . Some were singing Psalms, others fighting, others swearing, and some lay Drunk on the Deck. Seeing them in this strange Disorder, I spoke not a Word to any Body, but observing some Casks of Ball and Powder on the Quarter-deck, I began to put them into the Boat; whereupon two of the Men came to me, crying "Damn ye! You shall not have them, for the Ship is lost and it is ours." A third came with a Bayonet swearing he would kill me . . . [throwing] the Bayonet at me, but miss'd his mark, and I immediately got into the yawl and returned to the Shore.'

What had been the ship's company of HMS *Wager* now disintegrated into factions under the influence of the personalities which strove to exert influence. Cheap had been found accommodation in a small abandoned hut erected by the indigenous population, who came in due course to stare at the castaways, and here he tried to maintain his status as a post-captain, propped up by some of his officers and Captain Pemberton of the infantry. To some extent the maintenance of his distinction in rank worked to Cheap's disadvantage, for it automatically alienated the seamen – as did their knowledge that the pay of both commissioned and warrant officers continued, though theirs did not. The argument that the men's pay had ceased was aired, but countered by a contrary obligation that it remained the duty of all hands to look after government property, which included the boats and whatever they might salvage from the *Wager* as she slowly broke up under the onslaught of the sea, most importantly the tools, chandlery, rope, timber, oil, flour, wine and salted provisions. This imperative was to some extent frustrated by Boatswain

King, however, who remained on board with a handful of men, all drinking to excess and vandalizing the ship. When the weather again worsened King demanded to be taken ashore, but the surf was too bad to launch a boat – whereupon he fired two shots at Cheap's refuge from a quarterdeck-gun.

Meanwhile, as the cold wind and intermittent rain only added to the general misery and hunger, attempts were made to organize an encampment, which soon included the inverted cutter, in addition to Cheap's refuge. The men began what was to become a daily routine, foraging for shellfish and a wild celery that was found to bring rapid relief to the symptoms of all but the most advanced cases of scurvy. Several of the officers had saved muskets, and in the succeeding days shot wild fowl and even the crows that fed on the battered corpses that were coming ashore from the wreck. One ship's boy had to be restrained from eating the liver of a sailor that lay exposed by a gash in the dead man's side. Meanwhile a store tent was erected and put under the guard of the midshipmen. Cheap's injury was much improved and with Hamilton, the purser and the surgeon, all of them under arms, he ensured that what Bulkeley brought ashore was safely stowed away. But there was no issue of rations, and the men were left to fend for themselves. Almost immediately thefts from the common stock began, and the midshipmen charged with guarding it at night were already exhausted from the day's work of getting provisions out of the wreck.

The *Wager* was now almost submerged, except for her extremities, her remains now lying so low that on the 20th, by cutting away the bulwarks, they managed to float the longboat off the chocks in the waist and haul it ashore. That same day Boatswain King came ashore drunk and in looted finery. Cheap met him, raised his cane, and beat King to his knees, then threatened him with a pistol; King abased himself, and Cheap contemptuously let him go. That day they received their first visit from the Patagonians, who paddled into the bay and traded some mussels and two dogs for some cloth, wine, a hat each and a soldier's uniform. The dogs were roasted and enjoyed, but the worst scurvy cases were irreversible and death was hastened by exposure and hunger.

On 25 May, eleven days after the wreck, Cheap authorized the first issue of provisions, two days later Lieutenant Baynes, reappeared. Cheap dismissed Baynes, believing that the first lieutenant could have saved the ship if he had hoisted the main-topsail. Baynes vacillated in his loyalty, but his chief interest lay in saving his own skin. Cheap's insistence upon meeting any salvage party and taking from them under threat of armed force what they had brought ashore was greatly resented by the more moderate of the men. None of these circumstances improved the situation, and beyond securing the stores and provisions Cheap seems not to have exerted any real leadership, nor made any attempt to mollify the fears of his men. Instead the role of leader gravitated towards the most resourceful and energetic among them: emerging as the most naturally dominant was John Bulkeley.

On 3 June, as most of the men were recovering hogsheads, bales and odd items from the beach, where the prevailing westerly gale and its accompanying rain had driven them, ten deserted. They were all bad hats; one was suspected of murder, and an informer told Cheap that they had hatched a plan to blow him up with a keg of powder, a trail of which was found laid. They made themselves another camp some miles away, and Bulkeley tried to persuade them to return for he needed the skills of Armourer Russell and Carpenter's Mate Oram. Securing a pardon for these two from Cheap, Bulkeley concerted a plan with Cummins to enlarge the longboat.

On Sunday 7 June the work of getting stores out of the fast-breaking-up hull of the *Wager* went on, not without deep resentments. Midshipman Cozens was having difficulty rolling a cask of dried peas up the steep beach, and stopping near Cheap complained of the labour in an impudent manner. He had taken a drink while aboard the wreck, and Cheap accused him of being intoxicated. Cozens was a popular young man with a normally equable temperament, but drink made him cantankerous; to impudence he now added insolence and refused to move the cask, bawling out for help from the men. He then told Cheap to 'Remember Captain Shelvocke.'

Cheap struck Cozens with his cane, provoking a torrent of abuse, whereupon he had Cozens confined in a tent under one of Pemberton's soldiers. Going to Cozens later that evening Cheap found him still abusive; Cozens concluded his diatribe with a scathing denunciation of his commanding officer: 'Though Shelvocke was a rogue, he was not a fool,' Cozens railed, 'and by God, you are both!'

Cheap was about to strike Cozens again but the soldier remonstrated, and in due course he released the midshipman, blaming the outrage on alcohol. Two days later Cozens was drunk again and swore at the surgeon, William Elliot, who rounded on him and tied his hands behind his back. Next day Cozens approached Thomas Harvey, the purser, about a man's rations, and Harvey nervously raised a loaded pistol and fired. Only the quick action of Young, the cooper, in knocking up Harvey's arm prevented immediate bloodshed, but the shot alerted all hands, and as Harvey shouted 'Cozens is come to kill us!' Lieutenant Hamilton, who had been with Cheap, rushed out of the hut bawling, 'Mutiny!' with Cheap behind him crying, 'Where is the villain?'

Cozens immediately swung on the captain, and when he was within arm's length Cheap shot him. With Cozens bleeding, conscious but unable to speak through a shattered jaw, Cheap mustered all hands. 'I have sent for you to let you know that I am still your commander and intend to remain your commander. Let every man go to his own tent.'

The surgeon refused to operate on Cozens, so his mate asked the army surgeon to assist; but Cheap refused permission, and the surgeon's mate, also named Elliot, extracted the ball from beneath Cozens' eye. Cheap thereafter refused Cozens any care, saying 'if he lives, I will carry him a Prisoner to the Commodore, and hang him.' The wretched Cozens lingered until 24 June when he died, raving. The lack of care for Cozens outraged the seamen, and far from proving Cheap steadfast in his respect for discipline only distanced him further from the crew, in particular Bulkeley and Cummins. Cozens had been widely liked and, as the cooper wrote, though 'a conceited busy fellow, that was not a sufficient Reason for Killing him.' There is circumstantial evidence that Cozens had been manipulated and set up as a champion of the men by King, who knew what he was like with spirits inside him. To his note of the death and burial of Cozens, Bulkeley added: 'There have died sundry Ways since the Ship first struck, forty-five Men; seven have deserted from us, and still continue away; [there] remain and now victual'd one hundred Men.' Midshipman Byron recorded that Cozens' death 'contributed to lessen [Cheap] in the regard of the people.' Overall Byron was loyal to Cheap, but he is the most disinterested of the account writers, and also a more penetrating psychologist than his commander. Though they 'disguised their real sentiments for the present, [the men] were extremely affected at this catastrophe of Mr Cozens . . . '

From this point thefts from the stores increased, exacerbating the breakdown in order. Every man's hand appeared to be turned against his shipmate, and incidents occurred daily – Bulkeley 'turned the Boatswain out of our Tent for breeding Quarrels', while two marines caught stealing each received 400 lashes spread over two days. Food and warmth became the preoccupations of everyone: the privations endured upon that hostile shore are almost unimaginable. Men were still dying, one, John Anderson, from falling into the sea while foraging for limpets. Boatswain's Mate Phipps had a lucky escape when the raft upon which he was hunting duck capsized. He managed to scramble to a rock, but it was two days before another wildfowling party in the yawl found him, frozen half to death.

All the while Cummins and the tradesmen were engaged in lengthening and decking the longboat. This task occupied many weeks of patient skill, and was perhaps the most marvellous accomplishment of those wretched and divided men. On Thursday 30 July 'departed this Life Nathaniel Robinson, the last private Man of the Invalids . . . ' – that is to say, the

Greenwich pensioners. The same day Bulkeley formed the opinion that the only means of escape lay in making a voyage in the longboat east through the Straits of Magellan and then north to Brazil. Cheap, meanwhile, if he was meditating anything was considering making an attack on the nearest Spanish settlement or heading for the rendezvous with Anson off Socorro – never mind the fact that the appointed time was long past. Bulkeley by contrast was drafting an agreement to be made by those who volunteered to accompany him on his proposed passage to Brazil, for he was aware of the need for some sort of legal framework to relieve the survivors from the burden of duty and enable them to exercise their right to save their own lives. Most signed it, including the midshipmen and Pemberton and his colleagues; only the warrant officers close to Cheap did not. Then a deputation led by Bulkeley took the document to Cheap, who considered the matter for two days before returning it, claiming it had given him sleepless nights as he worried over the danger of the passage they were contemplating. Cheap, perhaps chillingly reminded again of Shelvocke, was all for seizing a Spanish vessel at Valdivia, but Cummins remonstrated with him, and Cheap's resistance provoked the comment that they were in this grimmest of situations because of his – Cheap's – refusal to listen to his officers – meaning Bulkeley. He stopped just short of accusing Cheap of incompetence, but the captain took refuge in only himself knowing the contents of his secret orders; it was pathetic. It was also the end.

For a few weeks there was a stand-off as work progressed on the longboat; at the same time, the stores were perceptibly diminishing. Beyond what they could forage, they were staring at starvation. Matters degenerated further, and argument and counter-argument wore round in circles. Bulkeley and Cummins did not trust Cheap once he was afloat; they were determined to work south, he to go north; there was some evidence that Cheap was attempting to suborn some of Bulkeley's party by means of drink issued by the purser. Bulkeley drew up another 'paper', an agreement that it was their intention 'to go from this Place through the Streights of Magellan, for the Coast of Brazil, in our Way for England', and expressing his anxiety that 'We do, notwithstanding, find the People separating into Parties, which must consequently end in the Destruction of the whole Body.' He added, for good measure, that 'as also there have been great robberies committed on the Stores, and everything is now at a Stand; therefore, to prevent all future Frauds and Animosities, we are unanimously agreed to proceed as above-mentioned.' To secure this unanimity Baynes was presented with the paper and asked to secure Cheap's signature.

Quite uncharacteristically, Baynes now declared himself uncertain of the captain's intentions, and proposed that they put him under arrest for the killing of Cozens. With the approbation of the people he would then assume command, whereupon their 'affairs will be concluded to the satisfaction of the whole company, without being any longer liable to the obstruction they now meet from the captain's perverseness and chicanery.' Baynes also stirred up an animus against the purser, as Cheap's creature; in sight of the winning horse, he was backing heavily.

The matter came to a head on 28 August at Cheap's hut. Some matters relating to the punishment of two marines for theft had been dealt with and all were expecting Baynes to raise the matter of Cheap's agreement to the proposal; he did nothing. Cheap however appeared to give a lead, saying that it was no time to dispute the way home when they were in no position to proceed. He protested his indifference to the route, claiming that he had no plan himself beyond a concern for 'the welfare of all. Whichever way you go I will take my fate with you.'

Again there was silence then Bulkeley took a copy of the paper, read it out and asked Cheap to sign it, upon which Cheap lost his temper and closed the meeting. As they withdrew the delegates proceeded to Captain Pemberton's tent. The military officer was not impressed by Cheap, and suggested that although not a naval officer himself, he thought that Cheap could be supplanted by Baynes, and that he would support such a move. The idea was greeted by cheers that brought Cheap out of his hut, to be again confronted by Bulkeley and the others. He asked whether Baynes would deprive him of his command, and the first lieutenant denied it. There was some shilly-shallying and then Cheap summoned Bulkeley and confronted him with a pistol. The gunner withdrew sharply and sent a message that he would not negotiate with an armed man, despite the fact that those outside were armed. Cheap tossed aside the pistol and emerged from his hut.

An agreement in principle was reached and the day ended affably, the men having been promised an increase in the brandy ration, though all the officers knew supplies would not last long. Meanwhile, as trivial but provocative incidents exacerbated the delicate situation, they received another visit from the Patagonians, and work on the longboat proceeded. The stores were almost gone, and two of the deserters came in requesting pardon. On 6 September marines again robbed the stores, then fled before they could be caught. Two days later a group of men agreed to sail in the yawl 'for the Easement of the boat now building'. On the 24th Bulkeley left in the barge to carry out a survey to the south. He returned four days later to find factions re-forming, 'the debate of which', as Midshipman Byron noted 'generally ended in riot and drunkenness.' Worse, Baynes informed Bulkeley that Cheap had changed his mind, and intended to enforce his authority. There was nothing more than that – no plan – and Cheap's latest volte-face appeared to have antagonized all but Lieutenant Hamilton of the marines.

The longboat was almost completed but Cheap now made difficulties over storing it; in particular, he refused to issue any gunpowder, on the grounds that it was Crown property and in his particular charge. It was now that Captain Pemberton addressed them to the effect that they would be within the law to arrest Cheap for the murder of Cozens, and indeed that it was a duty laid upon him (Pemberton), failure in which would lay him open to account; moreover, they might all by their passivity be deemed accessory to the foul deed. The matter was carried, its purpose concealed from Cheap. Baynes was in full acquiescence, and early on 9 October Cheap and Hamilton were arrested, the latter as a preventive measure. His hands bound, Cheap poured vilification on them all. Boatswain King, whom Cheap had struck, responded with a torrent of abuse. Cheap then called for Baynes, who informed him with his characteristic courage that he was acting upon Captain Pemberton's orders. Cheap then said that he would not go south on any account, and was confined with Hamilton.

There was no unanimity over the arrest of Cheap. John Young, the cooper, thought that Bulkeley and Cummins, 'the principal Agitators in the Project of going homewards through the Streights', although 'influenc'd by honest Motives . . . to engage the Captain to act as the common Interest required', ought not to have laid 'violent Hands upon him'. Young considered this to be 'altogether indefensible, it was undeniably an illegal mutinous Procedure.'

On Monday 12 October the enlarged longboat was launched and named the *Speedwell*, with or without conscious irony is not known. At noon next day, with fifty-nine men aboard, a further dozen in the cutter and ten in the barge, the little flotilla set sail. To the end Cheap ridiculed their plan, spoke of going north to meet Commodore Anson, and deplored a scheme that would certainly 'lead so many brave fellows to face ten thousand difficulties'. The first of these presented itself before they had cleared Wager Bay, when the *Speedwell*'s little topsail split – but it did not deter them. Cheap had taunted them with prospect of a hanging, to which Bulkeley had replied that he would rather be hanged in England after being tried and found guilty of any crime than go northward and risk the worse fate of a Spanish prison.

They sailed under Articles which condemned David Cheap, giving reasons for their disaffection, and bound them in due obedience to Baynes as a matter of form. Hamilton and William Elliot, the surgeon, remained with Cheap, more because they were apprehensive about the voyage than out of loyalty, and the yawl was left with them. They were later joined by some of the deserters, whom Cheap pardoned. Bulkeley also left behind a substantial share of what remained of the provisions. Incredibly, after all the rancour between them, Bulkeley and Cheap apparently parted with a 'melting Farewell' and, Young went on to say, 'To hear Bulkeley's moving Account, you would have thought he was painting the last Separation of David and Jonathan.'

The voyage started with a series of trials. During one the barge was sent back for some canvas which had been left behind; in it were Midshipmen Byron and Campbell, the latter of whom suggested that they should return to Cheap and take their chance with him. Motivated by self-preservation or, in Byron's case it seems, loyalty, they all agreed. 'The Conduct of these people surpriz'd and vexed' those in the *Speedwell* and the cutter.

The little *Speedwell*'s crew made an incredible voyage, enduring extreme hardships, 'encountering everything that was most terrible: the furious Waves frequently threatening to overwhelm us; the Rocks often menacing immediate Destruction; and the Prospect of the horridest Tormentor, Famine, continually before our Eyes. All these impending Evils . . . enhanc'd by the indolent listless Temper of some among us, who were, thro' Fatigue and Despair, become regardless of Life, and could scarcely be moved to do any Thing toward their own Preservation; or by the Inquietude and Turbulence of others, who were ready to Mutiny, tho' they had hardly Room to breath[e], if their brutal Demands were not instantly satisfied.

'Add to this, that being so closely pent up, the Steams of our Bodies and filthy wet Apparel infected the Air about us to such a Degree, that it was almost intolerable, and enough to cause a Pestilence.'

The appalling conditions encouraged discontent and a querulous mood prevailed, exacerbated by separation and the loss of the accompanying cutter. A few days later, on 8 November, a number of men apparently requested to be left ashore with their portion of the provisions to take their chance either of finding the cutter or returning to the north. Bulkeley drew up another document saying they departed of their own free will, which they all signed, though there is more than a hint of coercion in the Gunner's account. Despite the reduction in the party there were still sixty men in the *Speedwell* when on the 10th they entered the Straits of Magellan. They were by now reduced to the utmost privation; men and boys were daily dying of starvation, and though they bartered a little with the Tierra del Fuegans they acquired insufficient food to restore them to health as they wound their way through the tortuous passage, losing ten days by following a dead end.

A week later, however, they were through, and on 16 December they reached Seal Island, where they killed more seals than they could cope with. Unfortunately, three days later the last of the flour was shared out on the insistence of the majority of the men, who were by now in a black mood. On 6 January 1742 the purser, Harvey, died, prompting Bulkeley to note that: 'He died a Skeleton for want of Food. This Gentleman probably was the first Purser belonging to his Majesty's Service, that ever perished with Hunger.' Clark, the master, followed a week later; by this time Bulkeley was lamenting that they had only 'stinking seal' on which to subsist. Sighting land, they anchored in what they named Freshwater Bay, and a party swam through the surf and hunted seals, some of which were hauled off to the *Speedwell*. But an onshore wind then sprang up and 'forced' Bulkeley and the others to send a cask ashore filled with 'all manner of Necessaries' before heading out to sea with those on shore making 'Signals wishing us well'.

On 18 January they landed again and made contact with some fishermen, receiving some 'good Jurk-Beef . . . with good white Bread', and on the 28th the thirty remaining men landed on the shores of the Rio Grande in Portuguese territory and were given every assistance by the governor of the province. They had made a passage of over 2,000 miles during which, Bulkeley opined 'no Mortals have experienc'd more Difficulties and Miseries than we have.' Certainly it was a remarkable feat of endurance. In due course and after prolonged delays most of the survivors took passage to Rio de Janeiro and then to Lisbon from where they were repatriated aboard HMS *Stirling Castle,* arriving on 1 January 1743. Baynes arrived home a little earlier and made his deposition on the loss of the *Wager*.

Meanwhile, although the Austral summer was well advanced the loyalist party endured more bad weather on Wager Island, and it was mid-December before they set off north in the barge under Cheap and the yawl under Hamilton. They were in trouble almost immediately, before they had doubled Capo Tres Montes, and lost the yawl along with one man. Those remaining were too many to be accommodated in the barge, and four marines were left ashore by Cheap. Their condition was apparently so poor that they put up no resistance to the prospect of death. But even now they were unable to make much progress, and dispiritedly they returned to their encampment, where a fortnight later they were befriended by some Patagonians. One of these men, whom they knew as Martin, agreed to lead them north. He wore a cross and appeared to hold some authority derived from the Spanish, he was deferential to Cheap, who enjoyed much better rations, but did not extend any liberality or courtesy to the others, a fact which was deeply resented, particularly by Hamilton, Byron and Campbell. Cheap appeared to revel in their discomfiture, and such was the unhappiness this engendered that six men deserted, taking with them the barge. By the time the party reached Chiloe in native canoes the remaining men had died, including the surgeon, leaving only these four alive.

Received kindly at Chiloe they were conducted on to Castro, Chaco and Valparaiso. Not having commissions, Campbell and Byron were here imprisoned, while Cheap and Hamilton were paroled and taken on to Santiago. Cheap eventually secured the midshipmen's release and they too joined their commander in Santiago, where for many months they enjoyed a not uncongenial life. The handsome Byron in particular benefited from the company of the ladies, who showed 'a strong disposition to gallantry'. Cheap was by now manifesting more signs of paranoia and began to ostracize Campbell, believing him to be attached to a young woman and contemplating marriage and baptism into the Roman Catholic church – anathema to a naval officer of the day. Cheap expressed his displeasure by giving Campbell only a paltry share of the money he had drawn against the English consul in Lisbon, far less than he advanced to Byron. Campbell, both furious and humiliated, detached himself from Cheap and went overland to Buenos Ayres with four Spanish naval officers to travel home in a Spanish man-of-war. Cheap, Hamilton and Byron embarked in a French warship, the *Lys*, in December 1744, arriving in London in October the following year. When Campbell finally followed he found that Cheap had, publicly and quite unjustly, accused him of having defected and joined the Spanish navy; apparently Cheap's rancour knew no bounds.

Cheap's return home stirred up a hornet's nest. Following the common practice, all the survivors were court-martialled for the loss of their ship. By being the first of the *Wager*'s people to arrive in England, Baynes had managed to exonerate himself – a talent for which seems to have been his only accomplishment – laying much of the blame upon Bulkeley and Cummins; who when they received their summons, thought they were to be executed. Bulkeley had already received Admiralty permission to publish his journal, which had generated public animosity against both him and Cummins, particularly in attracting the curious charge that they had stolen Crown property in the form of the longboat – refuted by the equally curious argument that they had, on Cheap's orders, 'destroyed' the longboat by cutting it in half. By this argument the resurrected and enlarged *Speedwell* was essentially a new and different craft. There matters stood for some time. Bulkeley had actually obtained the command of a privateer and was in action in her in the Channel when the notice of the impending court martial arrived at his lodgings, and news of it came as something of a surprise to him.

The court was convened aboard the *Prince George* at Spithead in April 1746 with Vice Admiral Steuart as president; he was principally concerned with arguments as to whether the *Wager* could have been saved. In its findings the court exonerated Cheap and his officers and crew for her loss, only reprimanding Baynes, the one officer against whom Cheap laid a charge, for not having informed him when land was sighted, and for failing to anchor when ordered to do so. The court clearly appreciated the dreadful condition of the *Wager* and the sick state of her crew, both of which were an embarrassment to the navy, and this undoubtedly influenced their acquittal of the *Wager*'s people. It is probably material to the case that by this time Anson, now a peer, had joined the Board of Admiralty (and had in fact signed Bulkeley's letter of marque and reprisal for the command of his privateer). Knowing well, as he did, the ship's condition and the circumstances in which she was lost, he may well have exerted some influence on the outcome. Significantly, the proceedings made no mention of mutiny; in the event Cheap proffered no charges, and made no objection to his arrest by his crew. There had been dark mutterings over the precedent of the officers of HMS *Ruby* arresting their captain after he committed a murder, so Cheap was compelled to let the matter drop. He had little to complain of. His acting promotion by Anson of 19 February 1741 was confirmed, and had he lived he would have climbed to flag rank; but he expired in July 1752, outlived by the discredited Baynes who died, still a lieutenant and on half-pay, in 1755. Byron was perhaps the most successful of this dismal bunch; by 1746 he had himself been promoted post-captain and in command of the *Dolphin* made a circumnavigation with the intention of surveying *Terra Australis*. He failed, and it was left to Cook to do so a decade later. By 1779 Byron was a vice-admiral, and fought an inconclusive engagement off Grenada with a French squadron under D'Estaing. Wherever he went his ships invariably encountered bad weather and he acquired the soubriquet of 'Foul-weather Jack', so perhaps he too was dogged by Kidd's curse of the *Wager*. Luckiest perhaps of the survivors was Midshipman Isaac Morris, one of those left by Baynes, Bulkeley and their 'licentious crew' in the *Speedwell* when they deserted the landing party in Freshwater Bay. He eventually succeeded in reaching home, and published his memoirs in 1755.

So were the actions of the *Wager*'s disaffected and ship-wrecked crew mutinous? Clearly legal opinion at the time thought not; it was considered that the cessation of their pay ended the obligation of the crew to their officers. In one of its more facile judgments history has anathematized the event as 'the *Wager* mutiny', whereas the importance of the incident lies in its consequences: within a short space of time three Acts of Parliament had been passed which bound the ship-wrecked crews of men-of-war to naval discipline and allowed them the continuation of their pay. As a curious footnote to this, it was not until 1943, at the height of the Battle of the Atlantic, when sinkings of merchant ships in convoy were high and morale among their crews correspondingly low, that the same duties and rights were extended to the seamen of the merchant service.

But other matters flowed from Anson's voyage and the loss of the *Wager*. As First Lord of the Admiralty Anson began a radical overhaul of the Royal Navy comparable with that undertaken by Pepys in the previous century. As well as the acts referred to above and the introduction of new Articles of War in 1749, there were other measures aimed at reform in the Dockyards, standardization of ship classes and equipment, and the overhaul of the organization of the fleet. Although the new Articles of War were in part a consequence of disorder in a British fleet off Toulon in 1744 analogous to the behaviour of Benbow's captains, most of the reforms carried out during Anson's period at the Admiralty were the direct outcome of his experiences in course of his circumnavigation.

5

'I AM IN HELL'

IT was inactivity that cost Cheap the respect, and ultimately the loyalty, of his people. Despite the psychological damage caused to him by the loss of the *Wager*, his lack of a plan and his procrastination passed the initiative to Bulkeley, the most assertive and pragmatic natural leader among his crew. As for the rest, once they had overcome the shock of desolation and learned how to scratch the means of subsistence from their bleak environment, they were sufficiently fortified to consider escape from their predicament and return to the world they knew. Cheap had, in effect, relinquished command, and his conduct would not stand close examination. With this in mind, he dropped the threatened charges of mutiny against Bulkeley and his close associates.

Many years later Admiral Sir Charles Napier declared a man-o'-war's crew to be the 'the devil in harbour' – where the bonds of discipline were relaxed and the demands of the ship lessened. It was up to an efficient captain to find tasks to occupy his men (not usually very difficult) and to prevent any injustices, real or imagined, taking too firm a grasp upon the crew's collective imagination and causing that 'combination' which seethed amid discontentment and preceded mutiny. In short, inactivity on the part of a commander might in itself precipitate rebellion and this was the more likely if the crew were left in idleness. It was this fatal conjunction, not the tyranny of a sadistic commander, that caused the most notorious mutiny in history: that, and the infamous conduct of a friend.

The mutiny aboard the *Bounty* has achieved a curious life of its own which would bear a closer examination by historiographers rather than historians. The way it has been manipulated to establish one agenda or another is of passing interest. In the 1830s Sir John Barrow, a long-serving and highly influential member of the British Admiralty's secretariat, employed it to anathematize the practice of rebellion against established authority. A century later Hollywood used the story to exemplify British tyranny – from which of course the United States had freed itself – though to ensure that the film did not offend too many audiences across the then British Empire, it concluded with a brief explanation of how such tyranny had been rooted out and, within a few years, the Royal Navy had defeated Napoleon and saved European civilization. As we shall see, greater tyrannies than that imputed to the wretched Bligh existed well into the era of Nelson; and despite the grandiloquence of Barrow's title, his *Eventful History of the Mutiny and Piratical Seizure of HMS 'Bounty'* fell short of its promise to reveal the mutiny's causes, even if it did dwell upon its consequences.

The real causes of the mutiny were very far removed from tyranny, and the first blame must be laid at the door of the Admiralty itself. Though Barrow so described her, the *Bounty* was not, at least in the strictest sense of the words, one of His Majesty's Ships. Technically that title belonged to a man-of-war, and the *Bounty*, like Cook's *Endeavour* and other vessels sent on special voyages, was an armed transport, a converted merchantman, the *Bethia*. As is well known, she had been fitted out to collect breadfruit plants in Tahiti and transfer them for replanting in the West Indies, where they were intended to provide a cheap nutritious food for slaves. To this end her officers' accommodation had been co-opted, thus reducing their living space – a small but significant niggle among other niggles that eventually culminated in full-scale mutiny.

The Admiralty was not keen on the *Bounty*'s mission, which King George III had been moved to initiate by a petition from merchants and planters with interests in the West Indies. Mindful of the cost of refitting the ship, the Admiralty and the Dockyard officers at Deptford skimped where they could on other expenses the Royal Navy was compelled to bear. One of these was in her manning: Their Lordships failed to appoint William Bligh a Commander. He had expected such an appointment, and it would have elevated the *Bounty* to equivalent status with a sloop-of-war, and given him two subordinate lieutenants to support him. The Admiralty had experienced difficulties in the command structure in earlier distant water expeditions. In the last years of the previous century their lordships had specially commissioned William Dampier to the *Roebuck* and Edmond Halley to the *Paramore*. Neither had been regular naval officers, both had been specially promoted on the basis of their expertises and both had fallen out with their first lieutenants, Dampier seriously and, (for him) catastrophically. By the late 1780s these precedents had been long forgotten, obscured by Cook's great successes. It was true that Cook had only been a lieutenant on his first voyage – but then Cook was a different man, a strong and dominant personality to whom lack of official status mattered little: 'he was our leader to whom we looked for everything,' Surgeon's Mate Samwell wrote aboard the *Resolution*. As in Halley's case, and most definitely in Dampier's, character was all: Bligh's character, or perhaps lack of it, was one of the factors that contributed to the trouble on the *Bounty*. In the event, Bligh was the sole commissioned officer on board his ship, saddled with a command structure far too flat to withstand shocks on such a voyage. It also isolated him, augmenting the traditional loneliness of a commander, and this in turn exacerbated the negative aspects of Bligh's personality.

Bligh was not in much doubt that he could expect neither patronage nor promotion from anything but his own unadorned endeavours; not to make too much of the pun, by this time in his life Bligh probably felt himself to be a blighted man. Promotion was of itself desirable; the failure of the Admiralty to commission him commander particularly irked him for another reason. He had been of valuable assistance to Cook on the great explorer's final, fatal voyage, particularly as a surveyor. In the aftermath of Cook's death, when the command passed to Lieutenant King, Bligh's contribution to the expedition's successes and his justifiable claims to subsequent recognition and advancement had been lost. It is clear that this rankled greatly.

All this simmered behind the fitting-out of the *Bounty* – and in this, in Bligh's words, the 'Government . . . have gone too frugally to work . . .' But being the man he was, once under way he did his best to rectify the deficiencies. His attempt to beef up the command structure by promoting his friend and protégé Fletcher Christian to the rank of acting lieutenant might, had they not fallen out, have had the desired result of distancing Bligh from small routine problems. As it was, Christian was self-serving, and lacked both backbone and loyalty; like many who receive a mark of favour, he became critical of his benefactor.

The deliberately assigned lowly status of the *Bounty* as a transport under a lieutenant-in-command also meant that the Admiralty were not obliged to assign a detachment of marines to her. It was not a mistake they made again, but in Bligh's case the decision deprived him of the strong arm of law-enforcement. Apart from acting as a man-of-war's police and maintaining sentries, the marines messed and slept betwixt crew and officers. A full-blown mutiny required the suborning of the marines if it was to succeed; if they were not there, so much the better.

Though he lacked commissioned officers Bligh was supported by several warrant officers, of whom the master was the most important. Mr Fryer was a not particularly distinguished sailing master, however, certainly not as efficient as Bligh himself had been while serving in that rank on Cook's last voyage, and there-fore vulnerable to criticism from a man who could not only do his job better, but did not scruple to say so. Fryer's lack of zeal was one of the reasons why Bligh leap-frogged him in appointing Christian acting lieutenant, for initially Christian was one of Fryer's two master's mates. Bligh's decision to favour Christian was only in part nepotistic, for they were friends and had sailed together in a merchant ship, the *Britannia*, which Bligh had commanded. Aboard the *Britannia* Bligh had observed Christian's practical abilities and gone to great trouble to teach him navigation and seamanship, of which he was a master, eventually signing Christian on as his second mate. Each therefore knew the other to be a competent and experienced seaman, and they were familiar with one another's method and style. Bligh relied upon this previous bond, but was to be cruelly let down. For his part, Fryer resented being passed over.

In addition to this trio, Huggan the surgeon turned out to be a drunkard, something that could have been discovered before the voyage, had anyone checked, while Mr Purcell the carpenter seems to have been a knowall. Other members of the crew were either of little help, particularly the young and inexperienced midshipmen, or of strong character. The former had been taken on by Bligh to ingratiate himself with their families, for he was ambitious and they, in peacetime, were desperate to enter the navy and advance their careers. As for the strong characters, under a weak command structure they soon found themselves engaged in trials of strength with Bligh himself.

A disciple of Cook insofar as he was able, Bligh took particular care of his small crew of 46 officers and men – which was just as well, for numerous delays meant they did not sail from Spithead until 23 December 1787. Bligh was now short of time, for he had been advised by David Nelson, the expedition's botanist and breadfruit expert, that there was only short period of time favourable to taking aboard his strange cargo in Tahiti. He therefore settled for the direct route to Tahiti, and in consequence found himself attempting to double Cape Horn in the teeth of the prevailing westerly gales at almost the worst season of the year. Christian had been promoted by this time, and on 10 March 1788 Matthew Quintal had been given two dozen lashes at the request of Fryer, for 'insolence and mutinous behaviour'. 'Before this,' Bligh noted in his log, 'I had not had occasion to punish any person . . .' By the standards of the time Quintal's punishment on a charge of insubordination was far from excessive, and there were others of similar lenity. One, Williams's sentence of six lashes for failing to heave the lead properly, was mild in the extreme given the importance of the task. One of Bligh's most loyal seamen, the sail-maker Lebogue, who sailed with him several times, including his subsequent voyage in the *Providence,* deposed that 'Captain Bligh was not a person fond of flogging his men and some of them deserved hanging who only got a dozen.'

By early April the *Bounty* was fighting her way round the Horn, confronted by a series of violent gales. The ship was continually beaten back, and made no westing in thirty days of unremitting struggle. 'Having maturely considered all circumstances, I have determined to bear away for the Cape of Good Hope; and at five o'clock on the evening of 22nd [April], the wind blowing strongly at west, I ordered the helm to be put a-weather, to the great joy of every person on board.' When the *Bounty* arrived at the Cape of Good Hope Bligh put in to restore and recruit his ship and crew, remaining there for 38 days. This seems a long time, and perhaps indicates a tendency on Bligh's part to excessive relaxation after the rigours of a hard passage. It is not impossible, however, that he had taken too much upon himself, and was simply exhausted. Whatever his reason, the additional loss of time was to prove fatal.

Bligh pressed on, making a similar though shorter stop in Tasmania, and the *Bounty* dropped her anchor in Cook's old anchorage in Matavai Bay on 26 October 1788. Bligh had lost only one man, James Valentine, who had died of blood-poisoning after Huggan used a dirty knife on him. He had also preserved everyone from scurvy. He knew, too, that since 'there was great probability that we should remain at Otaheite [Tahiti], it could not be expected that the intercourse of my people [i.e. the *Bounty*'s crew] with the natives should be of a very reserved nature.' Before they arrived, therefore, he ordered that every person should be examined by the surgeon, and had the satisfaction to learn, from his report, that they were all perfectly free from any venereal complaint'. Though he was naively complacent in his acceptance of a result which Huggan's incompetence rendered unreliable, Bligh's concern for the welfare of the native population does him credit. He was only too aware that miscegenation would be unavoidable, and that the innocent promiscuity of the Tahitians exposed them to infection. The sexual act was as natural to the Tahitians as taking a drink of water, and its connection with procreation imperfectly understood. Sailing months later, he noted that 'only two patients [were] on the venereal list'. None of these concerns troubled the crew or Bligh's libidinous young officers, but there is every reason to think that Huggan's examination had been superficial and inaccurate, for some weeks later he followed Valentine, succumbing to *delirium tremens*. There is some circumstantial evidence that Fletcher Christian at the very least had been receiving treatment for a venereal infection before their arrival, though whether this was advanced enough to have affected his mental stability and thus his conduct in the months ahead it is impossible to say.

What is certain is that Bligh failed to maintain discipline in any way during the long enforced stay at anchor while he waited patiently for Nelson to nurture the saplings of *Artocarpus Altilis*, the breadfruit tree. Apart from refitting the *Bounty* and setting his men to work on any of the multifarious tasks a ship demands of her crew, he might have sent surveying parties to further Cook's work. As it was he seems to have fallen victim to a calenture, perhaps a minor breakdown resulting from his position of isolation, while his crew indulged themselves to excess for a period of six months.

Incidents of indiscipline ought to have warned Bligh of impending trouble; for example, the ship's corporal Churchill and two able seamen, Muspratt and Millward, deserted with one of the ship's boats and some small arms stolen while Midshipman

Haywood was on watch at night. Haywood was turned before the mast and the three men, brought back 17 days later, were flogged, but not severely. Another man was flogged for striking a Tahitian and, perhaps worst of all, Fryer forgot to wind the essential chronometer, and the boatswain failed to air the sails so that they grew mildewed, a fatal condition for flax canvas. There were other such incidents, many of which were actually Bligh's direct concern.

Apart from the suggestion that he had a minor nervous breakdown, the most probable reason for his inactivity was that he found the atmosphere of licence intolerable, though he must surely have been tempted. There is no hint that Bligh indulged himself sexually. He was sincerely attached to his wife and knew the risks he would run, but equally he was no saint and must have been prey to the imperative of lust. His only answer was to shut himself away with his books, his log, and his sense of failure at having been beaten back off the Horn and compelled to endure this interminable waiting. In a man of short temper given to violent outbursts of criticism of his subordinates at the best of times, this restraint provoked a reaction that in hindsight seems almost predictable.

Thus it was that when on Saturday 4 April 1789 the *Bounty*'s anchor was finally weighed from the sand and the coral heads of Matavai Bay, her long after-space full of potted breadfruit saplings, Bligh was unhappy because the ship's company were not smart and matters failed to run smoothly. He expressed his disgust unequivocally.

He was not the only unhappy member of the *Bounty*'s crew. Few of them wanted to leave their lovers, and chief among these was Acting Lieutenant Fletcher Christian, who had fallen in love with a Tahitian beauty who was pregnant by him. The parting from her rent Christian's heart.

The *Bounty* headed for Tonga and Bligh flogged Able Seaman Sumner, only the seventh man to be punished in 16 months. Off Annamooka the *Bounty* topped up her wood and water and replaced one breadfruit sapling, which to Nelson's horror had wilted. On Sunday 26 April they weighed and proceeded, but the following day Bligh discovered that his private stock of coconuts had been tampered with. It is an indicator of his mental condition and his obsessive nature that he should count these and notice a minor pilferage; but he was the ship's commander, and all theft aboard ship is serious, since it breaks down the notion of mutual trust and mutual inter-dependence that exists in a ship's company. After an unedifying exhibition of bad language from Bligh, Christian eventually confessed, making light of an offence that might be defined as borrowing from a friend. To Bligh, Christian's action was not merely a theft and an insulting misappropriation of his personal stores, but further evidence of the disrespect of his officers. That the culprit was Christian, his protégé and the man whom he had befriended and advanced (with every expectation of permanent promotion on Bligh's commendation) outraged Bligh's sense of honour. For him it was the last straw. He was well aware that Christian had spent more time co-habiting with his *Wahine* than attending to his duty; well aware that Christian had done little or nothing to maintain the ship or the crew's sense of discipline during the months they had lain at anchor; well aware that he had gone native and behaved no better than an unlettered seaman, becoming, in the seaman's nasty but apt phrase, 'cunt-struck'. Perhaps Bligh had thought that after the unrestricted licence they had all been allowed, the order to weigh anchor would shake them all – and the officers in particular – back into the rut of duty. If so, the casual theft by Christian of his own coconuts – practically poor Bligh's only indulgence in that period of generalized lotus-eating – was evidence to the contrary. Christian was verbally humiliated in front of all hands.

For Bligh that ended the matter; but it bit deeper into Christian than any lash upon the bare back of a common sailor. For all his uncommissioned status, Christian was a gentleman; worse, he believed himself better-born than Bligh. When Bligh sent a conciliatory invitation to dine that night, Christian pleaded an indisposition. Instead, and with an almost adolescent peevishness and naivety, he discussed making a raft and slipping overboard; in the event he is thought to have drunk too much in the company of Purcell, the carpenter, a man who would enjoy stirring up trouble out of sheer mischief. According to Lebogue, the two of them imbibed until midnight.

Christian was on deck as officer of the watch at four o'clock in the morning of 28 April. He may or may not have had a hangover. 'Just before sun-rise, Mr Christian . . . Chas. Churchill, Ship's Corporal, John Mills, Gunner's Mate and Thomas Burkitt, Seaman, came into my Cabbin [sic], while I was asleep and seizing me tyed my hands with a cord behind my back, threatening me with instant death . . .' Thus began the most notorious mutiny in history, an impulsive, foolish conflict of character, Bligh the victim of his own temper and foul tongue, Christian, ultimately the greater victim, of his own immaturity and disloyalty – immaturity because there is no doubt that he had been worked on by those strong characters in the crew who wanted to return to Tahiti where, they thought, their existences as white gods would be infinitely preferable to a life in Britain or in her Georgian navy.

Few in number, the mutineers had seized the ship while two-thirds of the crew were in their hammocks and the other officers were confined to their cabins. Planning to put Bligh into the small cutter and cast him adrift, they were surprised to find themselves confronted by a number of crew members loyal to him, and com-pelled to hoist out the larger launch. All the while Bligh, in his shirt-tails, harangued Christian, attempting to arrest the utter folly and 'change the Tide of affairs', but he was told to hold his tongue or face instant death. Eighteen loyal men were hurried into the launch. As Bligh was about to be forced over his ship's side, he asked Christian 'if this was a proper return for the many instances he had received' of his friendship, to which Christian is said to have replied: 'I am in hell, I am in hell . . .'

Christian laid hands upon Bligh and was advised to blow his brains out, but he could not bring himself to commit murder. As it was his intentions were clear, for although he allowed Bligh and the eighteen men loyal to him to board the launch he refused them any means of navigating the boat apart from a quadrant and a book of nautical tables. There was no ephemeris, or almanac, without which the quadrant was almost useless in any hands but those of a man of Bligh's dedicated skill, though his clerk Samuel did secure Bligh's journals and commission, along with some other papers without which Bligh's 'honor [sic] and Character would have been in the power of Calumny without a proper document to have defended it . . . ' Sadly, Bligh lost his surveys 'and remarks [his written navigational notes] for 15 years past which were numerous.'

Fryer might have turned the tables, for he had a pair of loaded pistols in his cabin; Bligh whispered to him to seize the initiative but he failed, though he joined him in the launch. A few minutes later they were cast adrift, hastened on their way by pots of breadfruit saplings hurled derisively out of the *Bounty*'s stern windows. Bligh recorded all the details of 'the affair' in his journal, including a description of the mutineers, and began his astounding boat-voyage to Coupang in Dutch Timor, some 3,600 miles to the westward. They were on short rations, came under attack when they returned to Tofoa, and had little to sustain them. Bligh proved himself the hero of the mutiny. In the course of the perilous voyage he noted the position of the Fiji Islands, hitherto unknown to Europeans, and carried out a sketch survey of the Torres Strait. They finally landed at Coupang on 14 June 1789, having lost only one man, killed by the Tofoans; poor Nelson died of fever at Coupang. Bligh purchased a small schooner on a promissory note, commissioned her as a naval vessel, naming her *Resource,* and sailed onwards to Batavia, capital of the Dutch East Indies. From here he took passage home, arranging for his loyal crew either to accompany or to follow him in Dutch East Indiamen. Several succumbed to the fever prevalent in the swamp-surrounded city.

As is well known, Christian returned to Tahiti, where he and his men took aboard their mistresses and a few Tahitian males before losing themselves in the South Pacific, finally settling on

Pitcairn Island. Not all the men left aboard the *Bounty* were either mutineers or keen to follow Christian to the ends of the earth. Sixteen remained in Tahiti, where one killed two Tahitians and the troublesome Churchill before himself being stoned to death. All those who survived were however treated as rebels when on 23 September 1790 Captain Edward Edwards arrived in HM Frigate *Pandora*, in consequence of Bligh's eventual return to London. Several, including Midshipman Peter Heywood, immediately went on board the *Pandora*, where they found their former shipmates Haywood and Hallett, both now lieutenants, part of *Pandora*'s complement and appointed to identify members of *Bounty*'s crew. The remainder were rounded up and confined in a cage in the frigate's hold known as '*Pandora*'s box'. It was Edwards who proved the tyrant in this infamous tale, for he showed no compassion towards the *Bounty* men, despite the fact that they had yet to be tried. To his chagrin he failed to find the *Bounty* herself during a search begun after *Pandora* left Tahiti on 8 May 1791. Passing through the Torres Strait the *Pandora* was wrecked on a reef and thirty-one of her crew were drowned. Four of the *Bounty* men were also lost, still manacled in *Pandora*'s box but, like Bligh, Edwards and most of his crew also arrived safely at Timor in the frigate's boats. They too took passage in Dutch ships, joining HMS *Gorgon* at the Cape of Good Hope and finally landing at Portsmouth on 18 June 1792.

By the time the ten survivors of the *Bounty* were arraigned for court martial aboard HMS *Duke* at Spithead on 12 September, Bligh was carrying out his second, and successful, voyage to transplant breadfruit trees. He should have been the principal witness at the trial, but naval court martials were not then noted for their legal probity. Under the presidency of Vice Admiral Lord Hood, four men were acquitted but six were sentenced to death. Two of these, Midshipman Heywood and Boatswain's Mate James Morrison, were recommended to mercy and – in Heywood's case, thanks to the labours of his sister Nancy – were pardoned. Muspratt was also pardoned, on the very eve of his hanging. But on 29 October Millward, Ellison and Burkitt were hanged aboard HMS *Brunswick*.

Curiously, Lord Hood offered to take Peter Heywood into his flagship *Victory* as a midshipman; in fact he joined HMS *Bellerophon*, where his uncle Thomas Pasley was captain. He thereafter enjoyed considerable favour and some distinction, compiling the first vocabulary of the Tahitian tongue known in Britain. By 1803 Heywood had been promoted post-captain, and in 1816 he married a widow. His step-daughter Lady Belcher, believing that good fortune was a mark of virtue, 'was active in promoting the idea of his innocence and at the same time, blackening Bligh'. Heywood died, still a captain, in 1831. At the time of the mutiny he was been a high-spirited youth of sixteen who probably failed to grasp the significance of what was going on that fateful morning; but he need not have connived at the darkening of Bligh's reputation.

Romantic suggestions that Christian returned to his native land have been largely discounted, despite Heywood's claim to have seen him in Dock Town, as Devonport was then called. Some have theorized that Christian and his mutiny were the inspiration for Samuel Coleridge Taylor's *Rime of the Ancient Mariner*, the mutiny being Christian's 'albatross' – another facet of this curious tale that deserves the attention of the historiographer.

Only John Adams survived for long on Pitcairn; the other seven Britons who had elected to follow Christian fell victim to internecine strife. Adams was discovered on the island in February 1808 by Captain Folger of the American whaler *Topaz*. Amazed to find islanders who spoke English, he presented him with a handsome chronometer. The news was reported to Admiral Sir Sidney Smith, then commanding at Rio de Janeiro, but the Admiralty took no action. Great Britain was in the throes of the struggle with Napoleonic France and, by 1814, with the United States too. In this year two British frigates, the *Briton* and *Tagus*, searching for the USS *Essex* then on a cruise against the British South Sea whale fishery, called at Pitcairn, where they recieved an account of events from the now patriarchal Adams. In 1825 Captain Beechey in HMS *Blossom* on a surveying voyage also lay off Pitcairn, and Beechey too met the old man. None of these naval officers saw fit to arrest Adams, who recounted the history of the handful of mutineers who had landed on Pitcairn as pirates and burned His Majesty's Armed Transport *Bounty*. Only Christian's end remained specifically unaccounted for – and will remain so forever.

Bligh distinguished himself in those all-absorbing wars, though he was widely known as 'Bounty' Bligh. We shall catch one more glimpse of him, as post-captain commanding the line-of-battle ship *Director* in which he fought at the Battle of Camperdown in 1797, where he earned high praise from Admiral Duncan; he also commanded the *Glatton* at Copenhagen in April 1801, and received a commendation from Nelson for his part in that hard-fought action. It seems a pity therefore that he should have been involved with another rebellion, when in 1808, as Governor of New South Wales, he tried to break a corrupt monopoly among the colony's establishment. In both mutinies it was Bligh who, in the words of the naval historian Sir Geoffrey Callender 'clave to what was right'.

For all his faults – and they were all too human – Bligh was a supreme professional, one of the old and exclusive school of highly trained surveying officers nurtured by Cook who were part seaman, part cartographer, part anthropologist, part zoologist and part botanist. Bligh in his turn encouraged George Bass and Matthew Flinders, both of whom sailed with him in the *Providence* on the second breadfruit voyage. Although Bligh successfully delivered the saplings to Jamaica, the slaves refused to eat them.

William Bligh rose to be a vice admiral, died on 7 December 1817 and lies buried in Lambeth churchyard, a stone's throw from the Thames.

6

'A BUSINESS OF SUCH VAST IMPORTANCE'

ALTHOUGH the French Revolution had erupted in July 1789, war with Great Britain did not begin until February 1793, by which time the French occupation of the Low Countries, and particularly the port of Antwerp, was said 'to hold a pistol to London's head'. The nation's chief bulwark of defence was, of course, the Royal Navy, and it was in an advanced state of preparedness owing to a series of crises in the previous years. Nevertheless its mobilization caused widespread social disruption, first among the maritime population of merchant seamen whose services were conscripted by means of the press, and then as the result of coercive Acts of Parliament by means of which additional manpower was raised. Already alluded to, the most significant of these were the Quota Acts of 1795 and 1796, and one consequence of these measures was the introduction into the navy's ranks of numbers of men from a variety of backgrounds, few of whom readily adapted to the rigours of the sea-life that were seen as the norm by the mass of former mercantile sailors. Whether pressed or volunteers, these latter 'professional' seamen were, for the most part, steady men who accepted the inequities of life with greater equanimity than the land-lubbers whom expediency had placed among them. These wretches included a significant handful of educated and ambitious men who wholeheartedly embraced the new ideals of the pure Revolutionary creed, ideals that do not seem outrageous to us today but were dangerous to the established order of the day. The extent to which the long-cherished notions of British liberty differed from the revolutionary creed wafting across the Channel is a complex subject, for it was never a problem for radical intellectuals and it was an Englishman, Tom Paine, who voiced the rights of mankind most eloquently.

Certainly, expressions of revolutionary zeal did break out as the old order was challenged and political pamphlets were circulated among ships' companies, but to what extent it was merely a subject of discussion among the fleet's messdecks and to what extent it was a real motivator for change is difficult to gauge. The influence of revolutionary principles, like that of the influx of Quota Men, is probably over-cooked. What may more profitably be discerned is a tendency for the steady 'professional' seamen to simply resent being put upon by those set in authority over them who were occasionally either over-bearing or incompetent. This was the nature of the complaint raised in the *Windsor Castle* in 1794 when that ship was off Corsica as part of the Mediterranean Fleet. The crew expressed a dislike of Rear Admiral Robert Linzee, Captain William Shield, his first lieutenant and the boatswain. Perhaps not incredibly, as has been suggested by some, the then Commander-in-Chief, Vice Admiral Hotham, acceded to the men's request and sent the ship a new captain, John Gore, and a new first lieutenant and boatswain, though understandably he refused to remove his fellow flag-officer. Matters changed shortly afterwards when Sir John Jervis (later Earl St Vincent) superseded Hotham: Jervis was a punctilious though fair martinet.

Matters ran otherwise in the case of the mutiny aboard HMS *Defiance* in 1795 when she was lying in Leith Road in company with other men-of-war, 'manned principally by fishermen, [who proved] stout resolute dogs'. Bligh himself, now a captain and in command of HMS *Calcutta*, helped suppress the mutiny, boarding the line-of-battle ship at the head of a detachment of fencible troops. A complaint about Acting Lieutenant Malcolm's habitual drunkenness and brutality had been accompanied by another of less weight, about the amount of water in the grog and the inedible quality of the ship's cheese, and a more significant one, about a lack of shore-leave. The mutineers were savagely punished, with four sentenced to be hanged, four to be flogged with 300 lashes each, and three with 100 each. The four condemned men were pardoned at the last moment and given a lesser punishment. There was no mechanism for airing reasonable complaints, and unless a wise and senior officer got to hear of the affair and headed trouble off, as Hotham had done, their expression was likely to end in tragedy.

Another such challenge to the absolute power resident in a captain was made in 1796 when the seamen of the frigate *Shannon* petitioned the Admiralty for the removal of their 'tiriant [*sic*] of a Captain', whose ill-treatment was 'more than the spirits and harts [*sic*] of true Englishmen can . . . bear for we are born free but now we are slaves.'

While Hotham's response may be judged as either humane and justified or as being an instance of unparalleled weakness (Captain Shield demanded a court martial and was, perhaps predictably, acquitted of any fault), another mutiny was long remembered by the seamen of the fleet as an example of sheer bad faith. On 3 December 1794 HMS *Culloden* lay at Spithead under orders to sail. She was ageing and had recently been aground; this had caused excessive leaking and there had been talk of docking and recaulking her, but Captain Thomas Troubridge ordered the ship unmoored. The desirability of the precaution of docking had been made plain to Troubridge, but he was an impetuous officer, did not consider that the *Culloden* leaked excessively and decided that the men could pump her. He was therefore affronted to find, when he gave his order, how some 250 of her crew, together with half a dozen marines, felt so strongly about the unseaworthiness of their ship that they barricaded themselves below decks, declaring that they would return to their duty on promise of a docking, or of wholesale transfer into another, safer ship. They, who had the labour of keeping the *Culloden* afloat, feared the condition of the ship; Troubridge considered his people's disobedience as being of more importance. He lost his spectacular temper, called out the marines and threatened to evict his crew at bayonet-point. There followed a lengthy stand-off during which several admirals whom the mutineers might have been supposed to respect visited the *Culloden* in the hope of persuading the men to go to sea. Finally, Lord Bridport received a letter: the mutineers would give up if their ship was docked and they were transferred to another or 'all the people present between decks [were] draughted [*sic*] on board different ships or, as you lordship shall think proper; and your lordship's word and honour not to punish any man concerned in the present business, or to mention it or remember it hereafter.' This missive was ominously signed using a word new to Bridport and his colleagues but redolent of Franco-Jacobin associations: *Delegate*.

The mutiny was finally ended when, upon instruction, Captain Thomas Pakenham visited the men under a truce. Precisely what was said is a mystery, but Pakenham was an Anglo-Irishman known throughout the fleet for his complex ideas of equality and the Rights of Man. Interestingly, this was not seen by his superiors as any deficiency or threat to his loyalty, for 'Mad Pack' had distinguished himself at the Glorious First of June in *Invincible*; on the contrary, his notions were regarded as rather an endearing, eccentric trait, an aristocratic foible. However, it was assumed that he could would be able to cajole the men in language they would understand, while his Irish background would draw their sting and win over that part of *Culloden*'s crew who espoused Jacobin or Republican views. What the *Culloden*'s people believed – what the whole fleet believed afterwards, and what the Admiralty never sought to repudiate – was that they had been granted the amnesty for which they asked Pakenham during their meeting on 11 December. Trusting Captain The Honourable

Thomas Pakenham, they dismantled their barricade and obeyed the reiterated command to go to their stations.

But Troubridge was not to be thwarted. Hardly had Pakenham departed than 'with great resolution and firmness' he 'seized the principal mutineers'. They were swiftly court-martialled. Of the ten he arrested, two were acquitted and eight condemned to death. Three were eventually pardoned but five were hanged, as was the custom, by their own shipmates from the arm of the foreyard on 13 January 1795. Asked afterwards if he could recognize a potential mutineer, Troubridge declared: 'Whenever I see a fellow look as if he was *thinking*, I say that is mutiny.'

However, if an efficient fighting force were to be maintained, dissension was never a thing to be tolerated. It was not the weakness of the mutineers' case that provoked the reaction of authority, but the challenge to that authority by the *Culloden*'s people. The seamen's dilemma was that only rarely had any reasonable appeal to their superiors been met with anything but affront. There was simply no mechanism for addressing complaints. But trouble was coming. By 1797 the Royal Navy had expanded four-fold, and about 110,000 seamen and marines were enlisted. Their continuing obedience was essential to the defence of the realm at a time when Britain was increasingly faced with threat of French invasion – despite a victory over the Spanish fleet obtained in February off Cape St Vincent. 'Without order and discipline', the recently ennobled Admiral Earl St Vincent famously declared, '*nothing* is achieved.' Most of the old school of seamen perfectly understood this; but they also believed that their interests and rights, such as they were, were entrusted in and ought to be catered for by the Board of Admiralty and the government of the day. That was part of the *quid pro quo* of loyal service.

The problem was that, in the face of a long war, this reciprocal duty of care seemed now singularly absent from Their Lordships' conduct, let alone the government's. Over a long period during which they did their duty, the seamen of the navy nevertheless began to nurse and nurture a number of significant grievances over and above the concerns of individual ships. Chief among these was the matter of pay; this had remained unchanged in value since 1653, when it had been overhauled by Cromwell, yet the cost of living had risen dramatically. Pay had been a cause of disaffection long before 1797, but two years earlier the army had received a significant increase and the seamen of the fleet thought that in common equity, it should have been accorded them too. They were 'naturally expecting that they should in their turn experience the same Munificence but alas no Notice has been taken of them nor the smallest provision made for their Wives an[d] Famillies . . . ' Subsidiary grouses concerned the method by which the remission of allotments to their dependants might be effected, and the necessity of obtaining ready cash by discounting their wages through visiting usurers.

This arose from their second complaint, the lack of shore-leave, which left them dependent upon such middle-men. Even in the large fleet anchorages where ships might wait for many weeks, shore-leave was invariably denied the crew of a man-of-war for fear of desertion. This fear produced other consequential abuses, such as the immediate turning over of the crew of a decommissioning ship into one newly commissioned, which saved the authorities the difficulties of recruiting a new crew and also sanctioned certain sharp practices in paying off the old. Moreover it was combined with others which denied men advances before sailing on protracted voyages, particularly those designated by convention as 'foreign' – which in those days meant south of the Equator. Seamen were regularly years in arrears of their full wages, and there were occasions when proper wage bills were never paid in full when ships paid-off, the original crews having died, been transferred or killed. Their dependants, of course, received nothing at all.

The lack of liberty was countered by allowing 'wives and sweethearts' access to a ship by boat – along with the usurers, itinerant vendors, liquor-sellers and others eager to strip Jack of the few shillings he could muster. This however, simply led to unbridled licence and venereal infection on a grand scale, and did little for the self-esteem of a class of men who did not care to be treated like animals put to the rut. History does not relate what the real visiting wives, faithfully carrying their marriage lines, thought of an arrangement that resulted in exposed copulation between the guns, or the dubious privacy of overnight stops in their husbands' hammocks (the dawn ejection from which they were spared if they 'showed a leg'), A well-regarded seaman might receive 'a twenty-four hours' liberty ticket to go on shore, while all the soldiers (. . . [who] got furloughs to go to the far end of the kingdom, to see their wives and families . . .) had orders to look after us, and even got three guineas reward for nabbing us when we overstretched the time.'

The seamen's third grievance was over the matter of food. At sea, food was (and is) most important. There was something almost sacramental about meal times, and a good captain bore this in mind. Discontentment over rations was a serious matter which could undermine morale and loyalty. Specifically the men objected to the 'fourteen-ounce pound', the missing two ounces of the pound allowed them in their regulation diet (which in the pre-refrigeration era was nutritious if monotonous) were held back as a purser's perquisites, though officially written off as 'Leakage and Waste'. The men also considered that in the great fleet anchorages such as Spithead, off Portsmouth, Plymouth Sound and, in the Thames Estuary, the Nore, they ought to receive fresh provisions.

Moreover, if a man was sick, wounded or hospitalized, he received no pay until he was fit to return to duty, the state taking his pay as recompense for looking after him. He might apply for a pension from the Sick and Hurt Board if he was invalided out of the Service. Venereal disease was regarded as a self-inflicted injury, so if a man underwent treatment he was obliged to pay for it himself, the sum being deducted from his wages.

Finally, there was the issue of punishment. For the regulation of life on board a crowded man-of-war the professional seaman had little argument against the necessity of a ruthless discipline. Though they were often considered harsh, the severity of punishments, was in the main accepted. What rankled were the petty aggravations of minor physical harassment such as the excessive use by petty officers of a rope's end or officers of a rattan cane in 'starting' slow members of the crew about their duties, to which we have already made reference. Worst of all was the licence given to midshipmen, 'mere boy[s] escaped from the school or the nursery [and to] the hobbledehoy hands of a young raw master's mate . . . '

The one advantage to the sailors of being detained in anchorages such as Spithead and the Nore was the means it afforded of communication between the ships. The business of the fleet required a constant stream of boats plying hither and thither, and while some were shore-craft, most were the ships' own barges, gigs, cutters and launches. At the behest of captains and officers, boat-crews often lay alongside other men-of-war, and by this means the very thing denied them on active service at sea – close association – was possible. This was but one step away from the sinister 'combination' of which the authorities were so fearful; yet the grievances among the various squadrons of the British fleet were in any case so well articulated and aired that they should have come as no surprise to the Admiralty. Earl Howe, who had commanded the Channel Fleet during the battle known as the Glorious First of June (1794), was well aware of discontent in this, Britain's principal squadron. He was a man of vast influence and commanded great respect at all levels of society, not least among the seamen of the fleet, to whom in the aftermath of the battle there is evidence to suggest he had 'hinted if he did not actually promise' that he would attempt to ensure they had a pay rise. Over the succeeding months, now running into years, the Admiralty itself had received a dribble of memoranda intimating discontent in the fleet, chief among which was a warning that the low rate of pay for an able-seaman – nine pence per day – was fast becoming a dangerous source of trouble.

The crisis approached in mid February 1797. A French attempt to invade Ireland and stir up rebellion against the government in London had just been dispersed, by bad weather rather than the valour of the Royal Navy. On 14 February Jervis and Nelson were engaging the Spanish off Cape St Vincent when Admiral Lord Howe, convalescing from the gout at Bath but still C-in-C of the Channel Fleet, received 'several Petitions, purporting to be transmitted from different Ships of the Channel Fleet. They were all exact copies of each other, limited solely to a request for an increase of pay, that the Seaman might be able to make better provision for their families, decently expressed, but without any signature.' Howe did nothing, afterwards pleading 'I could not reply to applications which were anonymous.' He also explained disingenuously that he had 'reason to think that they were fabricated by some malicious individual who meant to insinuate the prevalence of a general discontent in the Fleet.' This view was unwisely espoused by the naval hierarchy: nothing was done, despite a banking crisis in early March that affected the price of necessities across the nation which though in one sense it emphasized the immediacy of the seamen's claim, was weakened politically by the fact that it affected entire population.

On 10 April Lord Bridport relieved Howe, who retired from age and infirmity. Three days later Bridport was expressing anxiety about an application for a rise in pay that he heard had been made by the seamen in his fleet. 'If this should be the case,' he told the Admiralty, 'it would be very desirable for me to know what steps have been taken in consequence thereof . . . as I yesterday heard that some disagreeable Combinations were forming among the Ships at Spithead . . . '

Lord Spencer, the First Lord, responded with a similar expression of anxiety; but the time for prevarication was passing, and the Board and its admirals were surrendering the initiative, too intent instead on identifying ring-leaders and ordering captains to remain watchfully in their ships, to stifle any communication with the shore and to snuff out the first whiff of mutiny. At this time, the matter of pay was the sailors' sole remonstrance. Petitions went to the House of Commons, but soon the admirals were receiving reports that a general and precisely orchestrated insurrection was being planned, the seamen having received no response to their petitions, and that this was likely to occur simultaneously with the order to send several of the line-of-battle-ships to sea.

By Easter Sunday, 16 April 1797, when the order was passed to Admiral Gardner to move eight ships a few miles away to St Helen's Road, several ships were in open defiance. They informed Bridport that they wished for their petitions to be answered before they would weigh, at the same time respectfully assuring him that all normal duties for ships at anchor or moorings would be carried out. Bridport despatched Rear Admiral Pole to London to attempt a resolution, but Their Lordships, realizing that the matter must be laid before the Cabinet, only informed Bridport that they relied upon him 'to restore the discipline of the fleet, and for carrying their [the Board's] orders into execution . . . '

It is a curious and notable feature of the mutiny at Spithead that, in the strictest sense there was no breakdown in *discipline*, for routines were punctiliously maintained, and indeed the ships' yards were manned and three hearty cheers given when the Grand Duke of Würtemburg made a state visit to the fleet accompanied by Spencer and the Lords of the Admiralty – all as if nothing were amiss. Over the next few days there was ample *disobedience*, however, captains were deprived of their legitimate commands and the ships remained where they were – but watches were kept, drunkenness was punished, marks of respect continued to be paid to officers, and 'there shall be no Liberty from Ship to Ship until all is regularly settled'. The mutineers largely took their own advice, and while there were some abusive scenes between fire-eating admirals like Sir Alan Gardner and the seamen, each ship's company was urged to 'Let no disorder nor tumult influence your proceedings.' That the fleet held together was to be demonstrated every morning and evening by each ship's company giving three cheers. As for the leadership, the council of deputies which met regularly aboard the *Queen Charlotte,* they remained a unanimous body largely characterized by a reasonable and respectful dignity. This action by the fleet, mutinous in legal terms though it might be, was certainly not the revolution the Establishment feared.

In London 'the very delicate subject of an increase in pay, which appears to have been brought forward and enforced in an unpleasant manner', persuaded Lord Spencer and a quorum of his Board of Admiralty to travel to Portsmouth even before Pole had arrived. Meanwhile at Spithead the marines had sided with the seamen, a fact which rattled Bridport. Nevertheless, he informed the fleet that their case had been laid before the Admiralty, and told them he was 'authorized to assure them that their Petitions will be taken into serious and immediate consideration, as their importance requires.' He concluded by expecting that 'the different Ships' Companies will immediately return to their Duty, as the Service of their Country requires their proceeding to Sea.'

Bridport's order made, by his own confession, 'little or no impression'. He was much put upon and, for a man of seventy years of age, greatly fatigued by the pass matters had come to. It was clear that he was powerless and that 'the whole Fleet . . . are determined not to go to Sea till their Grievances are redressed, unless they knew the French Fleet were on the Coast.' It is important to note, particularly in view of the use of the noun 'fleet', that in fact the ships which were paralysed were the heavy ships-of-the-line. The reconnoitring cruisers, largely numerous frigates but including lesser men-of-war such as ship and brig-sloops, were deliberately excluded, partly because they were already at sea and therefore could not be communicated with, but also because it was not in the mutineers' collective interest to make them part of the active element of the 'fleet mutiny'. On the 17th and 18th Bridport and his subordinate flag-officers and captains did what they could to persuade the seamen to see reason, only to be respectfully but firmly rebuffed. The men remembered the *Culloden*, and distrust kept them staunchly united under the terms of their joint oath. The deputies nevertheless ordered the *Romney* and *Venus* to leave the anchorage and sail as escorts to an outward-bound convoy, 'as we would in no wise wish to bring the Injury of Country [i.e., damage to trade] in our Cause . . . '

By now Spencer and his colleagues had arrived, and they met Bridport ashore. He stated that 'the only chance of bringing back the Fleet to subordination . . . was by complying with the demands . . .'. The Board agreed to a monthly increase in pay of four shillings to seamen and two to landsmen, and a continuation of that pay until a man wounded in action was well again or offered a pension. The decision was conveyed to the council aboard the *Queen Charlotte*, but the time necessary to gain the consensus of the fleet sat ill with Their Lordships, who fumed at all delay. Then when the consensus came it was no simple agreement but a full list of the men's grievances, endorsed by the names of two delegates from each of the sixteen ships-of-the-line involved. That it was accompanied by a paper assuring the Board that 'it is unanimously agreed by the Fleet that for this Day no Grievances shall be received in order to convince the Nation at large that we know when to cease to Ask as well as to begin . . .' was small consolation.

The timing was unfortunate, since it was perceived, justifiably perhaps, as an escalation carrying with it a hint of further demands to come, when the Board of Admiralty was, as it were, over a barrel. Much of what now passed hither and thither was concerned with terminology, a debate that has become depressingly familiar in trade union negotiations of a later age but was quite foreign to the patrician Spencer, his Board, and the admirals. Some of the seamen's enquiries and demands were fair (what was to be done about the marines' pay?), others less so (a call for seamen in 'the Merchants' Service' to double their contributions to the Chatham Chest – a relief fund for Royal Naval seamen from which they themselves, unless they were unfortunate enough to be pressed, derived no benefit). Other requests, such as that for a proper adherence to victualling scales and an improvement in their quality, though reasonable, were received as criticisms and seemed only to presage a litany of complaint against which, on the evening of the 19 April, Their Lordships determined 'that a stand must be made somewhere.'

They made their stand: *inter alia*, 'With regard to the Quality and Quantity of Provisions . . . it has ever been and ever will be

Our intention that they shall be of the best Quality, and being convinced that the Quantity now served is sufficient, We see no reason to increase it.' Upon such blatant complacency – since *everyone* knew that a 'true' pound contained sixteen and not fourteen ounces – does history turn. Worse, it was backed up with a threat: 'that should they be insensible to the liberal offers now made to them, and persist in their present disobedience, they must no longer expect to enjoy those benefits to which by their former Good Conduct they were entitled.' That this was accompanied by promise of 'the most perfect Forgiveness of all that has passed on this occasion' cut no ice.

The sailors were intransigent: by the 21st the Board had shifted its position a little, conceding the full payment of the increase and honouring the sixteen-ounce pound, the Prime Minister, William Pitt, having backed Spencer with an assurance that 'the amount of the expense is comparatively of no consequence'.

While various ships' captains reported that the Board's proposal had generally been met with enthusiasm and an agreement to return to duty, such reports were invariably accompanied by the provision that it must be approved by the delegates aboard the *Queen Charlotte*. From the seamen's perspective this was entirely in accordance with their desire to act as one, and on behalf of all other British warships, whether attached to the Channel Fleet or not. Their Lordships viewed this rival cockpit of power with very jaundiced eyes. Nevertheless, they acted swiftly to communicate the concessions and the instrument of forgiveness, appending only the sinister warning that 'if the men from the several Ships now assembled in the *Queen Charlotte* do not immediately accede thereto (they all being well known) they may rely upon it that they will be brought to condign Punishment and suffer the utmost vengeance of the Law . . . '

Despite a subsequent assurance to the contrary, the matter of free pardon now seemed to be in jeopardy. Moreover, Sir Alan Gardner indicated that the delegates aboard the *Queen Charlotte* had only half an hour in which to respond before the order was given to weigh anchor. Unfortunately Gardner's embassy, though successful, was carried out in the absence ashore of the delegates of the *Queen Charlotte* herself, namely John Hudlestone and Patrick Glynn, and Valentine Joyce and John Morice who represented the crew of Bridport's flagship, the *Royal George*. These men now arrived and raised the spectre of the *Culloden* and the assurances given to her men, stating that a pardon for the capital offence of mutiny could only come from the King himself. Since they had all identified themselves, they would all hang together, or hang separately. Gardner was the last man to reassure the men to the contrary, he was an unwise choice as mediator, since he had earlier, and in terms of unambiguous clarity, promised hell-fire to the mutineers. He was huffed ignominiously out of the *Queen Charlotte* with a unanimous chorus of 'Off! Off! Off!'

The delegates dispersed to report to their own ships but shortly afterwards the red flag, summoning the council, was hoisted aboard the *Royal George*, whereupon Bridport's long-standing flag-captain, William Domett, had Bridport's own flag struck in protest. The delegates' record of the affair is a model of caution, referring directly to the suspicions of dissimulation they harboured at the time of Gardner's visit: 'The Settlement of a business of such vast importance . . . ought to be attended with the greatest wisdom . . . as a security and bulwark against the fair Speeches of designing men . . .'

As Spencer went back to London and Pitt, later, to Windsor to see the King, news of mutiny in the ships at Plymouth began to circulate. Next day, Sunday 21 April, the fleet was granted the King's pardon. Although dissenting voices deplored the lack of any written confirmation of agreement to the grievances, things appeared to be getting back to normal, and in the days that followed ships at Spithead weighed anchor. However, news of parliamentary delay in processing an appropriate Act and the inevitably slow pace of implementing the improvements in provisions combined to provoke ongoing rumblings that inevitably fell out of so prolonged a period of disruption. As unpopular officers reasserted their authority with unnecessary vigour, further trouble loomed. At Plymouth Captain John Duckworth of the *Leviathan* had been writing to the Admiralty about 'the very great hardships we [captains] labour under from our salary's being quite inadequate', before going ashore to the Dockyard. His ship had just returned from the West Indies: her crew were forbidden to go ashore, and were owed two years' pay. Smouldering with resentment, they forced their officers to follow Duckworth ashore. Later they were read the Royal Pardon issued to cover the mutiny at Spithead, but in the meanwhile a delegation of them had sailed in a coaster to Portsmouth to determine the true state of affairs.

Spencer now thought Bridport should take his squadron to Plymouth with the aim of persuading the ships there that matters were in hand, but Bridport knew this was impossible. Moreover, the slow parliamentary process rekindled suspicions, and the men were growing increasingly fractious, so much so that on 7 May Admiral Colpoys aboard HMS *London* stupidly ordered some of his officers to fire into a group of mutineers, and several were killed. Colpoys, Gardner, ten captains and about a hundred 'tyrannical' officers were sent ashore, though Bridport and the remaining three-quarters of the commissioned officers were suffered to remain in post. Late on 8 May the wretched Bridport reported to Spencer that things were worse than ever, only to be told by Spencer that matters were proceeding smoothly, that an Act was expected soon in Parliament, and that an Order in Council would be forthcoming. As the mutiny at Plymouth began to fizzle out, that at Spithead seemed to burst forth with renewed vigour: nothing was *settled*.

In fact, it was on the brink of resolution. In desperation Pitt's ministry forced the Act through both houses, and it received the Royal Assent. Poor old Howe was rooted out of his well-earned retirement and sent, with all the trappings of almost plenipotentiary grandeur, to promise Bridport's men that the matter was resolved and to pledge the Admiralty's word. Bridport, no lover of Howe, stood contentedly and exhaustedly aside as Howe worked his magic. Howe acquiesced to a list of unpopular officers, about half of those ashore being replaced, and then took part in a series of celebrations, including hosting a dinner for the delegates of the fleet. It was a public relations triumph. 'Black Dick' Howe was the one man the lower deck trusted – for all that he had, months earlier, done nothing about their initial petitions.

News of the trouble had spread rapidly. At St Helena aboard HMS *Dordrecht* the crew

> rose upon their officers, and menaced them with general destruction. The utmost promptitude and vigour became necessary; and, seizing one of the ring leaders Captain [Charles] Brisbane placed a halter about his neck, and, apparently was proceeding to immediate execution. His object, however, being only to inspire terror, and to convince the crew that he was not to be intimidated, he relaxed from the threatened infliction of justice; but, while the cord was yet round the culprit's neck, he solemnly declared to him, that, if he ever again ventured to open his mouth against his king or country, or in disobedience to the commands of his officers, the yardarm should inevitably be his portion.

In boldly seizing the initiative – along with one of the ring-leaders – and then linking so high a crime as implied treason with simple obedience, Brisbane snuffed out the insurrection before it had taken hold. Soon afterwards he was summoned to sail for the Cape and there required to take command of the *Tremendous*, whose crew had mutinied and put Captain Stephens ashore under accusations of cruelty and mistreatment. The mutiny in Table Bay extended to another man-of-war, the *Sceptre*, but was put down when Admiral Pringle, the flag-officer on the station, concerting operations with General Dundas and Lord Macartney, the Governor of Cape Province, resolved on bold action. They issued an ultimatum that unless the mutineers surrendered in two hours, both ships would be sunk by red-hot shot from the shore batteries. Smoke was soon seen to rise from the furnaces in the surrounding forts, and ten minutes before the expiry of the deadline the mutineers hoisted the signal for capitulation. 'The delegates were given up,' recorded *The Naval Chronicle*, 'many of them were executed, others were severely flogged, and good order and discipline were once more restored on board the fleet.' Perhaps predictably after all this, Stephens, having applied for a court martial to clear his name, was acquitted.

Off Cadiz, where the Mediterranean Fleet was stationed, Nelson declared himself to be 'entirely with the Seamen in their *first* complaint [as to pay – my italics: RW]. We are a neglected set, and, when peace comes, are shamefully treated.' But that was as far as his sympathy extended. Sporadic mutinous splutters were quickly extinguished by Earl St Vincent, who took several severe measures to ensure that the ships under his command remained loyal. It was relatively easy for him to accomplish this, because most of his fleet were at sea under his immediate eye and there was not a man in any of his ships who did not fully comprehend the ruthless and unbending nature of 'Old Jarvie'.

Although he was an admiral of similar moral stature, to St Vincent (and, at six feet four inches, of considerably more in the physical sense), Admiral Adam Duncan was unable to prevent a second mutiny in his North Sea Squadron, precisely because it was *not* under his immediate eye. His command was spread out: some ships were blockading the Dutch coast while a large proportion lay at anchor off Great Yarmouth in contact with the shore, and thus aware not only of events at Spithead but of further rumblings at the Nore.

7

'DISCIPLINE IS PRESERVED'

HAVING left Portsmouth, Lord Spencer and his Board received news that mutiny had broken out aboard the ships anchored off the Nore, a sand bank at the confluence of the Thames and the Medway. They travelled accordingly to Sheerness, a naval dockyard at the mouth of the Medway, arriving shortly before noon on 28 May.

The French export of revolution to the Low Countries and the establishment of the Batavian Republic had required the formation of a British North Sea squadron to blockade the Dutch fleet, particularly in its main anchorage off Den Helder, a port tucked behind the fishing village of Kampenduijn – or Camperdown, as anglicized by the Royal Navy. Commanded by Admiral De Winter, the Dutch men-of-war were known to be close to completing preparations to sail on a military expedition. The squadron formed to contain this potential new enemy was required to operate off a largely lee shore. It was placed under the command of Admiral Duncan, whose fleet anchorage was Great Yarmouth Road some hundred miles directly to windward of Den Helder. Unlike Spithead and St Helen's Road, Yarmouth Road was not closely backed up by a dockyard: its support and sustenance came from the twin dockyards of Sheerness and Chatham on the Medway, about a hundred miles to the south-west. Here, at the anchorage of the Nore, lay the guardship HMS *Sandwich* and the reserves for Duncan, under Vice Admiral Charles Buckner.

In addition to carrying her own ship's company the *Sandwich* acted as a receiving ship, a floating repository for the press tenders and drafts of seamen destined for ships on active service. Her population was therefore divided, inherently unstable, and probably largely unhappy. News of the uprising at Spithead motivated disaffected elements among the men aboard the *Sandwich* and quickly spread to the other warships anchored in the vicinity. These were not a 'fleet' or indeed a squadron, in any sense of either word, being transients on their way to or from the dockyards, powder and sheer hulks of the Thames and the Medway. Nor was Buckner a squadron commander: he was a 'port-admiral' running a dockyard, though for form's sake he flew his flag afloat at the *Sandwich*'s foremasthead.

Almost as soon as they arrived at Sheerness the Admiralty Board members met a delegation from the ships at the Nore, to whom they explained the concessions made to the fleet as a whole following the settlement with the Spithead ships. Their Lordships assumed this assurance would pacify the men at the Nore, and the delegates gave an undertaking to consult the ships' companies and respond by noon the following day. Unfortunately, a gale blew up and boats were unable to return the men's answer until five o'clock; no agreement was conceded, and additional demands were made.

Frustrated, Spencer and his colleagues decamped for London, leaving Buckner with orders that no boats were to be suffered to land from the mutinous ships and all communication with them was to be severed. Their Lordships ordained that the mutineers should be isolated and left to stew until they came to their senses. Their additional demands were deemed inadmissible; they included more regular pay – that is an end to the practice of holding pay over and not paying seamen in full until a ship was decommissioned – an advance of wages for pressed men so that they could purchase necessary clothing from the ship's slop-chest, a repeat of the right to take leave in port, automatic pardon for deserters who returned to duty of their own volition, and the right to veto the appointment of officers known to the sailors for their incompetence, brutality or persistent drunkenness. Since the number of ships at the Nore was small and commanded little public influence – unlike the main battle-fleet of the Channel Squadron – Their Lordships considered that the matter would die out once the arrangements for implementing the agreement with the Spithead delegates had been processed.

In this they made a fatal calculation. Although two frigates, the *San Fiorenzo* and *Clyde*, slipped their cables and ran the gauntlet of the guns of the other ships, encouraging Spencer to think his strategy was working, word of the mutiny had already spread to those ships of Duncan's fleet anchored off Yarmouth. One by one these ships weighed and proceeded into the Thames; from a handful of men-of-war passing to and fro, the numbers of mutinous ships at the Nore rapidly increased. The presence of these at the mouth of the Thames had a most dire effect upon trade. If the presence of the enemy in distant Antwerp could hold a pistol to London's head, here was a weapon of a more sinister calibre, aimed from the Nore at closer range. Within a short period most sea-borne commerce came to a standstill. With the whole of London affected, and almost immediately hostile to the sailors' cause, the mutiny at the Nore assumed an altogether different complexion from that at Spithead.

Threats came ashore, and the air grew red with revolutionary implication: some of the ships' captains and officers were sent ashore. Sinisterly, the sailing masters were retained on board, for their pilotage skills. If the authorities did not bow to the mutineers' demands, London would be starved; and if that did not work, the ships would be carried off to France, or to augment De Winter's squadrons. There was none of the moderate termin-ology of the Spithead movement: all was threat and bluster. The government took alarm: troops were quickly moved into

Sheerness, and the forts there and at Gravesend and Tilbury were garrisoned, while Trinity House sent their buoy-yachts from Harwich and Deptford to destroy the buoyage marking the channels out of the estuary. Although one rebellious frigate was sent down the Swin to act as a seamark, the anchored ships remained at the Nore, among them the 64-gun *Director* commanded by Captain William Bligh.

Things were not going well for the delegates, despite the mayhem their action was causing ashore. They were led by Richard Parker who, although a Quota Man, had seen previous naval service and had been a junior officer. Like Captain Thomas Troubridge, Parker was a baker's son, and had been sent to Exeter Grammar school before going to sea. He had seen service in the Royal Navy and merchant ships before marrying and coming ashore. For a time he ran a school himself, but fell on hard times and re-entered the navy as a midshipman. Too old for a position he found irksome, he had been court-martialled for insubordination and dismissed; there were unspecific suggestions of mental disorder. He tried his luck ashore again, only to end in a debtors' prison. The navy, it seemed, would have him after all as part of a Quota Act detachment: he was rated able seaman when delivered by the tender on board the *Sandwich*. He emerged as the leader of the Nore mutineers largely because wiser heads sheltered behind his eager figure. Clearly anxious to make his mark, Parker became fatally conspicuous – and, as time passed and nothing was achieved, isolated.

The various occurrences on board and ashore need not detain us. Parties sent ashore for provisions were shot at by the soldiers now billeted in the locality. The delegates corresponded with Buckner and Buckner with Their Lordships, but the answer was always the same: 'No.' Attitudes ashore grew ever harder. In the offing were more than a hundred and fifty merchant ships delayed in their lawful voyages – held in thrall by fourteen sail-of-the-line, six frigates, and seven sloops-of-war.

On the morning of 9 June, with an ebb tide and fair wind, Parker, now appointed 'admiral' under the red flag of rebellion, gave the signal for the ships to weigh anchor. Aboard the *Sandwich* the sails were let fall and a gun was fired, the executive order for the rebellious ships to desert to the enemy. Not one moved. The plan of defecting conceived by Parker and the other delegates might have been an obvious ideological solution, but it ran counter to the instincts of Jack Tar, as Parker must have been aware: when he was rowed round the ships on the 8th, suggesting that the seamen should place themselves in the hands of the Dutch, the men aboard the *Nassau,* initially one of Duncan's more rebellious ships, replied 'No, we'll be damned if we'll leave Old England whatever happens to us.'

About mid-afternoon Lieutenant Robb aboard the 50-gun *Leopard* led a coup of loyal petty officers and seamen, seized the guns on the quarterdeck and forecastle and hoisted topsails. Cutting the cable, Robb headed for the Medway. Shortly afterwards *Repulse* followed. Unfortunately, both ships grounded on the mud and were subjected to gunfire from the mutineers, directed by Parker, who had boarded *Director*, the nearest ship to the *Repulse*. 'Send her to the devil!' Parker ordered, but his resolution failed and he next called for a flag of truce, until *Repulse* fired back. The tide was now flooding, and *Repulse* and *Leopard* refloated and resumed their short passages. In the ensuing hours Parker vacillated – probable evidence of the disturbed state of his mind – but he had no control over events, for a haemorrhage had begun. Next to go was the *Monmouth*, after which Parker, on the 10th, made a last desperate attempt to end matters by agreeing to the acceptance of the Royal Pardon. He was far too late, and the reply was predictable. During the night of 12/13 June the *Agamemnon, Standard, Nassau* and *Vestal* made up the Thames for Gravesend. During the day that followed the *Champion, Monmouth, Brilliant* and the sloops and storeships all capitulated under the guns of Sheerness. On the 14th the *Sandwich* gave up after the ship's company defied Parker and agreed to be commanded by their proper officers; those on board were released from their confinement, and the ship moved under the direction of Lieutenant Flatt. She was swiftly followed by the others, *Inflexible*, *Montague*, *Belliqueux* and *Director*. By 15 June all were back under Royal Naval control, their proper flags flying, rebellion at an end. Parker had given himself up and was incarcerated in Maidstone Gaol.

Of a large number of men tried only 59 were condemned to death, and the sentence was actually carried out on 29. A further 29 were imprisoned, 9 were flogged (with up to 400 lashes) and the remainder pardoned. Parker was of course hanged, the sentence being carried out aboard the *Sandwich* at 9.30a.m on 30 June. Paradoxically, it was his best moment. Denied a leave-taking from his wife, who had striven to speak with him, he jumped from the starboard cathead and obliged his shipmates to run him up to the foreyardarm, where he swung above the boats of the fleet, each manned by a representative group from each ship.

Matters returned to normal with almost bewildering swiftness. Aboard *Nassau* the log records the transformation: 'June 13: At 9 [o'clock] all Mutiny ceases and the ship's crew in a submissive and orderly manner surrender to their proper officers, who accept their resignation. June 14: Captain [Edward O'Bryen] returned and joined ship, on which the ship's company discovered the strongest inclination of regard and affection.' Twenty of *Nassau*'s men were court-martialled, but all except one pardoned in due course. Bligh, to his credit but not in general to the rehabilitation of his reputation, strove to avoid any of his crew being tried.

The only sinister postscript was an incident that took place off Faversham, from where a requisitioned coaster slipped to sea bearing several men who had escaped from the *Inflexible* in three boats. They are thought to have landed in France. Others, from the *Montague*, escaped to the Low Countries. Presumably the ring-leaders, they had abandoned Parker to bear the brunt of Their Lordships' displeasure. One wonders what became of them.

With an admirable detachment, Admiral Duncan had meanwhile maintained the blockade with several small cutters and luggers and two men-of-war. It is said that on 30 April, when the first whiff of mutiny was smelt aboard his flagship the *Venerable*, Duncan lifted up a would-be mutineer and held him over the side, roaring 'This man intends depriving me of my ship!' During the crisis Duncan's handful of ships off the Dutch coast frequently ran up signal flags, deceiving De Winter into thinking a fleet lay out of sight just over the horizon. As the mutiny fizzled out, the ships crept back to join him. In early October the Admiralty warned him that De Winter was preparing to sail and on the afternoon of 11 October 1797 Duncan's formerly mutinous fleet decisively defeated the Dutch off Kamperduijn. In the wake of the victory many of the imprisoned mutineers were pardoned, for in a close-quarter and furious battle Duncan's fleet had redeemed itself.

Although the fleet mutinies of 1797 redressed the principal and justifiable grievances of the seamen and marines, they also aroused in the minds of the Establishment and the middle classes, who saw a steady preservation of the status quo as essential in prosecuting the war with Revolutionary France, the spectre of Jacobin extremism. Jacobinism was thought to have influenced the delegates at Spithead, though with one possible exception (that of HMS *Pompée*, see below) there is little real evidence for it. There is, however, at least circumstantial evidence that it had infected the men at the Nore, a few of whom, as we have seen, escaped and are thought to have landed in the Batavian Republic of the former Netherlands. There were almost certainly men in the navy of the day who had read and espoused the views of Tom Paine, though to what extent they were able to rouse their staid and conservative messmates remains unknown. Throughout the realm republican sedition was encouraged by Corresponding Societies such as had fomented rebellion against British rule in North America a generation earlier, and membership of them was proscribed. Two marines in the frigate *Diomede* at the Nore were indicted for being members of the Nottingham Corresponding Society. One, George Tomms, who had threatened to carry his ship into an enemy port after murdering the officers, was sentenced to hang; the other, John Wright, was sentenced to 500 lashes and being flogged round the fleet, a portion of his punishment being administered alongside each man-of-war in the squadron.

However, a more potent and active agitation was created by a relatively small number of Irish nationalists whose own movement broke out in domestic rebellion at home in the following year. Ireland was not subject to the Quota Acts, and the numbers of Irish enlisted into the navy is now considered to have been relatively small. The *Defiance*, aboard which trouble had flared in 1795 and which had been one of 'the most troublesome' of the Spithead ships, was subject to another mutiny in 1798. This was nipped in the bud by loyal seamen who informed on a number of Free and United Irishmen who had sworn to 'agree to carry the ship into Brest . . . and to kill every officer and man that shall hinder us . . . and to hoist a green ensign with a harp on it; and afterwards to kill and destroy the Protestants.' In the aftermath twenty-four seaman and one marine were court-martialled and twenty were hanged, by far the largest number from a single vessel in that turbulent period. Further evidence that there was an active Irish network desirous of carrying off ships to help the French-espoused cause of Irish independence was afforded from the *Caesar*. Led by Bartholomew Duff, the *Caesar*'s mutineers consisted of 8 committee-men, 37 seamen and 11 marines. One, Michael Butler, said he should 'never die easy till I swim in English blood', a point of view not likely to endear him to many of his shipmates.

A letter from the Irish contingent aboard another Spithead ship, the *Glory*, had expressed fervent loyalty. Captain James Brine was undeceived by an informer: ten men were arrested and tried for mutiny, eight were hanged and two flogged and imprisoned for a year. United Irishmen had attempted to agitate aboard some of St Vincent's ships of the Mediterranean fleet, particularly the *Princess Royal*; in the months following the mutinies the Admiralty, in its wisdom, sent some ships out to join Earl St Vincent, knowing the old martinet would subject them to severe but scrupulously fair regulation. He received one ship from Spithead, the 74-gun *Marlborough*. Her captain had been changed at the mutineers' request but she arrived to join the Mediterranean Fleet with a party of Irishmen held under charge of mutiny. The *Marlborough* was anchored between the rest of the fleet, the mutineers were tried and condemned and the boats of the fleet, their single carronades loaded, assembled to witness punishment. Captain Joseph Ellison had informed St Vincent that his men could not be brought to hang their fellows; the admiral had stated the contrary. Under the guns of the fleet, with St Vincent having ordered that the *Marlborough* should be battered to the extremity of sinking her if her company did not do their duty, the Marlboroughs carried out the grisly business. 'Discipline is preserved,' St Vincent, watching from his flagship, is reported to have said. But it cut both ways; in distant London Captain Henry Nicholls, whom Ellison had superseded in HMS *Marlborough*, was awaiting Their Lordships' pleasure at the Admiralty. The burden of shame was too much for him. Placing a loaded pistol to his head, he blew his own brains out.

Although mutinies occured intermittently aboard a number of men-of-war in the period following 1797, the most serious of the post-Spithead rumblings were heard aboard the *Pompée* on 4 June after Bridport's fleet had left Plymouth and were at sea on blockade duty. What appears to have been a highly politically-motivated uprising took place among 'eighty-six young and inexperienced men' who had not been satisfied with Howe's mediation or the Royal Pardon, and were opposed to the war with France. The ship's former delegates were not involved, which suggests that this was an entirely new manifestation of rebellion, arising from entirely new and probably idealistic motives. A committee, allegedly composed in its third part of United Irishmen, attempted to coerce the *Pompée*'s company 'to obtain an immediate peace on the return of the ship to port'. Threats were made to hang any man who would not take an oath on the Bible and sign a paper, but this attempt to suborn the men was reported by steadier hands and Captain James Vashon was able to seize the initiative. Reporting to Bridport, he was ordered to return to Portsmouth. Here the mutineers were accused of combining to seize the *Pompée* and 'prevail upon the fleet to return to Portsmouth and petition the King to make Peace, and if it was not immediately done, to compel him to do it, to change the ministry and to have a new parliament. If,' Captain Vashon went on, 'they had not succeeded in bringing the fleet into their traitorous proceedings, then the *Pompée* was to have been taken to some point in France.'

That this plan owed more to a desire on the part of 'young and inexperienced men' to end their bondage in the Royal Navy and return to their homes and families rather than surrender to the French, may be imagined. But it is significant that a belief existed among these poor fellows that the French Republic with its Bill of Rights would welcome them with an understanding that offered a stark contrast to the heartless oligarchy of their native land. What actually happened in the event of such recourse will shortly be demonstrated. As for the majority of the Pompées, the mad intentions of the rebellious faction were set at nought by a Loyal Address signed by 510 of them. The three administrators of the traitorous oath, Robert Johnson, James Callaway and John Broghan, were charged along with three other members of their 'council'. Johnson and a man named Thomas Ashly were hanged, Broghan was solitarily confined for a year, one man was acquitted, and Callaway and another had their death sentences remitted. The actuality is that the numbers of Irishmen bent on making trouble, though now impossible to determine, was small. Of the 462 men charged with mutiny in the Royal Navy during the whole of 1797, only 106 had been born in Ireland, a figure that bears an almost exact correlation to the rough 20 to 30 per centage of Irish-born seamen in the fleet. Nevertheless, as is clear from the case of the *Pompée*, even a small number could cause disproportionate trouble, while their avowed and wild intentions, though impossible of fulfilment, provided the conspiracy theorists of the day with plenty of alarmist fodder.

While naval courts-martial invariably visited the severest and most exemplary punishment upon ring-leaders – 'condign', they would have called it at the time – they were not entirely heartless. No action was taken against the great majority of the inexperienced young men who were split up and distributed among the fleet where, presumably, most gave little further trouble. This was, after all, the same navy which within months had achieved the notable victories of Camperdown and Aboukir Bay.

In addition to those mentioned in detail, in the period immediately following the Spithead and Nore mutinies rebellion broke out in the British line-of-battle ships *Royal Sovereign, Saturn, Mars, Bedford* and *Ardent*, the frigates *Beaulieu* and *Phoenix*, the sloop *Calypso*, and the storeship *Grampus*. The social changes wrought by the upheaval at Spithead took time to filter through; even slower to change was the conduct of some officers. The great fleet mutinies presaged no alteration in the strict stratification of Georgian society – that was a given fact of life – but they were eloquent of the firm determination of the British sailor to maintain that which he conceived to be what his country owed him for his service.

It is of interest to note that nowhere in the grievances of the moderates at Spithead or the extremists at the Nore did flogging appear. Indeed, the delegates in both cases flogged seamen disobedient to their own code of conduct, and the value of proper discipline was appreciated by the senior, sober seamen whose hands directed the insurrections, whatever their weaknesses in other directions. Even in all its brutal severity and ceremony, flogging itself was accepted when it was deserved. When it was not, or when it was accompanied by vicious and unjustified cruelty, that was another matter.

Such a case occurred in September of that same year aboard a British man-of-war in the West Indies. It is a curious fact that those who rake history for stories of barbarism and brutality settle upon poor Bligh and his miserable *Bounty,* entirely overlooking Captain Hugh Pigot and His Britannic Majesty's frigate *Hermione.*

8

'AREN'T YOU DEAD YET, YOU BUGGER?'

ALONGSIDE her ship's company of about 180 men and a solitary woman, at least two of the unholy trinity of rum, sodomy and the lash that were popularly supposed to motivate the eighteenth-century Royal Navy were present aboard HMS *Hermione* in September 1797. The 32-gun frigate was commanded by Hugh Pigot, the 28-year-old son of an admiral who, a contemporary considered, had 'neither foresight, judgement, nor enterprise'. Pigot had joined his father's ship in 1782, aged twelve, and was promoted lieutenant eight years later. He was made master and commander of the fireship *Incendiary,* then in February 1794 of the sloop *Swan* on the West Indies station, before being posted into the frigate *Success* in September. In July 1797 he replaced Philip Wilkinson as captain of the *Hermione,* by which time he had earned himself the unenviable reputation of being 'one of the most cruel and oppressive captains belonging to the Royal Navy'. He had flogged one man eight times in ten months and killed at least two more with the lash; one took eighteen weeks to die. With him from the *Success* Pigot brought a number of his best seamen, for he possessed at least enterprise and energy and the intention to run what was called 'a smart ship', demanding an absolute obedience at stations as the ship was manoeuvred. Such corporate tautness could make for a very happy ship, provided the ship's company was motivated not by bullying but by pride. Fatally for Pigot and his officers, he knew only one way, that of the tyrant. The Successes well knew this and were unhappy at being transferred with Pigot; in consequence, they did not mix easily with the Hermiones, and brought with them disturbing tales of the new captain's vicious habits.

Hugh Pigot was a man who regarded himself as the embodiment of naval puissance. As far as he was concerned, might – the captain's inherent authority – was right. He also considered the slightest deviation from strict conformity with regulations and standing orders as a challenge to discipline, and therefore an insult to his person. This megalomania tended to transform the tiniest infringement into technical mutiny, provoking an over-reaction from Pigot and a mobilization of the entire canon of naval discipline.

One example of the extremity to which Pigot would go will suffice. David Casey was an experienced midshipman who had earned Pigot's good opinion – he had, 'more than once, recommended [him] strongly' – and was in expectation of promotion to lieutenant. During the summer months, as news of the fleet mutinies percolated to the West Indies, the *Hermione* was 'most actively employed . . . frequently severely engaged in cutting out and harassing the Enemy in Puerto Rico and . . . in St Domingo.' Casey had distinguished himself in these minor actions but the *Hermione*'s first lieutenant, Harris, had left the ship, probably as a result of Pigot's victimization. The remaining commissioned officers were rather inexperienced – in fact, all held only acting commissions. The only other senior officer, and the most experienced, was the master, Mr Southcott, who under his warrant was responsible to Pigot for the navigation, stability and stowage of the *Hermione*.

One evening, about a week before the mutiny, the *Hermione*'s crew were shortening sail and reefing topsails, as was customary just before nightfall, when a frigate was cruising. Midshipman Casey was at his station in the main top. 'Fancying . . .', he supposed, 'that we were not as smart as usual . . . [Pigot] got into a violent passion, at which moment he observed a Man going up the lee Main Top Mast rigging, and instantly in very hard language, desired to know the cause.'

By a convention intended for the general safety of the hands, men ascended the rigging on the weather side, where the wind tended to blow them onto the shrouds and ratlines and, with the ship heeling away from them, the climb was not only safer but easier. The topmen of a man-of-war were the cream of her seamen, priding themselves upon their agility and their scorn of danger. In a crack frigate, they were both likely and expected – especially by such as Pigot – to act on their initiative to aid the overall effectiveness of whatever manoeuvre was in progress. Casey accordingly 'answered in the most respectful Manner, that a [reefing] point remain'd untied, and a Gasket hung abaft the yard', two details that, had they been left unattended to, would undoubtedly have incurred Pigot's wrath, particularly the un-secured reef point, which would have been considered sloppy.

This was precisely the sort of situation Pigot relished and one cannot escape the conclusion, in view of the lengths to which he now went, that sadism was a powerful part of his psyche. The captain publicly abused Casey, calling him 'a damned lubber, a worthless good-for-nothing . . . and used many other severe expressions, that I cannot and do not wish to recollect . . . [but] to which I made no reply.' As he descended to the deck Casey was again verbally assaulted, at which his 'feelings were so excited from his dreadful and unmerited abuse, I replied that I was no such Character as he described . . . '

'Silence, Sir!' Pigot raged, 'or I will instantly tie you up to the Gun and flog you.' To which Casey unwisely replied, 'I hope not Sir, this is cruel treatment, Captain Pigot and what I don't deserve.' Casey was then ordered below decks under arrest. A little later, at about eight o'clock, he was summoned to Pigot's cabin where the captain was attended by Mr Reid, the new first lieutenant, Mr Southcott and the Purser. Pigot now subjected Casey to a further 'disapprobation' of his conduct, and told the midshipman that had the officers present not attested to his character he would have court-martialled him, and now pitied him his misfortune. Casey would never again be invited to dine at his table, Pigot went on, and unless he went 'down on his Knees the following Morning publicly on the Quarterdeck, he would flog me most severely.' Casey 'endeavoured to express' his 'sincere sorrow' and apologized 'in a submissive manner to make every possible atonement for real or imagined offence', but Pigot was not to be appeased by anything other than Casey's complete, degrading and abjectly public humiliation. During the night Reid and other officers attempted to persuade Casey to oblige the captain, though none of them tried to dissuade Pigot from his irrevocable course of action. In due course Casey was summoned to appear on the quarterdeck the following morning at eleven o'clock, 'the usual hour of punishment.' He publicly assured Pigot that he 'had no intention of offering him the slightest insult . . . was very sorry that he should think so and begged his pardon.' But it was to no avail: 'nothing less than going on my knees would satisfy, which he repeatedly insisted on my doing.' Refusing to comply, Casey was stripped, seized to the capstan and received one dozen lashes from the boatswain. He was then disrated and turned out of his mess, his naval career as an officer at an end.

The extremity of Casey's punishment, perceived as unjust by the crew, had its usual effect. The atmosphere aboard the *Hermione* now took on a sinister air, and the men aloft were particularly wary. On the evening of 20 September the men were again called to their stations to shorten sail for the night. Once again Pigot interfered, calling out through his speaking trumpet that the men were slow and he would flog the last man down on deck. This was doubly unfair, for the most nimble topmen were posted at the extremity of the yards, where they hauled on and secured the reefing earrings; being farthest from the stays, they would automatically be the last down. On completion of their task, the men edged in along the footropes and transferred to ratline and backstay to get down on deck for fear of a flogging. Almost above the heads of Pigot and Southcott at their posts on the quarterdeck, the three youngsters on the mizzen topsail yard slipped in their haste, lost their grip and fell. One broke his fall by landing on Southcott, knocking the master down and injuring him. The other two fell onto the deck at Pigot's feet, their bodies shattered and quivering with shock and pain. Pigot is alleged to have ordered the half-dead 'boys' thrown overboard, though Casey makes no mention of this detail.

The incident temporarily paralysed the men coming in from the main topsail yard who stared in horror until Pigot, quite unconcerned, ordered two boatswain's mates up into the Main Top 'to start [strike] the entire Topmen, which was accordingly and indiscriminately done, and on the following morning a *very severe punishment* of several Men, I believe twelve or fourteen, took place in the usual way, at the public place of punishment.'

Next day the *Hermione* had joined the brig-sloop *Diligence* and both were in chase of an enemy privateer which had been sighted earlier, standing north on opposite tacks off the western extremity of Puerto Rico. In pursuit of an enemy there was no routine shortening down as darkness fell, and at this time there were some topmen gathered in the tops. Since the previous evening the ship must have been alive with hissed comment and secret communication. The officers' steward and the second lieutenant's servant had got hold of some rum and this was freely circulated to men conspiring in the main top.

At about eleven o'clock on the 21st or 22nd (the accounts differ), with the third lieutenant, Mr Foreshaw (also called in some accounts Fanshawe or Fairshaw), officer of the watch on deck, three parties of mutineers came aft at the run, shouting, whooping and rolling cannon-shot ahead of them to knock off their feet any hastily mustering resistance among the officers and marines. One party made for the quarterdeck, the second for the gun-room off which lay the officers' cabins, and the third overpowered Marine MacNeal, on sentry duty outside Pigot's cabin. Forcing the door they burst in upon Pigot.

Pigot jumped from his cot. Unable to reach his sword, he grabbed a dirk and parried the attacks of several men led by David Forrester and Henry (or Hadrian) Poulson, who all took 'a Cut or Stab at him' with cutlasses or boarding axes. Pigot tried to call for his boat's crew, whom he supposed might be best disposed to defend their captain, but one of them was Poulson, who swore at Pigot. The mutineers pressed him and he fell back, bracing himself against a gun and calling for assistance. Fighting for his life, Pigot pinked Forrester on the foot as the men fought and stumbled in the darkness. He slashed one man's hand, but the response was a slash of a cutlass at Pigot's stomach. In his night-shirt, covered with blood, Pigot was gradually forced back to the sash windows that ran across the stern of the ship.

The sentry meanwhile called an alarm to the quarterdeck above, whereupon Foreshaw, 'a good humane young man', instructed Mr Turner the master's mate sharing the watch with him, to investigate. Aware of what was under way, Turner told Foreshaw to 'go himself'. Alarmed by Turner's attitude, Foreshaw ordered Quartermaster Osborn to alter course to close with the *Diligence* as a precaution, but was roundly damned, and disobeyed. The lieutenant at once knocked Osborn down and made to take the wheel, but Osborn's shout brought more men running after along the gangways from the forecastle.

Outnumbered and isolated, Foreshaw was attacked and wounded about the head. Forced to the ship's side, he was re-duced to pleading desperately for his life in the name of his wife and three children. There was a moment of hesitant weakness among the seamen, ended by a man named Thomas Nash who, arriving from the cabin, ordered them to 'heave the bugger overboard!'

As Foreshaw disappeared over the side, Nash rejoined Forrester, Poulson, and the others in the cabin. One man named Farrel shouted, 'Aren't you dead yet, you bugger?' and provoked the wounded Captain to respond, but then another man, William

Crawley, entered the cabin armed with a boarding axe and with a 'Here goes then!' succeeded in knocking Pigot down.

His cries for mercy went unheard. A seaman named Montell who had earlier wrenched McNeal's musket and bayonet from the marine, said 'You've shown no mercy yourself and deserve none!' He then lunged at Pigot and drove the bayonet into him. Pigot had by now dropped his dirk and collapsed. As some of the men smashed glazings out, others seized Pigot. The captain made one last, feeble remonstrance and was then hurled from his own stern windows into the *Hermione*'s swirling wake. Pigot's shouts could be heard for some seconds as the ship drew away in the pitchy darkness, but by then the party were emerging from the cabin wild with blood-lust and rum, howling that 'Hughey was overboard!' The ship 'was instantly in the possession of the Mutineers'.

The seamen who had made for the gun-room 'put the Second Lieutenant and [a] Midshipman to Death in the most savage manner, and as they dragged them up the Hatchway, apparently Dead, they continued Cutting and Stabbing them with various Weapons, till they reach'd the Main Deck, when they threw them overboard; the conduct of some of the crew was truly savage, and brutal, and cannot be described.' Casey, the witness, had been awakened from his berth of exile and found all in confusion as the mutineers broke into the arms chest. The injured Southcott attempted to escape to the deck above through the gun-room skylight, but was struck over the head and fell back as men advised him to stow himself away.

Lieutenant McIntosh of the marines was in his cot with yellow fever. He was being tended by Sergeant John Place when Lieutenant Douglas rushed in in his shirt and asked what all the noise was about. All was now confusion as the mutineers went on the rampage, searching for Douglas, whose unpopularity appears to have developed from a flogging he had initiated. Douglas was cornered, as was Midshipman Smith, and these two were chased, hacked to pieces and dragged on deck as Casey described. They too were thrown overboard, Douglas's body scarcely recognisable as human.

The mutineers demanded that Pigot's servant John Jones give them the key of the captain's private liquor store, and then Foreshaw reappeared. Instead of falling clear of the ship's side he had landed on the mizen chain-whales – extended platforms to which the heavy standing rigging was set up and which stuck outboard like shelves. 'Good God men, what have I done to harm you that I should be treated in this manner?'

But Foreshaw was guilty by association. Farrel and Nash, gaining the deck on the shouted news that Foreshaw had returned from the dead, lost no time in despatching him. As the lieutenant clung to the rigging Farrel struck one of his hands off with his boarding axe; he and Nash then threw the bloody wreck of the *Hermione*'s third lieutenant over the side.

Casey's earlier humiliation on the quarterdeck saved his life. It was almost the only forbearance the mutineers showed. It might have been supposed that after the first mad attacks their thirst for revenge would have been assuaged. It might also have been supposed that the vast majority of the crew, only learning the full horror of what all were now, willy-nilly, implicated in as they tumbled out of their hammocks, would have offered some resistance. Not so. 'The Scene now became dreadful, and the greatest confusion prevailed, all were more or less inflam'd, and excited by Spirits [rum], except about 45 or 50 of the principal Mutineers, who kept Sober and Steady, and opposed to taking any more lives.' As the future was being debated and Nash was emerging as the leader at the centre of the insurrection, the remaining officers were kept in a state of horrified suspense.

During this hiatus First Lieutenant Samuel Reid sought treatment from Sansum the surgeon, who with Mr Pacey the purser and Laurence Cronin the surgeon's mate remained in the gun-room, where Casey had also gone after refusing Nash's offer to join them. A little later Crawley and a handful of other mutineers came aft and took Sansum off to attend to some of the wounded seamen, including Forrester. Shortly after Sansum's return Cronin got up upon the gunroom table and, poking his head through the skylight so that he could be heard by the men

on the deck above and his colleagues below, began an inflammatory address. Cronin, a Belfast man, described afterwards by
Casey as 'a treacherous, drunken infamous character', appears
to have taken no part in the mutiny; although rated surgeon's
mate, he had been pressed able seaman out of a merchant ship.
Now his influence became fatal. Declaring himself an ardent
republican, he declared the men's actions to be entirely justified,
but said the mutiny would be incomplete unless all the officers
were disposed of. Dead men, Cronin implied, tell no tales.

Southcott was spared, partly because he was being guarded
by 'two of the principal Muntineers' – probably for his future
usefulness as navigator – partly by the tearful supplications of
'his Servant Boy', and partly thanks to the injury he had sustained
from the falling topman. The gunner and carpenter, both useful
warrant officers, were also spared; but in addition to Pigot,
Douglas, Foreshaw and Smith, the mutineers now threw
overboard Reid, McIntosh, Sansum, Pacey, another midshipman,
the Captain's Clerk, and the boatswain, William Martin. The
other junior officers – Master's Mate Turner, 'a clever and
disappointed man', one midshipman and, of course, Cronin,
joined the mutiny. The solitary woman on board was Mrs
Martin, the boatswain's wife. We know little about her, except
that she shared her bed that same night with a mutineer named
Redman.

As the final act in the mutiny itself, Nash called all hands to
wear ship. It was the intention of the principal mutineers,
possibly influenced by Cronin's flamboyant rhetoric, to take the
ship south and surrender her to the authorities at La Guaira on
the Spanish Main. By obeying this order and turning the ship
round, the remainder of the ship's company became accessories
after the fact and thus mutineers under the 20th Article of War,
having abandoned their duty – read to them every fourth Sunday
of the month – to use their utmost endeavours to suppress mutiny
or stamp out sedition.

During the passage the *Hermione* was in the greatest disorder,
many of the crew being 'continually in a state of drunkenness,

and frequently fighting' with Casey and 'those officers saved . . . in continual dread of being put to Death'. With Turner able to navigate, Southcott's utility and thus his life seemed doubtful; but Turner lacked the confidence to assume full responsibility, and was constantly sending down to Southcott for advice. Turner appears to have been part of the conspiracy, singled out as the officer best disposed to take command after the murder of Pigot, hence his attitude to Foreshaw at that critical moment. His leadership was probably only nominal, necessary for treating with the Spaniards at the behest of Nash and his confederates. All took an oath organized by Cronin that they would not recognize one another, nor call each other by the names by which they then knew each other: all were to take their chances under aliases, depending upon what the Spanish authorities made of their surrender.

The *Hermione* arrived at La Guaira on 27 September and Turner and two others, dressed as gentlemen by Pigot's servant John Jones, were pulled ashore in the barge. Terms of surrender were negotiated with the astonished Governor of the tiny port – an open roadstead on the coast of modern Venezuela. Casey, showing some of the stiff pride that had made him refuse Pigot's perverse humiliation, refused to be suborned by the mutineers. For a while his fate hung in the balance, but the presence of the Spanish authorities cramped the mutineers' freedom of action, and with the other surviving officers he was closely confined for a while at La Guaira before being taken the twenty miles to Caracas. After six months they were all paroled and exchanged in a cartel. This took them to Martinique, where they 'were received on board the *Prince of Wales*' and, after a further month during which the first of the mutineers was apprehended, sent home 'in the *Alfred* with a large convoy.'

The news of the mutiny had preceded them. By chance the *Diligence*, having lost contact with the *Hermione*, had on 20 October captured a Spanish schooner whose master was able to tell Commander Robert Mends of the arrival of a British frigate at La Guaira. From that moment the Royal Navy set about exacting retribution. The degree to which the Hermiones were made to pay for their crimes is uncertain. Some men undoubtedly escaped, some of them to the United States. One, William Bowen, was pressed out of an American ship into HMS *Minerve* but not recognized until 1802; after trial he was hanged. Another, John Coe, joined a French privateer which captured an American brig, into which Coe went as prize crew. They were in their turn captured by HMS *Aquilon* and Coe too was recognized, to be hanged at Port Royal at the end of 1798. Two years later, when Curaçao was captured, Poulson was found serving in a Dutch frigate; he was hanged on the *Puissant*. Others whose implication in the mutiny was technical had mostly hidden away; although condemned by court martial, they were recommended to mercy. In many cases clemency allowed them their lives, but Sir Hyde Parker, Commander-in-Chief in the West Indies, saw to it that the principals suffered when they were caught, and there was a bounty of $100 offered for every apprehension. Nash had shipped aboard an American schooner called *Tanner's Delight*. He had assumed a pseudonym but was fond of the bottle and boastful, and a shipmate betrayed him at Charleston in Carolina. He was extradited under the provisions of Jay's Treaty, tried and hanged at Port Royal in August 1799.

Pigot's desperate summons for his bargemen had a curious sequel. Forrester joined a privateer named the *Lydia,* from which he was pressed into the sloop-of-war HMS *Bittern*. Having thus rejoined the Royal Navy he became one of the captain's barge-man and as Thomas Williamson earned a good reputation. Then on 22 March 1802 he was recognized by Pigot's old servant, John Jones, and arrested. The prosecution's main witness, Mr South-cott, arrived from Plymouth and told the court: 'I know the prisoner very well. He was as active in the mutiny as any I saw.' Forrester confessed, and was hanged on 1 April.

Others were apprehended over the years that followed. One, James Duncan, addressed the ship's company of the *Puissant* just before they ran him up to the foreyardarm. 'About a quarter of an hour before he was turned off [i.e., hoisted and hanged], he

Although he never completed the circumnavigation for which he was famous, Magellan boldly suppressed a vicious mutiny among his subordinate captains.

FERNAND, MAGELLAN,

The first English circumnavigator and a seaman of great enterprise – Drake, like Magellan, had to put down a rebellion among his officers and did so with words that have echoed down the centuries.

Irritable and foul-mouthed, Bligh is better known among seafarers for his professional skills than his alleged tyranny.

A contemporary print of a truculent Parker presenting a list of the seamen's demands to Admiral Buckner at the Nore. Parker's assumption of equality with Buckner is shown by his pose and his sword and pistol.

Naval vengeance: the crew of HMS *Surprise* recapture HMS *Hermione* from the Spanish, after her mutinous crew had surrendered her in 1797 ending Captain Hugh Pigot's inexcusable reign of sadistic terror.

Captain Thomas Worth of the American whaler, the *Globe* – one of the many American and British merchant shipmasters who fell victim to the horrors of mutiny at sea during the nineteenth century.

A harsh disciplinarian who ought to wear the mantle history has conferred on Bligh. This wood carving of Mackenzie was produced at the time of his court martial.

The gruesome image of the American brig-of-war, USS *Somers*, with her young mutineers hanging from the main yardarm.

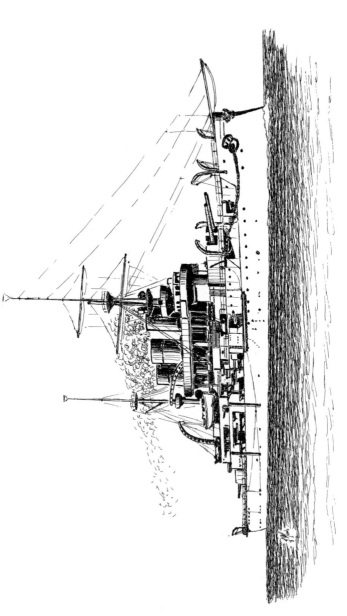

Second only to the *Bounty* in popular notoriety, the mutiny aboard the Imperial Russian battleship, *Potemkin*, was immortalised as soviet propaganda in Sergei Eisenstein's dramatic film.

Racial tensions aboard the Dutch squadron in the East Indies provoked a dramatic mutiny aboard *De Zeven Provincien*, the echoes of which reached the Netherlands.

The incompatibility between traditional naval management and young
'Hostilities Only' ratings was compounded by the appalling conditions prevailing
aboard the converted cargo-liner, HMS *Lothian*, at the end of World War II.

The cool Arnheiter, commanding officer of USS *Vance*, faces the cameras and
his critics. His operations officer said of him: 'This guy is paranoid'.

. . . said how justly he was condemned for being concerned in one of the worst of crimes, and warned them from ever being concerned in such an act of atrocity.' A seaman in the *Royal William*, the receiving ship at Portsmouth, was court-martialled and sentenced to two years in the Marshalsea Prison for having 'used reproachful and provoking speeches' towards a witness who had given evidence against Duncan. John Jones was certainly abused in this way. Sergeant Place and Mr Southcott, who by now had been commissioned lieutenant and later died a Master and Commander, were also frequently called as witnesses; courts being held over until Southcott returned from sea duty in the *Renard*.

Over a hundred of *Hermione*'s people eluded the navy's justice. Having given themselves over to the Spanish authorities, many were able to disappear. Some entered the Spanish colonial army, most escaped by going back to sea. The navy brought 33 of 'the Bloody Hermiones' to trial and hanged 24 of them, the last in October 1806, run aloft aboard the *Salvador del Mundo*, an ageing prize from Earl St Vincent's great victory by then lying off Plymouth in the Hamoaze. Most of the mutinous crew therefore survived, to live lives circumscribed by their aliases and their solemn oath. Cronin, its administrator, appears to have settled quietly in La Guaira, and the vicious Farrel to have returned to his native New York. Turner too disappeared, probably vanishing in the United States, which is where Mrs Martin is thought to have gone. Her lover Redman was caught and tried with a batch of his shipmates, having been taken out of a merchant ship. With several others, he was summarily hanged.

As for Casey, he continued the career Pigot had threatened to curtail and seems to have succeeded in blighting, for although he was promoted lieutenant in October 1799 he never rose higher. He subsequently served in a number of ships and saw action on several occasions, finally commanding a semaphore and signal station.

But it was not only murder that the mutineers had done: they had also handed one of His Britannic Majesty's ships-of-war to

the enemy. The *Hermione* became the *Santa Cecilia* in the service
of the King of Spain, and as such a permanent reminder of a
national humiliation; fortunately she remained in Spanish
American waters. Sir Hyde Parker was determined to recapture
her. The admiral felt the affair touched his personal honour, since
Pigot had been a protégé of his, but in addition to this personal
animus he was an admiral of the old, authoritarian school. He
bided his time, but in due course learned that the *Santa Cecilia*
was preparing to leave her mooring at Puerto Cabello to join a
small Spanish squadron at Havana. The dashing young Captain
Edward Hamilton of the 28-gun frigate *Surprise*, almost as strict
a martinet as Pigot though lacking his sadism, volunteered to cut
her out from under the guns of the considerable fortifications of
Puerto Cabello. Parker demurred; the place was heavily fortified,
and it was too dangerous. Instead Hamilton was sent to cruise
off Aruba, to intercept the *Santa Cecilia* as she made her way
north to Havana. Hamilton lay off Aruba for some weeks
without a sign of the *Santa Cecilia*. With the *Surprise*'s water
and provisions running low he decided to take a look into Puerto
Cabello, to ensure that his quarry had not eluded him. Sure
enough, the former British frigate remained secure under the
embrasures of the Spanish guns. The *Surprise* stood on and
offshore for three days, losing every property her name implied.
Then on the evening of 24 October Hamilton resolved to go in
and cut the *Santa Cecilia* out by boat. He and his officers made
careful preparations and, after dark but in bright moonlight, the
boats of the *Surprise*, led by Hamilton, pulled inshore to make
their attack. The Spanish were well prepared and the *Santa
Cecilia* was stuffed with men. As the British attacked and
clambered aboard, the defenders responded and the guns ashore
were manned. Despite the unfavourable odds, the Surprises
prevailed after a bloody hand-to-hand fight in which Hamilton
received a serious head wound from which he never afterwards
entirely recovered. The Surprises suffered no losses but inflicted
many upon the Spanish. Once they had the upper hand the
frigate's cables were cut, her topsails were dropped from the

yards, the yards were hoisted and all was sheeted home: once more under the British flag, *Hermione* crept out to sea under the gentle gusts of the *terral* as the Spanish artillery attempted to turn the tables with a brisk cannonade.

Their Lordships decided that the *Hermione*'s name had become so synonymous with mutiny that she must not resume it, now she had returned to naval service. She was first renamed the *Retaliation*, but this was considered too pointed; she then became the *Retribution*. She arrived back in Portsmouth in January 1802, only to be laid up as the Peace of Amiens briefly interrupted to hostilities. When war broke out again the following year she was not recommissioned. Instead she was taken round to the Thames and manned by the Royal Trinity House Volunteer Artillery as part of a cordon of ten similarly organized frigates which were moored to block the Thames and defend London against the expected French invasion. After the passing of the crisis in 1805 she went upstream to Deptford, where she was finally and ignominiously broken up. Within months the last of her mutineers to be caught had been condemned and executed.

The insurrection aboard the *Hermione* was the most terrible of 1797, that year of mutiny – and yet, for all its bloody consequences, perhaps the most justifiable. Men could be made to bow to the most appalling abuses, but there was a point beyond which they could not be pushed: and Captain Pigot had defined exactly where that point lay. If the blood of the *Hermione*'s innocent officers was upon the heads of Nash and his gang, it was also upon the bobbing head of Pigot as he died screaming with fury and pain in the wake of his hijacked frigate.

9

'AN EXCESSIVELY SEVERE OFFICER'

THE ruthlessness with which the Admiralty punished and hunted down mutineers was of course common knowledge on the lower deck of every British man-of-war. From Captain Edwardes' pursuit of the *Bounty* mutineers in *Pandora*, by way of the string of executions visited on Richard Parker and the crews of the mutinous ships at the Cape of Good Hope, to the piece-meal punishment of several of 'the Bloody Hermiones', the likely fate of any seaman contemplating mutiny must have been clear. Historians arguing over the extent to which French agents stirred up trouble have generally concluded by dismissing the notion, but it is undeniable that a strong sympathetic undercurrent in favour of republicanism had grown up not only in Ireland but in Scotland and England after the American War of Independence, and in a more extreme and urgent form, after the outbreak of the French Revolution. The Corresponding Societies may have gained less than a toe-hold in the Royal Navy, but some debate upon political systems certainly went on at the mess-tables slung between the guns throughout the British fleet.

Something of this sort of thing lay behind Cronin's desperate measure in surrendering *Hermione* to the enemy, albeit the

Spanish colonial authorities were somewhat farther from any republican model than King George's admirals. Perhaps their virtue, for Cronin and some of the others, lay in the fact that they were Catholic. Be that as it may, any crew contemplating mutiny after 1797 must have seen their only chance of success as resting in a surrender to the French. It was reasonable to assume they would be welcome in post-Revolutionary France, perhaps as the thin end of a long and effective wedge of desertion from Britain's Royal Navy: its 'storm-battered ships' were, as the American historian Alfred Mahan is so frequently quoted as observing, the only thing that stood between the French armies and the mastery of the world.

One of those 'storm-battered ships' was the *Danae*, a small 20-gun sixth-rate which had formerly been the French national corvette *La Vaillante*, captured in 1798. In the spring of 1799 the renamed *Danae* was part of a small squadron defending the Channel Islands under the command of Captain Lord Proby, heir to the Earl of Carysfort. By and large the officers of the Royal Navy were middle-class, a consequence of them having to learn their profession from the bottom up. Men like Lord Nelson, Lord Collingwood and Earl St Vincent earned their peerages for meritorious service, so that an aristocrat such as Proby was – like the able Lord Cochrane, son of the impoverished Earl of Dundonald – an oddity. Proby was described as 'promising', and although he showed signs of zeal, had received too-rapid promotion. However, his ship's station, with its fierce tides, strong winds and rocks and shoals – described by Lord Collingwood as 'having more of danger in them than a battle once a week' – was an appropriate training ground. It also offered Proby and his crew the opportunity to capture French vessels. Despite being desperately short of her full complement, the *Danae* did well on her first cruise.

On 29 April news reached Plymouth that Admiral Bruix had escaped from Brest with a squadron of men-of-war, and Proby was immediately ordered to the Breton coast. Here he pressed two seamen out of the crew of the British privateer *Tartar*. One was a 24-year old Liverpudlian named William Jackson, a man popularly supposed to have served Richard Parker during the uprising at the Nore, but whose name does not appear in the list of the Nore mutineers. Although a good seaman, soon made captain of the main-top, he was also quickly found guilty of several 'different crimes' and given forty-eight lashes.

Returning to Plymouth in August Proby, still short of hands, took aboard more men from the receiving ship. They were a dubious band, and formed a disproportionate percentage of his small crew. A number of them had just been captured with a French privateer, *La Bordelais*, which had been taken by a British frigate. At first thought of as renegades, these men claimed American nationality, pleaded plausible reasons for their plight, affirming that they had been aboard *La Bordelais* under duress, and added that they would be content to serve aboard a British man-of-war. One was named John Williams. Quite who or what these men were remains obscure, but the question of American nationality came to be a burning issue in the decade that followed. On the one hand, British seamen who had deserted to serve in American merchant vessels often claimed to be native-born Americans to avoid being pressed when British ships intercepted them in their anti-contraband operations; on the other hand, over-zealous British naval officers, often desperate for prime seamen, claimed that if a man had been born before the end of the American War of Independence he was technically British, and bound to serve in a British man-of-war. The argument resulted in war between Great Britain and the United States in 1812, but had rankled among sailors long before then.

Even this augmentation of manpower failed to fill the empty hammock-spaces in the *Danae* when she sailed on her third cruise, blockading Brest. Proby continued to press men – twenty-three of them – out of merchant ships. Shortly before Christmas the *Danae* went to the assistance of the frigate *Ethalion* which had run aground on the rock-girt approaches to Brest and was subsequently lost there, and early in the New Year she suffered damage which forced her to return to Plymouth for repairs. Significantly, Proby delayed the ship's sailing once the repairs had been effected 'since the ship's company wages were due near three months ago'. He thought it 'proper to get them paid now.'

The *Danae* thereafter continued to play her part in the Inshore Squadron, blockading Brest, harrying French coastal trade, and working with the heavier frigates in the chase of at least one French man-of-war, *La Pallas*. During this period she took on board a seaman named John MacDonald. Asked by the master of a British troop-transport to remove MacDonald as he was a mutinous and abusive man, Proby unwisely obliged. On 10 March he further compounded his folly. That day he seized the British merchantman *Plenty* which had been captured by the French; releasing her to her liberated crew, he retained her five-strong French prize crew.

To some extent Proby was a victim of his own success, for many of his best men were away in prizes themselves, and his continual attempts to recruit his crew only diluted the quality of those on board. In order to work his ship in so dangerous an area as off Ushant, he had taken the unusual step of turning up the so-called 'idlers' (officers' servants or other men such as the cook, who normally did not stand night watches but carried out 'day-work') to stand watches round the clock. The *Danae* now possessed a disparate crew which had never settled down as a proper 'ship's company'. One of the 'Americans' picked up at Plymouth was afterwards said to have been a former Hermione, while the presence of six Frenchmen, though in the long run it probably had little direct influence upon the conduct of a band of men uniting as mutineers, must have been unsettling, and was potentially dangerous to good order, particularly as the *Danae* remained cruising within sight of their native coast.

While the reasons why Proby's crew mutinied are obscure, we know that, quite apart from his polyglot crew, he had not been well served by some of his warrant and petty officers. The carpenter was court-martialled for drunkenness, disrespect and neglect of duty, and the master-at-arms had been sent to prison. Proby also appears to have been sparing of the lash, perhaps an odd folly, but conducive to an atmosphere of easy-going tolerance.

The disadvantage of such a regime is that too often it enables disaffection to increase where there are ill-disposed persons present. Too many among those now on board the *Danae* were at the very least finding life irksome, and some were combining, something else easy to achieve under relaxed discipline.

By the afternoon of Thursday 14 March 1800 enough had made their dissatisfaction known for the men from *La Bordelais* to be administering an oath on the Bible in the fore and main-tops. The ship had been working close in shore and lay in a haze with a light breeze between the Île d'Ouessant and Pointe St Matthieu, and the plan was for the conspirators to seize the upper deck and confine the remainder below. Importantly, no murder was to be done.

The following night was dark, and at about a quarter past nine the officer of the watch, the master, Mr John Huntingdon, was overcome and struck on the head with a cutlass. Midshipman Heron, also on watch, was hustled below. Proby, emerging from his cabin at the noise of the commotion, was likewise struck on the head. Hearing a disturbance, First Lieutenant Charles Niven and Lieutenant Stephens of the marines armed themselves and came to Proby's assistance; simultaneously the marines were turning out and one, Private Dowling, ran aft towards the after hatch. Meanwhile Huntingdon was thrown semi-conscious down the main hatch and the grating was secured over it. As Dowling tried to get on deck, two of the mutineers slammed the grating over the after hatch, and down below the second lieutenant and surgeon, arming themselves with pistols, found they too were prisoners. Proby and Huntingdon were wounded, and in addition to the officers about forty men were battened down with them. A search made for arms revealed that the arms chest had been taken on deck by the mutineers. In the succeeding hours all attempts made by Proby and his officers to negotiate with the mutineers were fruitless, resulting only in insults being offered by Jackson and MacDonald.

Proby might have immobilized *Danae* by chocking her rudder, to which he had access – but he might also have lost his ship as the strong tides cast her ashore upon the islets, rocks and reefs which lie between Pointe St Matthieu and the Île d'Ouessant, Ushant itself. It was soon clear to Proby that the *Danae* was heading for the mainland near Le Conquet, to the north of St Matthieu. The mutineers began lowering the stern boat, and as Proby threw the private signals overboard, Jackson with four seamen and a French sailor left the ship in the boat to parley with Capitaine de Frégate Julien, commanding the French national corvette *La Colombe*, anchored with a convoy off le Conquet. The *Danae*'s boat flew the tricolour superior to a British ensign reversed, in token of submission. Fearing a ruse, Julien held the men hostage and sent a boat of his own to determine the true state of affairs aboard the *Danae*, after which she was allowed to approach the road and anchor in company. As more boats now approached laden with troops to take possession of the *Danae,* one of the mutineers called out '*Vive la république française!*'

That afternoon Proby, taken aboard *La Colombe*, gave up his sword to Julien and made it clear in French that he capitulated, not to the 'rebels on board' his own ship, but to '*la marine française*'. At mid afternoon on 15 March, Proby and his officers were taken ashore to a torrent of abuse, particularly from MacDonald. At the same time Julien also placed thirty officers and men from his own ship aboard *Danae* and a few days later, with two British frigates in the offing, *La Colombe* escorted both her convoy and the *Danae* round Pointe St Matthieu and into Brest.

If the French were surprised at the ease of their conquest, it was as nothing to the surprise of the mutineers. On arrival, Proby and his officers were treated with every mark of the conventional respect that existed between the two nations. Officers were subject to exchange, and since there were more French naval officers in British custody than *vice versa*, a clutch of Royal Naval officers was most useful. Nevertheless, they were at first confined near the men, who were also held as prisoners. Much to the astonishment of MacDonald, Jackson and the other mutineers, no distinction was at first made between them and the loyalists, and they were in close enough proximity to their former officers to insult them; but worse was to follow. Far from being welcomed, the mutineers were denied the opportunity to serve in the French fleet, on the grounds that men who had betrayed their native land would certainly betray an adopted one. Protests that they were Americans and Irish were not believed, and were probably at least in part exaggerated (of the twenty who claimed to be Irish and twelve American, sixteen were listed as 'born in England'). However, after being interrogated for a few days the mutineers were turned out of Brest with a small sum of money and passports to go where they would. Three ring-leaders, Jackson, Williams and an undisputable Irishman named Feeny, together with the five Frenchmen taken out of the *Plenty*, were sent for to Paris by the First Consul, Napoleon Bonaparte, escorted by gendarmes.

Only twelve days after the arrival of the *Danae* in Brest, the exchange of her crew was under way. Although Proby and others spent some time in the prison at Valenciennes, three months after the loss of his ship he and those of his crew still loyal were being court-martialled for the loss of the *Danae* aboard the *Gladiator* at Portsmouth. There being no obvious reason for the rebellion, all were acquitted except the watch on deck, who were held not to have done their utmost in support of Mr Huntingdon, and were imprisoned.

The first of the mutineers had fallen into British hands five days before the court sat, though it was some time before he was identified. Most of the mutineers appear to have taken service in French privateers, scores of which were armed and commissioned to prey – very successfully – upon British merchantmen. On 12 June the corsair *Le Vengeur* was captured in the Bay of Biscay; her crew were imprisoned in the Mill Gaol at Plymouth and among them was John Marret, a French-speaking Jerseyman. On Sunday 24 August the prisoners were paraded and inspected by Lieutenant Niven, who having been sent to scour the prison hulks was now at the Mill Gaol. Marret was condemned aboard the frigate *Pique* at Plymouth and hanged a week later. Jackson also signed on a privateer, *Le Brave* of Bordeaux. *Le Brave* was chased by HMS *Anson*, but Jackson escaped justice and disappeared.

MacDonald was not so fortunate. He joined an American schooner at San Sebastian in December 1800 and by June 1801 the vessel was in London, and lying in the Pool, opposite the press tender off the Tower. Feeling safe with his American press-protection, MacDonald ventured ashore to visit the stews of Wapping, where, on the 3rd, he was recognized by the peripatetic Niven, and when apprehended unwisely blurted out that the mutiny was attributable to Lord Proby. Tried at Sheerness where Proby himself was chief prosecutor, MacDonald almost swayed the court in his favour. Claiming to be an American named Samuel Higgins, he stated that he had heard all about the mutiny from another of the mutineers, Jackson, whom he had met at Bordeaux. MacDonald had a document from the American consul at Lisbon certifying his American nationality and dated 27 December 1798, but such things were easy to come by, and the townsfolk of Hadden, Connecticut, from where MacDonald/Higgins claimed to hail, later denied all knowledge of him. In any case Niven, when pressed by the president of the court, was absolutely positive in his identification, and this was sufficient to hang MacDonald.

Another of the mutineers to find a berth aboard an American merchant ship was John Williams. He must have been a compulsive agitator, for a Mr Shanks, the mate of the *Statira* aboard which Williams had signed on as an able seaman, denounced him when the *Statira* lay in St Helier harbour, Jersey. Tried aboard the *Gladiator* at Portsmouth on 12 September 1801 he too was condemned to death, the weight of evidence too strong against him. Like MacDonald, however, he made a plea claiming American citizenship, and this time the American ambassador in London, Mr Rufus King, was minded to uphold the possibility, for political reasons. He 'wrote a most peremptory letter to the Secretary of State, Lord Hawkesbury, which was forwarded to the Admiralty (without comment), on the very day Williams faced his court martial.' It was left to Earl St Vincent, by now First Lord of the Admiralty, to sign the letter conveying 'His

Majesty's most Gracious and Free Pardon' to Williams, who now vanishes from history.

So too do most of the other mutineers. Some may have been killed in action when serving aboard privateers, some are thought to have become farm-labourers or soldiers. They had been paid some prize money for the return of the *Danae* to the French, but the ship was not recommissioned as a French man-of-war. She too disappears, after a period of service as a transport sent to the West Indies during the peace which had just then been signed at Amiens. A little over a year later war had broken out again, and the *Danae* mutiny was forgotten.

Captain Lord Proby was not employed at sea for some time, and served as a Member of Parliament for Buckingham until the renewal of the war, when he was posted into the frigate *Amelia*. In May 1804 the frigate was assigned to the West Indies where the senior officer, Sir Samuel Hood, sent her on to Surinam. Here, on the South American mainland, Proby's ship was infected with 'Yellow Jack'. At the end of October the *Amelia* anchored in Carlisle Bay, Barbados, her first lieutenant, master, surgeon and eight men already dead and her captain dying. Proby was taken ashore and died that evening. The reputation he left – that part of a person which might be said to embody a morsel of immortality – reveals no specific accusations of cruelty. Although some of the mutineers complained to the French of the floggings they had received, none of the three brought to trial mentioned harsh treatment, and his lordship's regimen was, as noted earlier, lenient. Of his last days, all spoke of his care of his officers and men. He was more sinned against than sinning, a victim of the Admiralty's desperation for seamen, and particularly unlucky in the accumulation aboard his small ship of an unsuitable crew, a proportion of whom were hell-bent on trouble-making and unwilling to accept the portion fate had dealt them.

Throughout the long wars with France between 1793 and 1815, during which time the Royal Navy expanded to almost one thousand commissioned ships-of-war, several of which experienced mutinies, only the rebels aboard the *Hermione* and the *Danae* were motivated to turn their ships over to the enemy. A brief outbreak of mutiny occurred in HMS *Gibraltar* during the Peace of Amiens, but it was quickly suppressed by the officers and marines of the ship, and the ring-leaders were hanged. After the renewal of the war in May 1803 the spectral motive of republicanism faded, for on 2 December 1804 France became a monarchy again, an imperial monarchy under Napoleon I, Emperor of the French. Neither for the first nor the last time were the idealists to be disappointed: even Beethoven, who struck out Napoleon's name from the manuscript of the Third Symphony upon hearing he had assumed a crown, substituting for it 'Eroica'.

To some extent the breakdown of the peace seems to have reconciled the seamen in the fleet to their fate. Clearly the war had to be won and they, poor fellows, would get no release until they had settled the matter. While sporadic outbreaks of disaffection continued, few matched the intensity of violence displayed aboard the *Hermione,* largely because the attitudes of officers, captains and, it has to be said, the Admiralty Board itself had shifted. It had become clear to the generation of sea officers who rose in the service during the formative period of the 1790s that harshness, though occasionally necessary, was not the foundation of good discipline hard-liners believed it to be, and that consideration for 'the welfare of the people', once appreciated, neutralized much of the resentment inherent in the older system. The truth was that a prolonged war brought officers and men into closer contact – though this has to be placed within a Georgian context – and although social distinctions remained, shared dangers and long service did much to erode the men's perceived grievances. It was a subtle matter, but it removed a great deal of the sting of prolonged naval service, in tandem with Lord Barham's revision of the Admiralty Regulations, introducing a more enlightened practices. As Charles Middleton, Barham had been a reforming captain, replacing the punishing regime of watch-and-watch, with the three-watch system, and proved a reforming First Lord of the Admiralty. For the old and usually exceeded order that 'no commander shall inflict any punishment upon a seaman beyond twelve lashes on his bare back with a cat-o'-nine-tails, according to the ancient practice of the sea' was substituted the more enlightened, general and encouraging admonition that a captain was 'not to suffer Inferior Officers and men to be treated with cruelty or oppression by their superiors. He alone is to order punishment to be inflicted, which he is never to do without sufficient cause, nor ever with greater severity than the offence shall really deserve.' At the time Barham was drafting these instructions the old punishment of running the gauntlet was abolished, but common usage ensured the survival of some of the casual punishments inflicted by petty officers, particularly midshipmen, which were often vindictive and spiteful and to which reference has been made. Most common among these was 'starting'. It might be specifically forbidden by commanding officers who took the trouble to issue their own personal and supplementary standing orders for the regulation of their ships, but it remained a grievance, grossly offensive to the *amour-propre* of long-serving able seamen. Unsurprisingly, it fomented mutiny.

In August 1808 the crew of the 36-gun frigate *Nereide*, having already sent one petition to Admiral Sir Edward Pellew, Commander-in-Chief of the East Indies squadron, sent another. Pellew, a very experienced admiral and a not inhumane man, was regarded as one of the finest and most capable sea officers in the entire British navy, but he was not without his faults. He did not react to this particular communication, perhaps because the round-robin received from the *Nereide* read like a seditious document of ten years earlier. Pellew was at Bombay (modern Mumbai) when the letter reached him from the *Nereide*, then cruising in the Indian Ocean. The ship's company stated that they had 'never before experienced such oppressive usage as we now labour under, under the command of Captain Robert Corbet, whose capricious temper on the least occasion will cause us to be beaten with large sticks'. Twenty-three men had already run from the ship – a difficult thing to do on the East Indies station, where there was virtually no refuge – and the Nereides were asking for a new ship or a new captain. Corbet's regime was comparable with Pigot's, floggings of up to 36 lashes on a regular basis for offences such as insolence or neglect of duty – charges often a little vague and subjective – every few days. Unrecorded in the ship's log were the endless startings by the boatswain Moses Veale and his mates, but hints of discontent and a fractious crew emerge.

Off the coast of Madagascar on 8 January 1809, having been ordered to weigh anchor at 7.20 a.m., the crew refused to obey the order and instead assembled on the forecastle to confront Corbet. The captain had paraded the marines under orders to load their muskets with ball and to fix bayonets. With considerable courage the crew's spokesman, Second Gunner Joseph Wilkinson, asked that the ship should proceed to the Cape of Good Hope, where, despairing of Pellew, the men hoped to find redress. Corbet ordered Wilkinson put in irons, then announced that on the first lieutenant producing the muster list he would call each man's name in turn to ascertain whether he would obey orders or not. There were loud shouts of, 'No! No! No!' but Corbet pulled out his watch and gave then five minutes to make up their minds. If at the expiry of that period they had not agreed to obey the order, the marines would be ordered to fire a volley. As a noise of dissension rose from the milling seamen, Corbet shouted for quiet. 'I shall have but two words,' he called, somewhat inaccurately, 'obey or not obey. What the devil, do you take me for a coward? You ought to know me by now.' As the watch ticked and the marines prepared to fire 'there was a cry of: "Obey! Obey!"' and the anchor was hove up.

Corbet arrested Wilkinson and nine other ring-leaders, but he also headed for the Cape. Arriving in Table Bay, he applied at once for a court-martial upon his prisoners. The court duly assembled, and the prosecution demanded a verdict of unlawful mutiny. In their defence the entire crew subscribed to a written statement in which they said that 'the treatment we experienced was such as it was next [to] impossible for men to bear . . . On the most trifling occasions and often when we did not know a fault had been committed we have suffered the most unmerciful starting that ever was inflicted, with sticks of a severer kind than is ever used in the British navy, some of which we have to produce in court if they [*sic*] think proper . . .' They went on to complain of flogging and the use of cat-o'-nine-tails with extra knots 'not in use in any other ship unless for the punishment of criminals of the deepest dye . . .' They had, they claimed, not mutinied, but made a relatively harmless demonstration to provoke an inquiry into their captain's conduct towards them. They had committed no act of violence; they had previously 'written for redress and we will have it.'

The members of the court, whatever their private feelings, found for the prosecution. The accused were adjudged guilty of mutiny – since no lesser offence existed to characterize such proto-industrial action – and all ten men were condemned to death. A recommendation to mercy was made, however, 'in consideration of a circumstance of a particular and favourable nature'. The character of the uprising saved all except Wilkinson who on 2 February 1809 was executed from the cathead of the *Nereide* and run up to the fore yardarm by his own shipmates, under the levelled muskets of the frigate's marines.

It was a wretched business, and worse was to come. On 4 February Corbet was told he would himself be court-martialled on the 6th 'for breaches of Several Articles of War'. In fact the court decided to disregard most of them – there were too many – in order to concentrate upon No. 33, which stated that 'If any Flag-officer, captain or Commander, or Lieutenant belonging to the Fleet, shall be convicted before a court martial of behaving in a scandalous, infamous, cruel, oppressive, or fraudulent Manner, unbecoming the Character of an Officer, he shall be dismissed from His Majesty's Service.'

By now the prosecution had done its homework, and Corbet was indicted for punishing men 'with such cats[of nine tails] as is customary in other ships in HM Service to punish a thief; and when the skin was broken to put salt pickle on their backs . . .'

Called as a witness, James White stated that he was started so severely that he 'could not lift my right arm to my head', and that after a flogging 'on my loins' [the upper back was supposed to receive the weals of the cat] he had passed blood for four months. Corbet broke in and demanded to be told if he had ever ordered White flogged on the loins, to which White replied, 'Yes, sir.'

Others deposed that they had been beaten not with rattans but with sticks as thick as broomsticks, so badly that they could not afterwards stand without support, and the court was told that such punishments were administered for failing to haul a rope taut to the satisfaction of the boatswain and for that old 'offence', being the last man off the yards. It was further alleged that Corbet had publicly threatened to lay wire in the yarns of the cat-o'nine-tails, and had told Veale to beat the men without mercy but not to break bones. The surgeon corroborated the medical evidence, and was forced to confess that he had failed in his duty to record the details in his journal as he was supposed to.

Corbet was breathtakingly confident in his defence. He claimed that this was the first time in twenty years' service that his conduct had been called into question, that eight of those years he had been in command, that he had simply followed the customs of the navy 'with impartiality and not more severity than the case requires', that he had 'used no new methods of punishment, no instruments unheard of or forbidden by law', and that he was not 'the odious character described'. Moreover, his conduct had occasioned 'no serious accident', and he had only been severe when 'circumstances rendered it necessary'. His problem had been finding the *Nereide* lax when he joined her, 'under discipline very contrary to what my ideas have pointed out to me as most beneficial to His Majesty's service.' He had noted 'a cabal formed in the main-top' and a 'sulky indifference to punishment' which encouraged him to persist in his duty. The adding of wire to the cat was only a ruse to terrorize the men, for he had had no intention of carrying out the threat, and he had never before seen the sticks said to have been used for starting that were laid before the court. It was, as the members of the court knew well, he said, impossible to subject a crew for eighteen months on detached service. His attitude was one of pooh-poohing the men's evidence as an entire fabrication. He then said: 'An idea has crept in and is gaining head that the punishment they call starting is not legal; I combat this opinion strongly; it has been one of the customs of the sea since I have known it. That it is illegal cannot I think be proved; that it is customary requires no proof. I court the public character of a strict and rigid disciplinarian. This honourable court I trust will have reason to distinguish it from that of a tyrant.'

The court's verdict was hung; it dismissed all other charges as 'malicious or litigious or vexatious' but found 'the charge of cruelty and oppression has been partly proved by punishment having been inflicted . . . with sticks of an improper size and such as are not usual . . .' But Corbet escaped condign punishment, the court merely sentencing 'the said captain to be reprimanded'.

It was an appalling decision, and might have been different had Corbet been tried at Portsmouth rather than on a distant station. So too might the verdict on Wilkinson, had the revelations about Corbet's conduct been made before the unfortunate gunner's execution. As it was, the Admiralty were in no doubt about the legality of starting: they immediately proscribed it. Starting was, Their Lordships rightly observed, 'disgusting to the feelings of British seamen'. Although the custom undoubtedly lingered on in some ships, it was no longer sanctioned.

Corbet did not return to the *Nereide*, which was taken over by Sir Nesbitt Willoughby, an officer noted for ruthlessness and cruelty but one who had been at the point of danger so often and consequently so frequently wounded – once in the opinion of the surgeons, mortally – that he had earned the soubriquet 'Willoughby the Immortal'. Willoughby found the *Nereide*'s gunnery highly deficient, a further indictment that might be laid at Corbet's door, but did little to improve it. As for Corbet, he was sent to command the *Africaine*, the crew of which almost mutinied on the spot and were only prevented from doing so by the intervention of Rear Admiral Sir Edward Buller. Legend has it, however, that they enjoyed a perverse kind of revenge.

At about two o'clock in the morning of 13 September 1810, the 38-gun *Africaine* was in action off the isle of Réunion. The two French national frigates *Iphigénie* and *Astrée* out-fought the *Africaine* while HMS *Boadicea*, five miles away and all but paralysed by lack of wind, was unable to work up to assist until it was too late. Early in the action Corbet was mortally wounded, and it was left to his first lieutenant, Joseph Tullidge, to fight on for two hours, by which time 49 of *Africaine*'s 295 officers and men were dead and a further 119 wounded and the ship was a wreck. Tullidge struck his ensign. No one mourned Corbet; rumours persisted that he had been shot by his own crew, for he appeared to have learned little from his reprimand and had governed *Africaine* in much the same manner as *Nereide*. 'It is the general belief', the historian William James admits, 'that the *Africaine*'s crew were disaffected, on account of the ill-treatment they had experienced from their captain. We regret to state that the more our enquiries have been extended on that point, the more they have convinced us that Captain Corbet was an excessively severe officer.' It was a pity, for Corbet had been given that first step on the path of promotion, that to master and commander, by Nelson himself.

All that might be said in Corbet's favour is that the final suppression of starting in consequence of the mutiny aboard the *Nereide,* along with the general amelioration in violent retribution for trivial misdemeanours, went far to ensure that the Royal Navy remained faithful to its task during the long and wearisome decade after Trafalgar. Against that, he must join with Pigot as a founder of a near-ineradicable myth that such brutality was commonplace in the Royal Navy of the day.

10

'A STRANGE PERVERSION'

THOUGH dissension surfaced from time to time until the very end of Britain's long war with France in 1815, the Royal Navy acquitted itself well. The swift demobilisation of both the navy and the army threw thousands of unemployed men onto the streets of Britain, creating a crisis comparable with that of the 1930s, and no doubt many seamen contrasted their post-war situation unfavourably with their period of naval service. There was at least one outbreak of mutiny after 1815, when no shore leave was given to the crew aboard HMS *Princess Royal* after a long period at sea, but those men retained by the navy during the century of the Pax Britannica were career sailors, and generally content with their lot. The social divisions between officers and ratings grew deeper, but an acceptance of such distinctions crept in. Revolutionary zeal largely evaporated as Britain became the workshop of the world and the pink of her empire spread across the map of the world, backed up by her navy, whose bluejackets became synonymous with world order.

The American navy had passed its baptism of fire during the brief but bloody war with Britain between 1812 and 1814 and, as any reader of Herman Melville's *White Jacket* will know, was run on lines indistinguishable in principle from those of the British Royal Navy. In 1800 Commodore Truxtun had mirrored the reforms under way in the Royal Navy in his statement 'Discipline is to be effected by a particular deportment much easier than by great severity', but the young Department of the Navy, established in 1798, recognized the dangers of mutiny, and an Act for the Better Government of the Navy, despite its loose, catch-all wording, pronounced death as the only meet punishment. Truxtun had a particular case in mind, however: he was conveying his disapprobation of the conduct of Captain James Sever, who had nipped a brewing mutiny in the bud aboard the USS *Congress*. Several men were condemned by court-martial, but senior officer Truxtun was persuaded that Sever's conduct was not unimpeachable, and commuted death sentences to flogging and dismissal from the service. At the time the seamen of the United States Navy were reacting to the events aboard the *Hermione*, some of whose crew had found their way into their ranks. American naval ratings, brought up on a diet of liberty and an aversion to all forms of tyranny, were prickly in defence of their freedoms.

In 1803, aboard the USS *President*, Captain Samuel Barron was handed an unsigned letter which complained of 'horrid usage . . . [which was] enough to turn a man's stomach . . . [and] at such a pitch as to exceed the *Hermione*.' Mention of that baleful name alarmed Barron, who promptly identified a culprit, or perhaps a scapegoat, named Robert Quinn. His punishment was Draconian. Condemned by a court martial, Quinn had his head shaved and branded with the word 'Mutiny', and was then flogged through the squadron assembled in Hampton Roads. As he was brought alongside the waist of the *John Adams* Quinn passed out, and the ship's surgeon, duty bound to examine the prisoner as he hung suspended from a tripod in the *President*'s launch, deferred the remainder of the punishment of 320 lashes to a later period, when Quinn should have recovered sufficiently. The *John Adams*'s purser noted his surprise that Quinn could survive his ordeal, concluding that 'It is to be sure the most cruel punishment, but the very existence of the Navy requires it.'

Quinn apparently did survive, at least for long enough that his death was not blamed upon his ordeal. The first American naval seaman to be executed for mutiny was William Johnson of the ketch *Dispatch* in 1812. Rather far gone in liquor, Johnson got into a fight with another sailor and then, fatally for him, abused first a midshipman and then a lieutenant who attempted to stop the scrap. As he flailed about wildly it took several marines to restrain Johnson, whose conduct was judged to be mutiny under the vague interpretation of the word in the Congressional Act. Johnson's fate established the precedent that mutiny could be caused by a single individual, and that a combination was not absolutely necessary.

None of these disturbances was of a scale to disrupt the regulation of the United States's small navy, but an interesting event occurred in the South Pacific that was in a small way a mutiny on the classical model. Captain David Porter's frigate USS *Essex* had carried out a successful raid against the British sperm-whalers, destroying some but taking others as prizes. Though he was an energetic commander – a man of 'delicate physique and impetuous nature' – Porter found time to linger in those distant waters and allow his crew shore leave at Nuku Hiva, where he assembled his prizes. He diverted himself with a 'handsome young woman of about eighteen' while his ship's company engaged in 'helter-skelter and promiscuous intercourse'. When word was passed to the men to muster to weigh anchor, murmurs of dissent and incipient rebellion filtered aft, whereupon Porter summoned all hands, laid his naked sword on the capstan, and announced that at the first sign of disobedience he would himself 'put a match to the magazine and blow them all to hell'. To add emphasis to his resolve, and despite the man's protestations of innocence, he called out one seaman and had him dumped overboard into a passing canoe. The *Essex*'s anchor was weighed and she left, heading for her Nemesis off Valparaiso.

Porter's departure left a number of prizes behind under the command of a marine lieutenant named John Gamble. Gamble was to make his way home if he had no word from Porter within five months. By 7 May 1814, he had heard nothing, and had no way of knowing that Porter and what remained of his crew were prisoners of the British. Gamble left Nuku Hiva in the former British ship *Seringapatam*. He had with him two midshipmen, thirteen American seamen, and a dozen British prisoners. Combining with the British, eleven of the Americans rose against Gamble, set him adrift with the two midshipmen and two loyal seamen, hoisted British colours and, heading for New Zealand, disappeared from history. In a small boat Gamble reached an island, only to be attacked by the inhabitants with the loss of the two midshipmen. Bearing away, Gamble eventually returned to Nuku Hiva, where he fitted out a second of the prizes still lying there, the *Sir Andrew Hammond*. With the small loyalist band left to him Gamble burnt the last prize and sailed the former whaler towards Hawaii, only to be captured by a British cruiser. It was probably just as well; although whalers were designed to be handled by a small crew, Gamble and his eight loyalists were by now scorbutic, and their captors almost certainly saved their lives.

That the seductions offered to seamen of all nationalities in the South Pacific were disruptive of discipline and conducive to mutiny is clear, but they proved to have another effect as the war receded and the benefits of free trade and a long period of peace ran in tandem with an explosion of enterprise and the dawn of the modern age. Steam and speed, railways and rapid communications had social spin-offs as simple as the promulgation of books and magazines in which the South Pacific and the life of a sailor were culturally detached from images of rum, sodomy and the lash. These subtle influences were experienced nowhere more intensely than in America, where opportunities seemed limitless. For those drawn to the sea, as was Melville's Ishmael whenever he felt depressed, the South Pacific beckoned romantically. By about 1820, the New England whale-fishery had turned its attention from the Atlantic to the Pacific, where in long, arduous but ultimately financially rewarding voyages the men of New Bedford, Martha's Vineyard and Nantucket hunted the sperm whale. One such youth seduced by this idyll who took to the sea aboard a whaler was Samuel Comstock. As a boy Comstock was thought of as odd by his family, and he matured into an unfeeling loner and trouble-maker: the term had yet to be coined, but he was in fact a psychopath. In his early voyages to sea, he thought of establishing himself upon a tropical island where he and those of the crew who cared to join him would rule as white kings. Many boys might fantasize about such an idyll, but Comstock persuaded himself that such an existence was possible. Among the oddities of behaviour noted by his family was his apparent indifference to pain; along with this he also seems to have felt no need to keep any rein upon his natural passions. In this he bears more than a passing resemblance to Jeronimus Corneliszoon of the *Batavia*, but without the Dutchman's pseudo-religious justifications. Comstock was an all-American product. An unstable character, wary of any humiliation, real or imagined, Comstock was skilful enough to serve as a competent boat-steerer, but temperamentally unfitted for a career at sea.

Nevertheless, by the end of 1822, when he signed on the whaler *Globe* as a petty officer under Captain Thomas Worth, Comstock had become an experienced seaman. He had however conceived a dislike for the whaling trade: he had attempted to work ashore, but falling out with his father had gone back to sea in high dudgeon. Worth was an acquaintance, and turned a deaf ear to rumours of Comstock's tendency to 'ride' the men in his watch with acts of petty tyranny. Worth himself was not a harsh commander, though he was prepared to take a rope's end to a man if he deemed it necessary. Indeed, the only complaint of any substance against him seems to have been of his tendency not to let the men have a proper meal period – a small matter to lands-men, but of crucial importance in a monotonous voyage which often lasted as long as four years. Writing home, Second Mate Lumbert spoke of Worth as 'a fine man', but he was apt to take matters into his own hands and manhandle recalcitrant seamen who were slow to obey orders.

Desertions from whalers, while common, had little to do with the regime on board, more with the blandishments of the shore.

The *Globe* was no exception: she lost six men in Hawaii, and Worth was obliged to sign on new men at Honolulu after an unsuccessful cruise on 'the Japan [whaling] ground'. These men were of poor quality, mostly drifters left on the beach by other ships, and easily worked upon by Comstock, who by now had developed an animus against Worth. When the *Globe* left Hawaii on 27 December 1823, Comstock had determined to take the ship and realize his youthful fantasy.

Events played into his hands. The meat Worth had reprovisioned with proved partially rotten: Comstock seized the pretext, and orchestrated the grumbling. Then on 25 January 1824 an incident occurred which provided him with his motive. Summoned peremptorily on deck as they ate, the men were provocatively slow to respond. One, Joseph Thomas, was singled out above the others. If he did not show more alacrity, Worth fulminated, he would be knocked to hell. Thomas responded, and Worth lashed out; Thomas dodged the blow and ran forward, to be caught by the mate, Mr Beetle, and brought aft, where Worth whipped him soundly with the tail-end of a buntline. Witnessing this, the crew moved forward, murmuring. Comstock followed, telling the disaffected sailors that if they wished to avenge Thomas, who had been struck upwards of a dozen times, he would support them.

In the forecastle the men now argued; their loyalty to Worth was badly shaken, but not all wanted to follow the demonic Comstock; some favoured desertion at the next island. Comstock's younger brother George wrote afterwards, 'I had been very well used [treated] by the Captain and had nothing to complain of, but foreseeing that there would be some noise yet between the crew and the officers I was determined to leave the ship to get clear.' They were approaching Fanning Island (south of Hawaii and near Christmas Island), and a plan was concerted to desert in one of the whale boats that night, during Comstock's watch. Comstock meanwhile had other things on his mind. He attempted to suborn Thomas directly; Thomas afterwards claimed to have prevaricated. Comstock knew that delay would lose him the initiative that Thomas's whipping had given him.

The *Globe* was not in fact entirely isolated, for she had been in company with another whaler, the *Lyra*, and the two masters, enjoying a 'gam' or gossip, had decided to sail in company, thus extending the area they could search for whales. Nevertheless, the watery wastes of the Pacific combined with petty tensions on board to blow matters out of all proportion, and while Captain Worth entertained Captain Joy, Comstock continued his dirty work. Reality was remote from Comstock's thinking; he was consumed with his own dark ambitions, and despite the presence of his own brother he carried out his plan on the stroke of the eight bells which divided 26 January 1824 from the 27th.

The *Globe* was shortened down for the night, and within sight the *Lyra* lay similarly snugged down. As a boat-steerer, 21-year old Samuel Comstock stood a watch in charge of the deck when lying-to, and as midnight approached he had his brother George on the wheel. George asked to be relieved, and Comstock told him to keep the sails full to avoid disturbing any senior officers. When George repeated his desire to be relieved, Samuel threatened him with his life. Cowed, George stood at the wheel as Samuel Comstock went below. Afterwards Comstock boasted of what now happened, saying to his brother, 'I suppose you think I regret what I have done; but you are mistaken – I should like to do such a job every morning . . .' Carrying an axe, Comstock led the way below, followed by Thomas Lilliston, John Oliver and a black man William Humphreys, who carried a lantern. All had been recruited by Worth in Honolulu.

In Worth's cabin Comstock stood over the master in his cot and brought his axe down upon his sleeping head. Payne then stabbed the mate, but bungled it, so that a shocked Beetle pleaded for his life. Comstock told him he was 'a damned rascal' but Beetle, recovering, got to his feet and seized Comstock by the throat. The lantern was kicked out and Comstock lost his axe in the ensuing struggle; Beetle almost succeeded in throttling his assassin but Payne handed Comstock his dropped hatchet and with it the latter smashed Beetle's skull. The mate fell into the adjacent steward's pantry and was left moaning. Second Mate

Lumbert and Third Mate Fisher were left under guard in their shared cabin as Comstock, crying 'I am the bloody man; I have the bloody hand, and I will be revenged', went back on deck, his enunciated paranoia hanging in the air.

Having relit the lantern, Comstock returned to the mates' cabin with a loaded musket fitted with a bayonet. Firing it through the door, he hit Fisher in the face. Then he opened the door and lunged at Lumbert. He tripped at this point and Lumbert grabbed him. The musket fell and was picked up by the bleeding Fisher, who thrust the bayonet at Comstock, holding it at his heart. There was a pause, then Comstock, lacking all fear, told Fisher to lower the bayonet. The third mate complied, and immediately Comstock recovered his weapon and stabbed Lumbert repeatedly until the second mate fell in his own gore. Comstock then quietly told Fisher that he was going to die, reloaded the musket, and fired into the back of Fisher's head.

Comstock now went on deck and ordered sail to be made, in order to distance the *Globe* from the *Lyra* as quickly as possible. Covered in blood, he dominated the *Globe's* deck. All were in fear of him. Appointed mates under him, Comstock's confederates took petty revenge on other members of the crew as they disposed of the displaced officers' bodies. Lumbert and Beetle were still alive when they were thrown overboard. Next day Comstock drew up a list of laws by which all hands were to be bound – but matters were far from being that simple. Humphreys and by implication others were later suspected of plotting against Comstock. A court was convened, and Humphreys was quickly tried and condemned to death. His elder brother William, later testified that Samuel Comstock 'always felt a strong dislike to coloured persons and was therefore willing to lay hold of any pretence to set Humphreys aside': the wretched mutineer was hanged.

Having taken the *Globe*, Comstock now sought his kingdom, finally deciding upon Mili Atoll, part of the Marshall Archipelago, where on Friday 13 February 1824 the *Globe* dropped her anchor. He began to plan Comstockville, laying out an entire town, at least in his imagination, and actually selecting a site for, of all things, a church. But the idyll was rudely shattered a few days later when Silas Payne remonstrated that he was too readily disposing of the ship's resources in charming the island's inhabitants. The men fell out ashore, quarrelling furiously in a tent made out of sails. Comstock returned aboard, took up a cutlass, and slashed the agreed 'laws' to pieces, theatrically gesturing to those men on board at the time and then going ashore again and walking away to contact the natives. His former shipmates were now both bemused and less fearful of him; Payne was taking a stand.

A little later Comstock appeared with a crowd of fifty natives and Payne set a guard, drawing several of the mutineers about him in anticipation of a show-down. Nothing further happened that day, nor the following night, but the morning after that Comstock reappeared. Confronted by Payne's gang with muskets levelled he shouted, 'Don't shoot me! I will not hurt you!' But he no longer had any power. The muskets fired and Comstock fell, Payne administering the *coup de grace* with an axe-blow to Comstock's head. Then Payne insisted on a bizarre ritual: Comstock was wrapped in the American ensign and buried with his cutlass and pistols, and a volley was fired over the open grave. Then the fourteenth chapter of Isaiah was read by Gilbert Smith: 'When the Lord gives you relief from your pain and your fears and from the cruel slavery laid upon you, you will take up this song of derision over the king of Babylon: See how the oppressor has met his end and his frenzy ceased! The Lord has broken the rod of the wicked . . . who struck down peoples in his rage with unerring blows . . . The whole world has rest and is at peace . . .'

After these obsequies, 'when the grave was filled, the surviving mutineers required of every man that he should dance upon it, so showing his approval of Comstock's murder, and his allegiance to the new authorities' – meaning Payne.

But with Comstock's perverse vision gone, no motive now existed for their continuing at Mili. Indeed several men, unwillingly roped in to the wicked and pointless rebellion, were already planning to leave. They were led by Gilbert Smith, and that night, as Payne and his close adherents enjoyed the company of the native women, Smith and his five confederates, who included George Comstock and Joseph Thomas, having preserved one compass, quietly cut the *Globe*'s anchor cable and hoisted what remained of her sails. As the sea breeze set in after dark the *Globe* sailed away to the eastwards, and after a long and uncertain passage during which Thomas proved himself the trouble-maker Worth had originally taken him for, they were rewarded by a landfall. On 5 June the peaks of the Andes were seen above the horizon and two days later, assisted by the crew of a Chilean vessel, they arrived at Valparaiso.

Initially they were held aboard a British cruiser while the American consul, Michael Hogan, investigated their cases, one by one. It was clear that Thomas was implicated in the mutiny, and he was in due course tried accordingly after the *Globe* had returned to Boston. As for Payne and the inheritors of Comstock's putative kingdom, the owners of the *Globe* and the United States government mounted an operation to discover them. In addition to carrying out a hydrographic voyage, Lieutenant John Percival, commander of the schooner USS *Dolphin*, was to search for the mutineers and bring them home to justice. After a rambling approach to the Marshall Islands during which Percival carried out his other orders, and a painstaking search of the archipelago island by island, Percival's men finally located just two survivors, William Lay and Cyrus Hussey. The two men had been kept separately on different atolls, protected as favourites and servants to two chiefs. Taken by the *Dolphin* to Valparaiso, they took ship home, arriving in New York on 22 April 1827.

The fate of Payne and the remainder, some of them innocent men, was bloody. Their intended life of lotus-eating was initiated by Payne and Oliver, who took native wives. Payne's did not stay beyond dawn on her wedding night, however; Payne chased after her, seized her, took her back to the camp and flogged her. Then he put her in irons. Next day they found that the tool chest had been robbed, and natives were milling about the periphery of the camp. That evening one of the natives appeared with a chisel. Payne unwisely grabbed him and bound him, further compounding his folly. Next day, 24 February, Payne sent out a punitive expedition of four men; it was ambushed and overwhelmed, and as it retreated the first of the white men was killed. The Milians now surrounded the camp and began to destroy the whaleboat which Payne was working on. Payne made signs for a parley, and after about an hour concluded an agreement in which he had been forced to surrender all the remaining goods from the *Globe* (perhaps he heard Comstock laughing from his grave). Moreover, Payne and the remaining crew members were to submit to being ruled by the Milians. For those like Lay and Hussey, innocent of any involvement in the mutiny, the situation was now desperate. Lay's hand was taken and he was drawn away by an elderly Milian couple. As soon as he was clear the Milians, men, women and children, attacked, scattering the *Globe*'s people so that they were cut down or stoned piece-meal, two of them at Lay's feet. Captain Worth's young and innocent cousin, Columbus Worth, was chased by an elderly woman who speared him and then stoned him to death. The others were stoned, including Payne.

Lay was protected at some risk to themselves by the old couple, and later discovered that Hussey too had escaped death, though not a stoning, and was being similarly cared for. Although allowed to meet occasionally, they did not see much of one another until the arrival of the *Dolphin* liberated them from their enslavement. Both men were later obliged to defend their conduct during the midnight mutiny, but only insofar as obtaining proper discharges was concerned, and they were treated with great humanity by the American naval authorities. As for Thomas, he was alleged to have caused 'Murder on the High Seas on board ship *Globe*' and appeared before magistrates who committed him to Boston jail pending trial before a circuit court. A week later the charge was altered to one of mutiny, of which he was, in the end, acquitted. Rumblings of accusation and counter-accusation as to who was and who was not a mutineer ran on among the relatives of several of the *Globe*'s dead crew. Hussey told his story, but America has preferred to bury the tale of the *Globe* and expunge it from the record – it runs contrary to the American dream, while that of the *Bounty* cheerfully maintains all the old prejudices of which the United States wished to see itself free.

Sadly, it was in its ambitious young navy that its own most reprehensible case of mutiny broke out. By the time Herman Melville sailed as an able seaman aboard the frigate *United States* and thereby obtained the material for *White Jacket*, others were animadverting upon the state of discipline and its maintenance in the American service. In 1841 a pamphlet entitled *An Exposition of Official Tyranny in the United States Navy* was produced by a former sailor. One of the examples cited was that of a zealous first lieutenant who had ordered the flogging of a marine aboard the *Independence* in July 1837. The ship was anchored off Brazil, and the sea-soldier had obtained some oranges from the shore. Having enjoyed the fruit, he dropped the peel into the spittoons situated on the quarterdeck. Lieutenant Alexander Slidell considered this a serious breach of discipline. Slidell, like most of his seniority and generation, did not have a great deal of experience at sea to his credit. The flat command structure of the contemporary American navy and its paucity of ships resulted in a frustrating lack of opportunity – a 'system of deathlike stagnation' was how Slidell described slow promotion into dead men's shoes. Even in the squadron of small vessels sent on the United States Navy's first Exploring Expedition in 1838, the senior officer was – shades of Bligh – only a lieutenant, Charles Wilkes.

Like Wilkes, whose job Slidell among others had coveted, Slidell had spent much of his naval service ashore. Indeed, a great deal of his naval time had been an extended furlough, during which he had become an accomplished author of several well regarded travel books – and indulged in a little discreet intelligence-gathering while collecting material for his *An American in England*. Another protracted leave followed his first period in command of the USS *Dolphin*, and during it he fulfilled the necessary conditions to inherit from an uncle who had died without issue. As one of these Slidell was obliged to change his name, and quietly metamorphosed into Lieutenant Alexander Slidell Mackenzie.

He had for some years taken an interest in the quality of the navy's intake. Generally speaking, the three decades following the end of the Napoleonic War were marked by an indifferent quality of seafarer, except perhaps in the Royal Navy where rapid demobilisation meant the British could pick and choose, but certainly in the mercantile marines of both Britain and America and, at least in the opinion of Lieutenant A. Slidell Mackenzie, in the United States Navy. The Service had become full of foreigners, he claimed, adding that recruitment of genuine Americans was not helped by the unpopularity of a 'harsh system'; the irony of this conclusion will become apparent. During his captaincy of the *Dolphin* he had himself acquired the reputation of a harsh disciplinarian: while a sentence of a mere 39 lashes for 'desertion and mutinous conduct' might be seen as lenient in comparison with the British equivalent, Mackenzie – for so we must now call him – punished with sedulous regularity. In those 39 lashes lie a key to the man's obsessive nature, because he flogged for *any* misdemeanour, the mere fact of a crime having been committed exposing a man, like the *Independence*'s marine, to punishment.

But Mackenzie went further. He was related to the Secretary of the Navy and expressed himself freely on the subject of the poor quality of seamen, advocating a system of apprentices sent to sea under training in a vessel dedicated to the purpose. Frustrated in his hope of commanding the 'Ex-Ex', as the Exploratory Expedition was colloquially termed, Mackenzie fished for another plum: command of a training brig. In 1841 he was promoted commander and a year later achieved his objective, being appointed to the command of the USS *Somers*, a new, fast, but over-sparred brig-of-war destined to end her life capsizing and sinking off Vera Cruz in 1846.

Though not a large vessel, she shipped a complement of 166 men and boys, half of them under seventeen years of age and among them a small number of midshipmen. One of these was

Philip Spencer, an odd youth not unaffected by the misplaced romance of piratical voyages and adventurous fantasies, but whose father was Secretary of War John C. Spencer. An unsuccessful operation to cure him of a squint had left the younger Spencer with 'a fixed staring look' and 'enigmatic smiles'. In addition to his strabismus he was subject to 'a strange flashing of the eyes'. Despite his youth and his Establishment background, Spencer had been in and out of trouble before joining the *Somers*. He had fought with a senior over a dispute that had its origins in a New York brothel, and had narrowly escaped court martial after a drunken argument with a British naval officer in Rio de Janeiro. He seems to have been utterly unfitted for a naval career, for in addition to being hooked on piratical yarns, he favoured the company of the men and boys, whose palms he read and whom he furnished with alcohol and tobacco. He also possessed a disconcerting knack of deliberately dislocating his jaw and, by a percussive 'contact of the bones, playing with accuracy and elegance a variety of airs.' When he did open up to his own messmates Spencer seemed quite irrational, even unhinged, doodling pictures of the skull and crossbones and muttering openly about the ease with which it would be possible to take over the ship and disguise her, and how he would delight in tossing the captain overboard. This he said to several people at various times during the trans-Atlantic passage. After the *Somers* left the African coast, the atmosphere on board was such that, hearing of it, the purser spoke of it to the first lieutenant.

On the forenoon of 26 November Lieutenant Guert Gansevoort (a cousin of Herman Melville) informed Mackenzie he had received information that 'a conspiracy existed . . . to capture [the brig] . . . murder the commander, the officers and most of the crew, and convert her [the *Somers*] into a pirate [ship], and that Midshipman Spencer was at the head of it.'

However extraordinary the situation appears, and despite the manic tendencies of its alleged instigator and chief conspirator, it has to be seen in context. Mackenzie had secured his position in charge of a vessel intended to produce highly motivated and professional able seamen on the grounds that he was an enlightened and reforming commander, though there was ample evidence to suggest otherwise. Either nepotism or simple neglect resulted in a failure to inspect the *Independence*'s and *Dolphin*'s logs, which would have revealed Mackenzie himself as verging on the insane. Whatever his state of mind, he dismissed Gansevoort's report 'with ridicule', his complacency presumably deriving from a belief that his harsh discipline was the correct and only way to force men and boys to submit.

Notwithstanding the fact that most of his crew were minors and it was his job to induct them into the ways of the American navy, Mackenzie had continued to flog. In the first three weeks of his cruise, as the *Somers* proceeded from the Brooklyn Navy Yard towards the African coast, Mackenzie ordered forty-three floggings. A catalogue which to others seemed like evidence of a failure of leadership was exacerbated by the conduct of Bosun's Mate Samuel Cromwell, who appears to have enjoyed laying-on and 'would strike with all his might as though it was pleasing to him.'

When they left Madeira, where ten boy seamen had been punished for failing to keep themselves and their mess clean, the severe regime continued. If the cat was withheld, a rope's end known to the American sailors as 'a colt' kept them up to the mark, punishing and mortifying them for both minor infringements of duty such as wearing grubby clothing, and more serious offences such as falling asleep on watch. In the single month of October sixty-odd punishments were administered and at least one seaman, William Fry, was confined in irons. When the *Somers* left Monrovia in mid November there was no improvement in the management of the ship, just a worn and resentful crew of late adolescents and a festering complement of older ratings who, far from passing on their skills to the youngsters, had been humiliated in front of them. What Mackenzie thought tightened the brig's discipline had in fact a cumulative contrary effect.

After Gansevoort left Mackenzie, having been instructed not to take further action but to keep a weather eye open, he observed Spencer in the foretop being tattooed by one of the seamen. When Spencer descended he fixed Gansevoort with 'the most infernal expression I have ever seen . . . It satisfied me at once of the man's guilt.' Thus squinted at, Gansevoort returned to Mackenzie's cabin, where the commander had himself been having second thoughts. Mackenzie decided 'to make sure at once of his [Spencer's] person'.

Mustering the hands, Mackenzie called Spencer out and made his accusation. 'It is all a joke,' Spencer responded. 'You are joking on a forbidden subject,' Mackenzie retorted, ordering Gansevoort to relieve Spencer of his dirk, confine him in irons, and kill him instantly if he made any attempt to communicate with any member of the crew. That night the officers wore side-arms, for a search of Spencer's sea-chest had revealed an incriminating list, written in Greek characters, of 'certain' supporters, along with those considered 'likely' and those 'doubtful'. The rest of the ship's company, Spencer had recorded optimistically, 'will probably join when the thing is done, if not they must be forced'. One of those not on the 'certain' list was Boatswain's Mate Cromwell, though an unidentified name which may have been his alias was. Nevertheless, Cromwell was soon attracting his commander's attention.

When the upper sails were being set the next afternoon the main topgallant mast carried away, and Mackenzie considered Cromwell might have had a hand in it: such a distraction could give conspirators a chance to act decisively. Moreover Mackenzie, increasingly paranoid, was now intercepting significant glances between Spencer, manacled on the quarterdeck, and Cromwell. The sadistic petty officer who had so joyfully implemented his draconian regime, Mackenzie now saw as a direct and potent threat to his very tenure of command. The coming night was, Commander Mackenzie decided, 'the season of danger' as long as Cromwell was unconstrained. He therefore ordered the boatswain's mate and an associate named Small fettered next to Spencer, under the eye of the officer of the watch.

Elsewhere men and boys gathered in small groups, fuelled by the endemic resentment Mackenzie had created. Some petty offences committed during a night of fear were the next morning punished in the usual way. With his crew mustered to witness the punishment of others while the three prisoners were confined at their feet, Mackenzie took the opportunity to address them. The announcement of Spencer's expressed desire to seize the ship surprised some, doubtless causing older hands to smirk, or to show relief that matters had been arrested. A few of the boys were seen to weep: the USS *Somers* was a profoundly unhappy ship. Satisfied and mollified, Mackenzie wrote later in his defence that he 'now considered the crew tranquillized and the vessel safe.'

But not all were pacified. Several men wanted to release the prisoners, considering that confining them in irons was unacceptable (though it was one of Mackenzie's few justifiable acts). Then men failed to muster at the changes of the watches. The *Somers* was close to a total breakdown in discipline – the very thing she had been conceived to rectify throughout the American fleet. In this 'insolent and menacing air' Mackenzie 'came to the conclusion that if the officers had to take care of any more prisoners, the safety of the vessel required that the first three should be put to death.'

Next day the weather became boisterous. In handling the ship and ordering the sailors aft at the run to tail on a rope, Midshipman Perry caused a precipitate rush that Gansevoort took for a possible attempt to get aft in a stampede and free the prisoners. The first lieutenant brandished his navy Colt, swearing that he would kill any man who came too far aft. It was the last straw for Mackenzie. Having privately determined on the death of the prisoners, he wrote a letter to each of his officers asking his opinion. 'Determined if necessary to do without counsel what I knew to be . . . my duty . . .', Mackenzie ordered the ship's marines to arrest four more men who had missed their watch musters and were on Spencer's list of names.

Gansevoort and the other six officers conferred and decided to examine witnesses. They took evidence under oath but uncovered only circumstantial indications of any real conspiracy beyond the fulminations of Spencer's imagination. Since the man who had blown the whistle on him, Purser's Assistant James Wales, was on Spencer's 'certain' list, little real hard evidence to support the passing of a death sentence could be gathered, though enough to make it clear that Spencer was deranged. Wales testified that Spencer had said that after he had seized the brig and killed Mackenzie he would 'with his own hands, murder the wardroom officers while they were asleep'. After this they would sail to some piratical island and, it was implied, live out a fantasy of native women and plunder. Alongside this idiocy, plain prejudice fuelled some wild assertions from others: the black cooks were a party to the conspiracy; Cromwell was a sadistic bastard and deserved death; Spencer, Cromwell and the others had been seen 'in combination' discussing some privy matter; Spencer had quizzed the marine sergeant about the state of the arms-chest and how many muskets were kept loaded. What was not attributable to Spencer's derangement could be laid at the feet of Mackenzie himself, as being due to the low state of morale of a persecuted crew.

The ruminations of the officers were hardly decisive. They had the ship to run, the prisoners to guard – they never examined them, but the following day, 1 December, they concluded in a written submission to Mackenzie that Spencer, Cromwell and Small were guilty of 'an intent to mutiny'. Whether the later story – that Gansevoort had told Mackenzie they had insufficient evidence to convict the three principal prisoners – is true does not matter. Gansevoort and several of the other officers were related to Mackenzie, and in any case owed him their professional allegiance. It was far too late to remonstrate as to the severity of the ship-board regime, of which they had become, however unwillingly, a part. They were not, like Fletcher Christian, 'in hell', but bound to continue in the manner they had started. Accordingly and appallingly, they concluded that 'they should be put to death in a manner best calculated as an example . . . upon the disaffected'.

Considering 'the pleasures held out to [the boys] . . . as accompanying the life of a pirate', and believing that 'at least twenty' more men still at large had thrown in their lots with Spencer, Mackenzie was keen to carry the officers' 'recommendation into immediate effect'. It was noon when Gansevoort reported to him with the officers' advice; an hour and three-quarters later, as the *Somers* ran before the steady trade winds on her way towards the West Indies, Gansevoort ordered all hands to witness punishment. With the marines paraded and the officers in full dress ordered to 'stab to the heart' any man who failed to lay his hand on the three whip tackles rove to the main yard arms, Mackenzie read what he conceived to be a just sentence to the prisoners, and gave them ten minutes to prepare themselves. He also called for a pen, paper and a stool and, settling down by Spencer, held a low conversation with him, simultaneously writing notes. What emerged from this extraordinary behaviour seems to have been a last-minute 'confession' which would clear Mackenzie of any charges of impropriety and sweeten the pill for the wretched midshipman's father, the Secretary of War. Gansevoort is thought to have heard Spencer ask Mackenzie if he were not acting too precipitately, but all that was heard for certain was a protest of innocence and of concern for the fate of his wife from Cromwell, and another from Small about his mother. This done, the prisoners were hooded, Spencer was noosed to the outer starboard whip, Small to the inner; Cromwell went to the port yardarm alone. Then Mackenzie gave the order and the *Somers*'s log records the event in terse naval language: 'At 2.15 p.m., fired a weather gun and ran the prisoners up to the yardarm.'

Before being dismissed the ship's company were called upon to give three cheers. They are reported to have done so lustily. That evening the bodies were lowered and buried formally, after which Mackenzie, before retiring to his cabin relieved but unwell, felt that 'I once more was completely commander of the vessel entrusted to me.' This seems hardly to have been the case: on the passage to and home from St Thomas, Mackenzie resumed his old regime of punishment. On 9 December eleven boys were given a dozen stripes of the rope's end for 'not going aloft to furl sails'. The inconsistency of Mackenzie's punishments is nowhere better exemplified than here, for failure to obey a lawful order is indeed mutiny and ought to have warranted some severer punishment which he could and ought to have delayed and submitted to a court martial when, to everyone's intense relief, the *Somers* anchored off New York in the East River on the night of Wednesday 14 December 1842.

Mackenzie still had the original four mutineers in irons and now arrested six boys and two seamen, shrouding the ship from the shore and sparking waterfront conjecture about 'a strange mystery' surrounding the brig.

Sending his report to Secretary of the Navy Abel Upshur, Mackenzie released a terse statement to a friendly newspaper. In so doing he sought additional justification for his conduct in not waiting to arraign Spencer and his confrères before a court martial by claiming not only the paramountcy of his duty to preserve his ship, but also his desire to ensure that nepotism and influence did not save Spencer. Mackenzie stated that it would have been unnatural for Spencer senior not to have intervened to save his son, a clear implication that such intervention would have been prejudicial to the good order of the United States naval service. Moreover, the commander went on moralistically, 'For those who have friends or money in America there was no punishment for the worst of crimes.' Such conduct goes far beyond William Bligh's loss of temper and provocatively intemperate language. In all other respects Bligh was supremely fitted for his job; here Mackenzie exposes himself as an incompetent. Many of his detractors saw Mackenzie as himself a sadist, though not of the Pigot mould. It has been pointed out that in one of his earlier books, *A Year in Spain*, published in 1829 when he was still Alexander Slidell, he had recounted how his coach had been attacked by brigands, who murdered the driver and postillion. Significantly, he had been unable to intervene, though he recorded that he could 'distinctly hear each stroke of the murderous knife'. After the apprehension, trial and conviction of the robbers, Slidell attended the hangings and on a subsequent visit to Spain was drawn by curiosity to observe a garrotting 'a spectacle full of horror and painful excitement, still I had determined to witness it. I felt sad and melancholy, and yet, by a strange perversion, I was willing to feel more so.'

Spencer's father reacted with a blistering attack on Mackenzie and the illegality of his summary act, igniting a national scandal. A formal naval court of enquiry was held aboard the receiving ship *North Carolina* moored in the Brooklyn Navy Yard. 'As all the mutinies on record have been provoked by injustice toward the crew, or by gross tyranny, or incapacity, on the part of the commanding officer, it concerns me to show that no such causes existed on the *Somers*,' Mackenzie declared to the court. However inaccurate this statement was in fact, it is clear that he was distancing himself from the images of Bligh and Pigot, whose names were then synonymous with mutiny aboard a man-of-war. The mute testimony of the *Somers*'s log, itemising over 2,250 lashes being laid on the backs of predominantly boys over a period of some six months (one fourteen-year-old recidivist named Dennis Manning had received 101 of them), told another tale and rocked Mackenzie's complacency. But despite Secretary of War Spencer's attempts to clear his son's name and foul Mackenzie's, despite the attempts made to portray the incident as 'a phantom' of Mackenzie's fears and the prejudiced perjury of witnesses, at worst a 'plot . . . in embryo', the court found for Mackenzie. His 'immediate execution of the ringleaders [was] demanded by duty and justified by necessity'. Mackenzie now sought a formal court-martial to avoid being charged with murder in a civil court, something Cromwell's family, as well as Spencer's, were threatening.

Again the hearing was held aboard the *North Carolina*. Mackenzie handed his sword to the court of fourteen senior captains and a judge advocate, and submitted his conduct to examination again. The proceedings began. Sergeant Garty of the marines was a convincing witness to the reality of the threat of mutiny, and to the subsequent danger of a rising to release the manacled prisoners. The court pondered whether Mackenzie could have taken the *Somers* to a port where the support of another American warship could have been called upon? That was unlikely, and Mackenzie raised the spectre of the dishonour attaching to appealing for help from the ubiquitous British Royal Navy: 'A naval commander can never be justified in invoking foreign aid in reducing an insubordinate crew to obedience.' Mackenzie's defence was prolix but concluded that 'Necessity stood stern umpire.' He implied that he had not flinched from his unpleasant duty, that he had thereby personally risked a civil suit for murder in the execution, literally, of his public duty. It was a bravura performance; the court agreed. 'The intent . . . to supersede lawful authority', the judge advocate summed up, 'or resist it, or to bring it into contempt' was of itself an act of mutiny. Mackenzie's sword was turned hilt towards him on the table. His conduct had been 'prudent and firm', he was acquitted and free to go. The sentence never received President Tyler's confirmation.

In the aftermath Mackenzie, wearied by his ordeal and peremptorily and 'mortifyingly' removed from command of the *Somers*, dropped the charges against the remaining prisoners. Surgeon Leacock, a contributor to Gansevoort's council, blew his brains out in the *Somers*'s wardroom and the Bowery Theatre dramatized the incident, about which New York buzzed for months. Practically every American literary figure of the age seems to have become embroiled: Washington Irving was already a friend of Mackenzie, James Fenimore Cooper became an enemy, while Richard Henry Dana was sympathetic to Mackenzie's dilemma. In Herman Melville's Captain Vere one is able to perceive a full, sanitized and compassionate exculpation of Mackenzie. Melville was careful, however, to ascribe the death of poor Billy in *Billy Budd* to the unjust and tyrannical horrors of the British navy from which Vere could not escape, being held like a fly in the web of Admiralty. Perhaps it was as well that the novelette, Melville's last work, was not published until 1924, long after his death – by which time the British at least had learned that, in Rudyard Kipling's words, 'Blood was the price of Admiralty'.

Mackenzie resumed his literary career as he waited to go to sea again, writing a biography of Captain Stephen Decatur. He was summoned to serve in command of the USS *Mississippi* during the war with Mexico, and died in 1848. Gansevoort rose to command but was suspended, charged with intoxication, though he died a commodore after seeing action in the Civil War.

The *Somers* affair was a nadir in the history of the United States Navy, but there were other disturbances such as that at San Francisco in 1846 aboard the USS *Warren*, an 18-gun sloop, another aboard the frigate *United States* in the Mediterranean in 1848, and a nasty insurrection in 1864 among two hundred naval ratings taking passage aboard an American merchant ship, the *Ocean Queen*. The ratings were on their way to Panama, to cross the isthmus by train and relieve men in American men-of-war on the Pacific station. Their mutiny was scotched by the prompt action of the draft's senior officer, Commander Daniel Ammen, and Captain Tinklepaugh, the master of the *Ocean Queen*, whose ship also bore a full complement of passengers of both sexes. Having shot the ring-leaders in a fight, Ammen was relieved of the remainder by the Union cruiser *Neptune* off the coast of Cuba, where she was protecting shipping from the Confederate commerce raider *Florida*. Like Mackenzie, Ammen requested a court-martial to remove the threat of a civil suit for murder, and he was freed with a verdict of justifiable homicide.

There was one other official echo of the executions aboard the *Somers*: the Department of the Navy were compelled to grasp the nettle of proper training. As with the events following the loss of the *Wager*, the unhappy *Somers* may be said to have in the end made her contribution to the improvement of her Service. As a consequence of her disastrous cruise, and three years before Mackenzie died, the United States Naval Academy was established at Annapolis in Maryland.

11

'INSOLENCE, DRUNKENNESS AND NEGLIGENCE'

DURING the latter half of the eighteenth century and up to its loss of the monopoly of trade between Britain and the East in 1813, Britain's greatest private merchant-owners were the Honourable East India Company. Mortality was a greater danger aboard an East Indiaman than mutiny, so their commanders – for so the captains of East Indiamen were styled – were compelled to make good the losses of British sailors by the employment of Indian or Chinese, or by picking up indifferent seamen in odd locations. Discipline sometimes broke down when they were wrecked, which was not infrequently in consequence of the poor charts then available, the lack of knowledge of the natural dangers strewn across their route and the lingering difficulties of establishing longitude. As a precaution, and for their passengers' comfort, East Indiamen invariably shortened sail at night, which made their voyages tediously protracted. This measure did not always work – the grounding and subsequent loss of the *Hartwell*, Captain Edward Fiott, on Boa Vista in the Cape Verde Islands in August 1787 being a case in point. The wreck was not attributed to poor navigation, however, but blamed on 'the bad discipline of the crew, who four days before had behaved in a most extraordinary manner'. Quite what this constituted is now uncertain, but a similar example is provided by the fate of the *Fame*, a chartered ship which on a homeward voyage from Calcutta to London was cast ashore and lost in Table Bay. The ship 'was standing out of the Bay [when] the wind fell light; the ship's company refused to make sail, and, in consequence of this dastardly and villainous conduct, the ship drove on shore and was wrecked. Mrs Mills, a lady passenger, of Calcutta, was drowned. These scoundrels declared [in court] the ship should not leave the port, and many of them are now watermen at the Cape of Good Hope' – which, since it was known as the 'Tavern of the Seas', was probably where the mutinous sailors most wanted to settle.

Personality clashes were not uncommon on these long voyages, and frequently boiled over when the ship was anchored off a port. In such circumstances matters could be dealt with ashore, where the charge of mutiny was ambiguous. In 1798 Second Officer Reid assaulted Commander Colnett of the East Indiaman *King George* when both were ashore at the Cape of Good Hope. Reid was arrested and court-martialled aboard the naval guardship, HMS *Stately*, and sentenced to two years' imprisonment. Had the same incident occurred afloat he would have suffered death.

The quasi-naval nature of the East India Company's service in distant waters made it possible for courts of inquiry composed of its own officers to sit and hand out sentences. In 1787 the East Indiaman *Belvidere*, part of the so-called 'China Fleet', lay anchored off Whampoa, some miles below Canton in the Pearl River. Her commander was sick ashore with dysentery and the ship was in the charge of her first officer, Mr Dunlop; he found himself confronted with a major uprising by his crew, who it seems were demanding the release of a man confined for insubordination. There may also have been a grievance that the crew had been refused leave to go ashore at Canton (invariably denied because of difficulties with the Chinese authorities, though several sparsely inhabited islands in the river were made available for recreational purposes). Dunlop summoned help from the other Indiamen at anchor and fought off the mutineers with his sword. Commodore Dundas, the senior captain present, convened a court of inquiry which sentenced the ring-leaders to be flogged round the fleet, and others to severe floggings. When Dundas was himself subjected to a civil action on the return of the fleet to London, the Company paid his expenses; he was not only acquitted, but praised by the judges.

Prompt action by East India commanders seems frequently to have put paid to the irruption of small mutinies among disaffected seamen. As in the *Belvidere,* the spark of solidarity was often kindled by the apprehension of a known trouble-maker. In 1804 Commander Timins extinguished such an insurrection aboard the *Royal George* with his pistol. The ship was off the coast of Sumatra and had experienced a tropical thunderstorm during which fierce squalls had laid the ship over and 'the fore topgallant mast [had been] shivered with lightning'. Next morning the crew refused to come on deck. Timins having armed all his officers, brandished a pair of pistols and confronted the crew. They were brought to heel, Timins promising to redress a minor grievance which had been exaggerated into a major issue.

Aboard the *Minerva* Commander Kennard-Smith used his sword to similar effect when the crew rushed the quarterdeck where a man was about to be flogged, and in 1823 Commander Mitchell of the *Bridgewater* found himself in similar circumstances. This mutiny appears to have arisen from the insubordinate behaviour of one man, Thomas Jones. Jones had been insolent to the *Bridgewater*'s fourth officer, but had so worked upon the men's fears that his arrest brought the entire ship's company to his support, confronting Mitchell and his officers with a wholesale breakdown in obedience. With his officers in support, Mitchell drew his sword and waded in, cutting three of the ring-leaders down and seizing a fourth, whereupon the rest fled and later returned to their duty sufficiently contrite to mollify Mitchell. One possible cause of these almost casual mutinies may be revealed in a letter written in 1830 by the first officer of the East Indiaman *Susan*, Mr Henry Hyland. Hyland signed on an able seaman named John Murray, and he deliberately provoked trouble by inciting his fellow shipmates to refuse to obey orders while the *Susan* lay at anchor off Port Louis. In the ensuing days Hyland 'observed Murray to be active in stirring the sailors up to disobedience of orders, asserting that he did not go to sea for wages, but that he depended upon getting damages in law, by provoking the captain and officers to strike him; and that he generally got from £50 to £100 damages'. Such trouble-makers were justifiably known as 'sea-lawyers'. Murray suborned two other men, who gave Hyland such trouble that he 'was obliged to keep them in irons until I got into St Helena, and I then delivered them over to the civil power.' Murray himself dodged such a fate, but equally failed to provoke Hyland or his fellow officers during the rest of the voyage. In a last desperate throw, however, he waited until the *Susan* was working her way up the Thames with a pilot on board before confronting Hyland on the quarterdeck. Shouting abuse, Murray shook his fist in Hyland's face and claimed that as they were in pilotage waters he could not be charged with mutiny. Busy with working the ship, Hyland had 'to pass over such conduct in the best manner I could, and would subsequently have had him committed for trial, was it not for the *excessive trouble, expense*, and *loss of time* attending such a prosecution' [Hyland's emphasis].

Commander Christopher Biden, who commanded the East Indiamen *Royal George* and later the *Princess Charlotte of Wales*, collected a large body of evidence, including Hyland's, adding to the sorry tales of insubordination aboard East Indiamen further incidents on the British-flagged and -officered 'country ships', often Parsee- or Anglo-Parsee-owned, which traded between India, the Malay peninsula and China.

Although a High Tory and typical of his generation and type, who enforced obedience to lawfully appointed masters irrespective of grievances, Biden was not insensible to the plight of the common sailor, particularly his vulnerability to licensed abduction by the naval press-gang. The purpose of his endeavours was to promote a proper code of regulation for the merchant service in order to improve its general quality, and he began to attract a number of like-minded reformers to his cause. As he ably adumbrates, most mutinous conduct arose not from any deep-seated tyrannical cruelties but from trivial causes, the malevolence of individuals, or the deprivation of reasonable liberties. Others were quick to point out that the commanders of Indiamen were not themselves free of blame, for by and large merchant seamen were not actually averse to discipline itself – though the justice of its dispensation was another matter. Aside from mutiny on board ship, merchant seamen had struck for better wages when ashore, notably in the English north-east coast ports in 1792, 1806 and 1815. These incidents have a curious similarity to the naval mutinies of 1797, in that the seamen were conscientious about their own discipline. Biden recounts how in 1815 the 'seamen in the ports of Newcastle and Sunderland preserved the most systematic order and very severe discipline. Any seamen of their party who missed muster (which took place twice a-day) was paraded through the principal streets of the town, having his face smeared with tar, and his jacket turned inside out. He was afterwards mounted on a platform attached to poles set up in triangles for the purpose, where he remained at the mercy of the mob.'

The removal of the East India Company's monopoly in 1813 was followed by other major changes in the maritime world. The first was a new method of measuring tonnage which gradually transformed sailing ship design, greatly improved speed and opened the way for innovation; the second was the repeal of the British Navigation Acts in 1826, which rapidly opened up the world's trade to competition. It was this expansion that had stretched British resources and led to the decline in the old Honourable Company – a term now used with the utmost irony. A corresponding invigoration and expansion of the British Admiralty's Hydrographic Department also brought about a swift improvement in charts, with a corresponding improvement in the safety of navigation. But this general air of technical progress did not extend to the area we should today call Human Resources.

It is clear that insofar as crew discipline was concerned, by the 1830s matters had slid from bad to worse and the East India Company in particular had seriously degenerated. Neither commanders nor their crews were, it was asserted, up to the mark. The former were often guilty of a 'supercilious pomposity' and treated their crews 'like animals'. The crews, on the other hand, showed evidence of 'insolence, drunkenness and negligence'. However polarized this point of view, one commander at least seems to have been from the same mould as Pigot and Slidell Mackenzie, and generated a tirade of criticism. A naval officer, having studied the events aboard the East Indiaman *Inglis* in June 1829, opined that 'The India Company are the shabbiest set of shipowners whose vessels traverse the oceans.' This was strong stuff, but the *Inglis*'s captain, a Commander Dudman, was a foul-mouthed bully who verged on sadism, sanctioning 'some disgusting occurrences' aboard the *Inglis*. When his crew remonstrated with him over their brutalized existences, he saw fit to flog them without mercy. Matters came to a head when Dudman ordered a ship's boy to attend to duty better suited to an able seaman, forcing the reluctant youth to go out on a spar from which the lad fell into the sea and drowned. Once again the troubles of a single individual provided the spark to dry tinder: the crew rose against Dudman. In due course, although brought to justice and found guilty, the mutineers were given lenient sentences, and the case brought the plight of seafarers generally into the public arena. It soon became clear that it was not just among the prestigious Indiamen with their traditional place in the British public's imagination, that matters had deteriorated, but that things were rotten elsewhere in the British merchant fleet. The debate spread beyond the courts and the waterfront, bringing an an era of reform that began with the first of a series of regulating Merchant Shipping Acts of Parliament – the provision of proper wage-scales, victualling allowances and standards of competency, administered by the Board of Trade and Plantations – and culminated with the prevention of excess profits being made from overloaded and unsafe 'coffin' ships, provided for by the Act of Parliament sponsored by Samuel Plimsoll in 1876.

Under the new conditions that emerged after the end of the 'Great War' against Napoleonic France the United States merchant marine expanded alongside the British and, as will be seen, both suffered from similar malaises. As the dynamic nineteenth century unfolded, mutinies became increasingly common aboard merchant ships other than East Indiamen, both British and American. In the large mercantile marines, possessed by these nations at the time, the hierarchy was flatter than that in men-of-war, making confrontation with authority easier. Merchantmen had always suffered from the curse of occasional disorder but usually the matter was smoothed over or solved by quick, summary intervention, often by the master himself but usually by the mates. In the absence of proper regulation a master dominated a fractious crew or an incorrigible individual by sheer force of personality; on occasion, a mate would lay out a rebellious crew-member, scotching incipient mutiny before it had gathered any momentum. Often this was taken too far by tough young officers being over-zealous and over-bearing with members of a crew, dominating them with pre-emptive violence for the smallest infraction of conduct. 'The second mate struck the man at the wheel in the face because he was half a point [about 5.6°] off the course . . .' was how an old shell-back recalled one circumstance in the steady disintegration of discipline aboard a sailing ship. 'The helmsman knew better than to do it, but he let go of the wheel and she came up all standing and shook the main and fore topgallant masts out of her. Hell broke loose . . .'

During this vigorous age of expansion and exploration a crew often had cause to complain about poor food, overloaded ships, or lack of faith in the master and mates. Often a 'hard-case' mate would terrorize a crew simply to keep them jumpily obedient, a practice known as 'hazing'. The same old seaman told how 'The third day out [from New York] we went aft in a body and complained about the food, which was the very worst any of us had ever had. The Captain told us the food was good enough for a bunch of wharf-rats, and he said some other things that I cannot put on this page, ordered us forward, and as we did not move fast enough to suit the mates, they waded into us with belaying pins and beat us up plenty. If we hit back, that would be mutiny, of course.'

In addition to the old problems always associated with sailing ships, early steamships also bred anxiety. Their boilers had a disturbing propensity to explode, while the gangs of 'firemen' signed-on to tend their voracious appetites for coal were drawn from the roughest fringes of waterfront society. These men often feuded among themselves or sought to terrorize the remaining crew, presenting their officers with intractable problems. Equally, masters and mates were sometimes driven to ruling their crews with extreme vigilance, most especially after the discovery of gold in California, Australia and New Zealand in the mid-nineteenth century, events that dramatically increased the number of passengers travelling the seas. As ships arrived in ports near the gold fields with excited 'diggers' and prospectors eager to get ashore and make their fortunes, it was often the case that among those landing were the entire crew. In response to this crisis, masters often forced the local constabulary to lock up their crews on trumped up charges for safe keeping, the men being released to sail the ship away after she had completed cargo-work.

The most mysterious mutiny of them all – motivated, it must be presumed (in the absence of any real evidence), by a lust for rich pickings – occurred aboard the *Madagascar* in 1853. The ship was one of a thoroughbred type of sailing vessel known as 'Blackwall frigates', from the famous yard on the Thames. These fast cargo and passenger ships serviced the gold fields and bore the growing number of emigrants to Australia, making rapid passages in which the public began to take an interest. Their masters became household names and their passage-times were followed in the newspapers, but they mostly attracted attention when they were lost, homeward-bound, laden with gold and with happy and successful prospectors. One such was the *Madagascar*.

She was due to leave Port Philip, near Melbourne, in July 1853, under Captain Fortsecue Harris, a competent and popular master who was well regarded by his passengers. Just before the sailed, police officers arrived and apprehended two of the passengers in connection with a recent robbery. A great deal of gold dust was discovered in their baggage but this, the men claimed, was the fruit of their labours at the diggings. More to the point, the protracted delay to the *Madagascar*'s sailing resulting from the consequent legal proceedings caused Harris a further problem. Harris had fully manned his ship, but the lure of the gold fields led to desertions. Finding himself in a common predicament, Harris sent his officers to recruit any likely hands from among the unemployed men ashore – men who had tried their luck in the gold fields and failed, men who might have thought easier money lay aboard the delayed *Madagascar* than at Ballarat.

As she lay at anchor awaiting the resolution of her problems, an outward-bound vessel, the *Roxburgh Castle,* arrived with a lady passenger, her three children and their nurse. Mrs de Cartaret was intending to join her husband, a prominent member of the Melbourne Bar. Sadly, as she read the Melbourne papers which came aboard with the pilot, Mrs de Cartaret learned she had been recently widowed; she immediately asked the *Roxburgh Castle*'s master to arrange for her to transfer to the next homeward-bound ship – the *Madagascar* – and this was duly accomplished.

Captain Harris finally sailed towards the end of July. Thereafter he, the *Madagascar*, her crew, her passengers and her cargo vanished. Weeks later she was posted missing at Lloyd's, and there the matter rested. More than thirty years later a persistently enduring rumour surfaced: a dying woman in New Zealand who sent for a clergyman had told how she had been a nurse and had taken passage aboard the *Madagascar*. After the ship passed into the South Atlantic, the woman stated, a savage mutiny took place during which most of the crew and a few of the passengers seized the ship, murdered Harris and all his officers, and confined all but the youngest and most attractive women below. The boats were then lowered, all the gold found aboard the ship was put into them, along with water and provisions, and the *Madagascar* was set on fire. After a protracted and difficult passage, only one of the boats, bearing five men and six women, reached the Brazilian coast, where it capsized in the breakers and the conspirators lost most if not all the gold. The survivors struggled ashore and were swiftly reduced by yellow fever to two men and herself, who had been Mrs de Cartaret's children's nurse. What happened in the intervening years, and how the woman reached New Zealand, was never made clear. That the poor creature had been obliged to live a degraded life was hinted at by a further revelation that one of the survivors was later hanged in San Francisco for murder; beyond that – nothing.

It was not unknown for ships to be overwhelmed and founder in the Southern Ocean, or to run into icebergs and sink, but there was usually corroborative, albeit circumstantial evidence, of other ships having experienced heavy weather or ice in the estimated position of the lost vessel which had been posted missing. It is more likely that the *Madagascar* was overwhelmed not by the forces of nature but by the malice of man. If so, the rising was comparable with the horrors aboard several slavers, such as the *Amistad* or the *Creole*, or convict ships like the *Lady Shore*, and may not have been mutiny, pure and simple. The horror and indignity of the young woman is only to be guessed at, but the burning of the ship and her passengers is equally dreadful – if that is what took place. The obscurity of the fate of the *Madagascar* simply emphasizes the isolation of a ship at sea, where the rule of law, howsoever arbitrarily administered, is preferable to the rule of lust and disorder.

The mystery is compounded and the waters muddied by another version of the story which places the death-bed revelation in Brazil in 1883 – a more credible location, given the alleged position of the *Madagascar* at the time of the mutiny. However, the focus returns to New Zealand with yet another account which states that a Maori reported witnessing the loss of a Blackwall liner on Stewart Island. This version is accepted in New Zealand as the real account of the loss of the *Madagascar*. Perhaps the truth lies somewhere between: the position of the ship has been mixed up, and the old woman did die in New Zealand and had been badly used by some survivors. That undesirable characters were on board Harris's ship is entirely probable, as is the likelihood of their trying to seize any available gold. While one can speculate on what happened, any of these resolutions seems plausible, and all offer insights into the curious nature of shipboard life, with its necessary hierarchies and its carefully contrived social checks and balances. The end of the *Madagascar* has a metaphorical quality which stands for all mutinies. In the end, despite any provocations, the greater good is achieved in standing by the ship, since the artificial constructs of order and discipline are not conceived for the aggrandisement of the commander but for the survival of the entire company embarked.

A similar rising occurred the following year when her crew was seduced by the amount of gold in the lazarette of the *Sovereign of the Seas*. Built in the United States, she had been the largest merchant ship in the world and flew the American flag, but by 1853 she had been chartered by the Black Ball Line of Liverpool for the Australian emigrant trade. It was when she was homeward bound from Melbourne on her first voyage under the British ensign that the mutiny attempt was made. Captain Warner was equal to the occasion, however, and quickly mastered the situation and confined the mutineers to irons. where they were kept during the greater part of the vessel's remarkable 68-day passage to Liverpool.

Occasionally a political motive might influence a crew, especially in time of hostilities when allegiances were tested. On 29 December 1856, during the Second Opium War, the Chinese crew of the British-registered coastal steamer *Thistle* mutinied while the vessel was on a passage down the Pearl River from Canton to Hong Kong. Eleven European officers and passengers were decapitated by the Chinese crew, who wore the badge of Imperial Commissioner Yeh, the Emperor's Viceroy and a man opposed to the British insistence on their right to import opium into the Middle Kingdom.

The gold rushes subsided but a steadier emigrant trade continued, and was taken over by steamships. Steam power, with its augmentation of a ship's crew by firemen and engineers, and the establishment of regular, scheduled passenger routes, increased the numbers of people aboard a merchant ship. This in turn had implications for the social order on board, and for the job of a master and his officers.

In times of dissent, one thing a ship-master could rely upon was the presence of a Royal Naval ship in most waters of the world: if he could contact her, he could demand assistance to quell any crew trouble. As the century progressed and more nations joined the imperial camp it was a duty assumed by most national navies, and provision was made in the emerging internationally agreed codes of flag signals for a ship's master to summon help if his crew was mutinous. Having offered armed assistance to quell mutiny, even a junior commander of a minor warship was empowered to convene a Naval Court. This, calling on the help of any other independent British master in port, could try and condemn mutineers, though its powers of sentence were limited. Indeed in 1877, when the crew of the Peruvian man-of-war *Huascar* were caught up in a revolution, took control of their ship and raided trading vessels in the Pacific, HMSs *Shah* and *Amethyst* engaged the rebel warship. Although the *Huascar* escaped, later to be taken by the Chileans, her piratical activities were thereby curtailed.

An alternative available to a master faced with mutiny was the civil power. When in 1870 the crew of the Whitby-registered brig *Bussorah* mutinied during a passage in the North Sea, her master and his mates took the ship into the Humber, besought the help of the local police and hauled the mutineers before the magistrates, who handed down prison sentences.

While many insubordinate acts aboard merchant ships were often based upon a justifiable grievance, there remained those acts of wanton criminality that were either the result of careful plotting, or almost spontaneous and opportunist rebellions. The latter were the most common and were characterized by a reckless disregard for consequences, which in almost every case, had not been considered. An example of the former was that occurring aboard the American schooner *Plattsburg* in July 1816. The *Plattsburg* was bound from Baltimore to Smyrna in Turkey laden with coffee and $42,000-worth of specie. Although only Captain Hackett and the owner's supercargo, his agent responsible for cargo matters at Smyrna, were supposed to know of the shipment of specie, word of it had leaked out along the Baltimore waterfront. Among the thirty hands were eight conspirators led by a seaman named Stromer who had signed on with malicious intent. Their first move was to provoke an act of insubordination in which the mate was overpowered. It took the intervention of Hackett with a belaying pin to break-up the fight and restore order. This incident brought under the conspirators' influence several unsuspecting seamen who espoused Stromer's cause while remaining entirely ignorant of his intentions. Stromer next persuaded the black steward to add poison to the officers' coffee, but this proved insufficient.

As the *Plattsburg* ran into thick weather east of the Azores, the conspirators hatched their next plot. A call at the change of the watch one night that a ship had been sighted through the murk compelled the two mates to peer anxiously into the darkness. As they searched distractedly for this chimera, Stromer struck both men. The mate went out cold and was pitched overboard; the second mate Stephen Onion escaped the worst of the assault and ran aft into hiding. Hackett had been roused by the shouts of the mates, and as he came on deck was immediately knocked out and flung overboard, as was the supercargo. Onion was now enticed out of hiding, promised his life if he co-operated in navigating the schooner, and the *Plattsburg* altered course for the English Channel, the North Sea and Norway.

Thus far the criminals had masterminded a near-perfect crime, and they shared out the money between them. But matters began to disintegrate when, on arrival off Kristiansund, the crew started an extravagant debauch that must have attracted attention and soon had them spending money like water. Off Copenhagen Onion was able to escape. He alerted the American consul, who arranged for the seven mutineers to be arrested. Afterwards they were transported to Massachussetts, tried, and hanged on Boston Neck in February 1819. Two others were located in Europe, but with no extradition treaties in place they escaped justice. Stromer also vanished, escaping entirely with what remained of his ill-gotten gains.

A similar plot was hatched by a seaman named Charles Gibbs who signed on the American brig *Vineyard* in New Orleans in November 1830, having got wind that she was carrying a consignment of specie. Captain Thornby had in his charge $59,000 dollars intended as payment to a Philadelphia merchant named Stephen Girard, along with a mixed cargo of cotton, sugar and molasses. Gibbs began to canvass support among the small crew, drawing about him a coterie that went into action early on the morning of the 23rd. Called on deck, Thornby was struck down and thrown overboard. After a struggle Chief Mate William Roberts followed him, though Gibbs stopped short of murdering the two men who had refused to join him. The *Vineyard* was off Cape Hatteras and Gibbs, altering course away from Delaware Bay, headed for Long Island, dividing the specie among his fellow mutineers. On 27 November the *Vineyard* was hove-to about three miles off Coney Island, the two boats were then lowered, and the brig scuttled. Pulling ashore one boat capsized in the surf, drowning three men, one of whom was an innocent. Gibbs and the others landed and buried their haul, but before the could disperse they were discovered by a wild-fowler named Johnson who offered them shelter – they were on Barren Island, just off the main coast. Gibbs and his cronies fell asleep, whereupon an agitated crew-member named Brownbrigg, who had not been party to the plot, told Johnson what had happened.

Thoroughly alarmed, Johnson plied Brownbrigg with liquor until he too was asleep, then launched his punt and made for the mainland to inform the authorities. Apprehended and tried, all received sentences, for although the boy, Brownbrigg, turned state's witness, he had heard of Gibbs's intentions and had failed to alarm the *Vineyard*'s master. Gibbs and another seaman who had actually murdered Thornby and Roberts were hanged.

But it was the senseless, ill-considered and vicious mutiny that became all to tragically frequent, mutiny in which there is not hint of glamour, only a depressing display of man's inhumanity to man. Two years earlier, in November 1828, the New Bedford whaler *Sharon* was cruising after whales in the South Atlantic. Short of hands, Captain Norris had been obliged to sign on six men at Ascension, and they formed a disproportionately large clique aboard the ship. Sighting the spouts of whales Norris ordered two boats lowered in pursuit, and all his American crew, including the mate, Smith, went off after the cetaceans. Norris was left with his cook, a Portuguese boy, and three of the men engaged at Ascension.

Having successfully killed a whale the two boats began the laborious business of towing the carcass back towards the ship, signalling their success and expecting Norris to bear down towards them. Instead, nothing happened until they were close enough to see the Portuguese boy in the rigging, waving frantically, while the islanders were on deck, hefting whale lances. The seamen were for leaving their prize, pulling smartly for the *Sharon* and boarding her in overwhelming numbers, but Smith demurred. If Norris was dead, as the Portuguese lad was shouting, *he* was in charge – and he was not to be hurried. The trouble was that he put off taking action seemingly indefinitely, angering one seaman named Clough who insisted that they go to Norris's aid. The master, Clough said, might be badly wounded, and they were bound to retake the ship. Darkness fell as the boats paddled after the ship, Smith still indecisive and Clough ready for action. After dark Clough, with considerable courage, dropped over the whale-boat's side and swam towards the distant

Sharon, hauling himself inboard through an open stern port. He had hardly done so when he encountered one of the mutineers. Defending himself with his sailor's knife he succeeded in besting his assailant, only to be attacked by a second mutineer just as he had located a musket. Clough despatched this man with the musket, whereupon the third islander, having come to the assistance of his mates, saw what had happened to them and fled.

Clough now summoned the boats and drew the boy down from aloft. He had recaptured the *Sharon* single-handed. The third mutineer was located and secured in irons; the *Sharon* continued her voyage and returned to New Bedford, where Clough received rapid promotion and Smith was sent out of the ship. Clough's resolute initiative and courage turned the tables on an impromptu plot, and was in sharp contrast to the fatal vacillation and capitulation to events displayed by both Smith of the *Sharon* and Third Mate Fisher of the *Globe*.

The isolation of a merchantman at sea occasionally seems simply to have presented resentful men with an opportunity they were incapable of resisting. On 5 August 1838 the crew of the American brig *Braganza*, on passage between Philadelphia and Genoa, was approaching the Straits of Gibraltar when the mate was attacked, his skull opened, and he fell mortally wounded. The master, Captain Amel Turley, who had his wife and some passengers in his care, was overpowered and thrown overboard. The second mate escaped below, where the mutinous crew confined the remainder. In due course the mutineers, having robbed the afterguard of their valuables, put them in a boat and abandoned them. Fortunately they were picked up by a British vessel on her way to Glasgow.

Meanwhile, the *Braganza*'s dying mate had been tossed into the Atlantic and the vessel made sail to the north-east and worked through the English Channel and into the North Sea, where she was deliberately run ashore on the coast of Hanover near Emden. Fortunately the mutineers were apprehended, and except for one who committed suicide were in due course brought to trial in New York. All were found guilty, though one escaped execution by suicide, and one was commended to mercy on account of his immaturity. The remainder were hanged on Gibbet Island off New York.

That such petty felonies seem to have been the motive, or perhaps only a pretext, for mutiny owes much to the degeneracy of many seamen in sailing vessels during the nineteenth century. With the exception of diehards who sailed in the elite tea clippers, and after their replacement by steamships transferred with their favoured ships to the Australian wool trade, the best and most reliable men went into steamers, where a more regular life prevailed. Often it was the case that a polyglot crew shipped aboard a sailing ship by a desperate master after doing a deal with a crimp were just eager for trouble. Often they had been cheated of wages earned on a previous vessel, and mutiny seemed their only way of avenging themselves on a harsh world. They did so without any apparent consideration for the consequences, often committing acts of senseless violence and brutality. Such, among many others, were the outbreaks aboard the British sailing vessels *Flowery Land* in 1863, the *Manitoba* in 1871 and the *Lennie* in 1875. Casual murder of the master and mates often accompanied these senseless uprisings, and the mutineers, lacking any sustainable plan, were usually brought to justice. Not infrequently one of their number turned state's or Queen's witness, or they were compelled to retain a loyal officer if only to navigate their vessel. The seized ships were usually scuttled once in sight of land, and the consequent losses prompted owners, shippers and consignees to muster the forces of law and order across the globe to apprehend mutineers. As for the criminals themselves, they were incapable of hanging together and so, in Benjamin Franklin's memorable phrase, they were hanged separately.

The case of the *Lennie* is typical. She was one of a large number of sailing vessels that earned their living and profits for their owners alongside steamships in the second half of the nineteenth century by being able to compete in the market place because of their low running costs; these were minimal compared with those of steamers, and made lower still by canny owners,

agents, crimps, masters and mates. Since they carried homo-
genous cargoes whose arrival time was not critical, further economies could be achieved. In all this cost-cutting there was no
benefit at all to the common sailors who manned them, and these
men were often, quite literally, the sweepings of the waterfront.

Registered in Nova Scotia, the *Lennie* flew the British red ensign
and was commanded by a Canadian, Captain Stanley Hatfield, who
was under orders to make a passage from Antwerp to New Orleans
in ballast. To save money Hatfield did not ship a crew until he was
ready to sail, although by 24 October 1875, when the main body of
the crew was expected, he already had aboard an innocuous Irish
mate named Joseph Wortley, a Scots second mate called Richard
MacDonald, Constant van Hoydonck the Belgian steward, and a
Dutch steward's boy with the French-sounding name of Henri
Trousselot who was only fifteen years old. That morning a
boarding-house runner arrived with the crew from London,
garnered among the 'hotels' and brothels of Wapping's Ratcliff
Highway. These eleven men were signed on under the eye of the
British consul and Captain Hatfield and then taken aboard the
Lennie, which was to sail the next morning. Reinforcing the polyglot
nature of those already aboard the vessel, the eleven newcomers
consisted of three Greeks, four Turks, an Italian, an Englishman, a
Dane and an Austrian. Most had given false names and/or false
nationalities on the Articles of Agreement at the consular office.
The Italian, named Giovanni Caneso, 'seemed an intelligent man',
spoke fluent English, signed on as George Green, and was appointed
boatswain. One of the Greeks, named Cargarlis, had served an
eight-year-stint in prison in Marseilles and had a hold over at least
one other crew member from the outset.

Two days out, Cargarlis was one of two men who came aft and
requested an issue of tobacco. Hatfield was unable to supply it,
stating that he had not bought any on board for sale, and that the
men had had an advance of wages and enough time to lay in a
private stock if they so desired. Carting their resentment at this
mild rebuff back to the forecastle, the two began abusing Hatfield,
Cargarlis allegedly declaiming that there would be trouble 'if any

of those useless ornaments aft start their monkey tricks on me'. Several men voiced their support of Cargarlis, others wandered out on deck to distance themselves from his wild talk.

Thereafter the ship settled into her routine, working her way down Channel and out into the Atlantic, so that by the night of 31 October she was crossing the Bay of Biscay. The night was dark and blustery and Hatfield decided to put the ship on the other tack 'at eight bells', when the watches changed and all hands were on deck together. This was customary in short-handed sailing ships, minimizing the disruption to the crew's routine of four hours on watch and four hours off. Hatfield would have been within his rights to call for all hands immediately if he deemed the alteration absolutely necessary. He was clearly anxious, but instead of mustering the hands at once, which would undoubtedly have provoked a degree of grumbling, he ordered Wortley to ring eight bells a quarter of an hour early. This not only deprived the watch below of fifteen minutes' sleep, it meant their watch was extended. It was a silly decision. As soon as the watch below realized what had been done, they interpreted Hatfield's concern for the ship as an act of spite, and it was with an air of deep hostility that the second mate's watch came on deck to join the mate's as they stood waiting at the braces.

When Wortley reported all hands at their stations, Hatfield ordered the helm put hard over and the main and mizzen yards trimmed. Half-way through the turn the yards ceased to swing, the ship bucked into the wind and the *Lennie* 'missed stays', falling back onto the former, starboard, tack. Hatfield, furious as the two mates reported the braces had fouled and not run clear burst into a tirade against the sloppy seamanship of the crew. It was no more than might have been expected of any master in the middle of a manoeuvre, but one of the Turkish seamen named Caludis dropped the brace and rushed at the master, striking him full in the face. Hatfield hit the deck, rolled over, got to his feet, and grappled Caludis. There was a moment when order might yet have been restored, but suddenly Cargarlis was alongside the Turk and drove his knife into Hatfield, swiftly eviscerating him as he fell again. Seeing what had happened MacDonald gave out a roar of horror, but the two mutineers quickly turned upon him and, as he tried to escape, stabbed him to death.

Several men now hid, including the mate, who made for the foretop – but suddenly shots rang out. The two mutineers had hidden pistols. Wortley was driven out of the foretop and fell to the deck, breaking his headlong drop by grabbing at the rigging. However, once at the feet of Cargarlis he too was swiftly butchered. The two men now dominated the deck and overawed the remainder, who sheepishly did as they were bid. The steward and boy were locked in the after accommodation under the poop. Woken by the fracas on deck and realizing that he was a prisoner, van Hoydonck went to Wortley's cabin and secured the dead mate's revolver, loading it and hiding it. He also removed the brace Hatfield kept in his own cabin, and hid them with some ammunition. Van Hoydonck and Trousselot now nervously settled down to await the outcome. At six in the morning the mutineers crowded into the saloon, demanding that the steward, who had some knowledge of navigation, should see them into the Mediterranean. They had 'dealt with' Hatfield and the two mates and were now determined on reaching Greece, where they could sell the empty *Lennie*. They promised to cut van Hoydonck into the deal if he acted straight.

Having secured an agreement that little Trousselot would not be harmed, van Hoydonck agreed to sail the *Lennie* wherever they wanted, provided that they would all obey his orders as to the handling of the ship. Van Hoydonck had shrewdly and courageously judged that the mutineers' plan had been extemporized only moments before, and that the perpetrators were not men of the keenest mind. He therefore set himself the task of saving his own life and on the pretext that they must avoid any pursuit, ordered a course set which would close the French coast. The mutineers, who had no knowledge of their precise whereabouts, swallowed all he said. They were further deceived by the false positions van Hoydonck pencilled on the chart as in due course he brought the *Lennie* to anchor off Sables d'Olonne, where he and Trousselot threw bottles containing messages requesting assistance out of the saloon ports under the cover of darkness. Caludis and Cargarlis were told they were off Cadiz, and only waiting suitable conditions to pass through the Strait of Gibraltar unobserved by British naval forces stationed at the Rock. Van Hoydonck then proceeded to do nothing, provoking the mutineers – who by now had enlisted most of the remainder of the crew – to demand what he was up to. Incredibly, the story van Hoydonck now spun them, about waiting for an overcast night with fog and a light westerly breeze, was delivered so effectively that he convinced the mutineers to go along with him. Some division began to manifest itself among the mutineers as the steward eventually headed again for the French coast, where a pilot cutter intercepted them.

They claimed their chronometer was stopped and they had lost their way, but the presence of the strange vessel apparently aimlessly standing on and off the coast had become known to the French authorities. Several of the crew, including Cargarlis and Caludis, decided to abandon ship, and went over the side in one of the boats. On landing they claimed they had been ship-wrecked, and a kind-hearted lady named Madame Diritot fed and boarded them. She also told them that they were not in Spain, but not far from La Rochelle in France. They agreed on a story with which to bamboozle the authorities as they sought to sign on a ship at La Rochelle, in happy ignorance that one of van Hoydonck's bottled messages had come ashore at Sables d'Olonne. The appearance of ship-wrecked seamen without a ship-wreck raised suspicions at La Rochelle, suspicions compounded by the arrival of the police report from Sables d'Olonne. All were arrested. On 11 November the French corvette *Le Tirailleur* put to sea and soon located the *Lennie*, still at anchor. A boarding party secured the five remaining mutineers and accepted van Hoydonck's version of events. The *Lennie* was towed into the Loire and berthed at Nantes, where an enquiry began. After several weeks during which the difficulty of establishing the identities of several of the mutineers delayed matters, the case was turned over, with the accused, to the British authorities, and on 28 February 1876 eleven men were charged with the murder of Hatfield and his officers at Bow Street. Van Hoydonck and Trousselot appeared for the Crown. On 7 April three of the men who had attempted to avoid being caught up in the mutiny were released, and the rest were committed for trial. These were arraigned at the Central Criminal Court on 4 May and before the first day was over two more had been released, one on a technicality. Of the six men left in the dock, four were found guilty by the jury and the other two acquitted, deemed simply to have been caught up in events after the murders had been committed, and to have gone in fear of their lives as a consequence.

Van Hoydonck deservedly received the trial judge's warm praise and was awarded an *ex gratia* payment of £50. He later received other monetary presents and several awards for courage; Tousselot was also fêted. The four condemned men, who included Cargarlis and Caludis, were hanged unlamented at Newgate on 23 May.

A similar recovery of a seized ship by a number of dissenting crew members had been made almost simultaneously aboard the *Caswell*, while another in the *Wellington* ten years later was defeated by the weather when the mutineers, unable to handle the ship, asked for assistance and were towed ignominiously back to Plymouth. It was not surprising for a master and his officers to be in possession of firearms, and was common in many merchant ships – anti-piracy small-arms were maintained in a few British ships into the 1960s. A century earlier, in 1860, the former East India Company ship *Tudor* carried 'fourteen carronades on the main deck. There were stands of arms in the saloon, cutlasses, pistols and muskets . . .' Faced with a minor insurrection among 'some half a dozen men from Glasgow, rough blackguards and insubordinate . . .', Captain Armstrong, 'a smallish man, with a florid complexion, blue eyes and a rather more than sufficient nose', defied the mutineers led by one

Alexander Braid as they attempted to storm the poop with a double-barrelled gun. A few male passengers appeared from the saloon with loaded pistols while several seamen, the boatswain and his mates, led by the officer of the watch, appeared on deck well armed. Braid and his fellows were 'overpowered after a struggle, and placed in irons.'

But while arms in the hands of seamen, as aboard the *Lennie,* were not unknown, they were invariably a portent of coming trouble. Another notorious mutiny in which guns were taken aboard by the crew, and which like the mutiny on the *Lennie* captured the public interest because it ended in the English courts, was that aboard the *Veronica.* This wooden barque was another Canadian vessel, owned in New Brunswick. In October 1902 she was 23-years old. Commanded by Captain Alexander Shaw, an easy-going master, her crew were once again a polyglot mixture. Acknowledged to be the finest of her seamen was an Irishman named Patrick Doran; the other ten were Germans, Canadian, Dutch, a Swede and an Indian, the cook being a black man named Moses Thomas. Thomas, a Dutchman named Smit and three Germans named Rau, Flohr and Monsson were the only survivors, and it was from their confusing evidence that the court had to determine the course of events.

The *Veronica* left the Gulf of Mexico bound for Montevideo loaded with timber. She was last seen off the Florida coast on 24 October, and all was reported well on board. At the end of the year her five 'survivors' were taken aboard the Liverpool-bound steamship *Brunswick*, Captain Browne, from the island of Cajueira off the coast of Brazil; they claimed to be genuine distressed British Seamen, whom Browne was duty-bound to adsist. They had, they said, been ship-wrecked. Gradually however the *Brunswick*'s crew grew suspicious of their story, suspicious of the well-caulked boat they had had on the beach, of the fact that Smit was wearing his shore clothes, and of the lack of evidence of their having been in contact with the fire they claimed had consumed their ship. They also kept themselves to themselves, eschewing the bonhomie shipwrecked sailors might be expected to share with their rescuers. Then, on the tenth day after leaving Brazil, Moses Thomas asked to speak confidentially to Captain Browne. He told him the story peddled by Rau was a pack of lies. Shaw summoned his chief officer, made Thomas repeat his version of events as he wrote the cook's words in the *Brunswick*'s Official Log Book, got Thomas to sign this statement and his chief officer to witness it. Then he ordered the other four 'distressed British Seamen' clapped in irons. On his arrival in Lisbon Browne reported the case to the British consul and received instructions to carry the men on to Liverpool, whither the *Brunswick* was bound. Here the men were arrested. Thomas was kept under close police observation, and in due course the suspects were brought to trial. Eventually the occurrences aboard the *Veronica* were revealed to a horrified yet fascinated British public.

Apparently Able Seaman Gustav Rau had conceived a hatred for Doran based on the fact that the Irishman was a first-rate seaman who enjoyed the confidence of the officers and got all the sailorizing jobs in which technical skills were required. In the hermetic world of a ship such pragmatic favouritism could work on an unstable mind, in unpropitious circumstances, and this is what seems to have happened to Rau. The German sailor had seen previous service in the Imperial German Navy, from which he may have been dismissed but from which he had certainly acquired an authoritarian air, and he was able to orchestrate the factions that inevitably developed in a mixed-nationality crew during the prelude to the affair that followed. Rau led a German clique which included Smit and ridiculed the rest of the crew. Meanwhile Doran and his mates ignored any warning signs, attributing them to the normal unpleasant atmosphere that prevailed aboard a vessel manned like the *Veronica*. Doran and his shipmates were quite unaware that Rau had told his own cronies he had heard the officers discussing a plan to throw all 'the Dutchmen' over the side. This brought into play a racial prejudice prevalent at the time which lumped Germans and Dutchmen together colloquially as 'Dutchmen', and was calculated to inflame his fellow-Germans, whose country had not long been welded into a unified nation. Rau offered no explanation as to why Captain Shaw and his officers would want to deprive themselves of half their deckhands. Was it necessary he should, with Doran so fine a paragon of his profession? Rau decided that they ought to seize the ship before it was too late, reminding his men that they had two revolvers between them. With his diabolically inclined inferiority complex at work, he wanted Doran and a Canadian knifed before they went aft to deal with Shaw and the mates. Young Flohr demurred and Rau dropped the matter until three days later when, with the ship making little headway on the equator, he and Doran had a blazing row. Rau then suggested that when Doran was middle-watch lookout and the mate, Mr McLeod, had the deck, they should strike. Again Flohr cried out against the plan, and Rau began a systematic terrorizing of the younger man. Early the next morning Rau accosted Doran on the forecastle, and split Doran's skull with a belaying pin. Flohr and Smit afterwards carried the wounded man away and shut him in a locker. Aware that something was amiss, McLeod came forward from the poop and saw the forecastle deserted. 'Where's the lookout?' he called, only to be felled by Rau and Smit, as a horrified Flohr looked on. McLeod, probably still living, was thrown overboard.

Rau led his men aft, he and Smit bearing revolvers, to seek out the master and Second Mate Abrahamson. The latter, thinking he was being called for his watch, sat up from sleep only to be shot at by Rau. Leaping from his bunk, Abrahamson ran past Rau and into the saloon, calling out to Shaw that he had been shot. Rau and Smit seem then to have gone to the poop to deal with the man at the wheel, a Swede named Johannson who was a chum of Doran's. Rau ordered Flohr to kill the Swede, but again Flohr failed, and Johannson ran forward while Flohr took the helm just as Shaw appeared on deck, confused as to what was happening. 'Where's the mate?' he asked. 'Why has the second mate been shot?'

Seeing Shaw, Rau shouted that he had been looking for the master, threw a belaying pin at Shaw and then shot at him.

Clutching his side, Shaw made for the companionway to the saloon, where he and Abrahamson were battened down. Rau now headed for the galley, determined to execute Thomas. Fortunately Smit restrained his maddened leader, pleading the usefulness of the cook and extracting a promise from the terrified man that he would stay away from the poop where the master and second mate were confined.

Forty-eight hours after Shaw and Abrahamson had been made prisoner, during which they were held without food or water, Rau allowed them a drink in exchange for the charts and instruments. Three days later he convinced his fellow mutineers that the two must be disposed of. Assembling his men on the poop, Rau released the wounded men. Abrahamson emerged first, to be confronted by Rau, Smit and Monsson, all armed with revolvers, the third having been looted from Shaw. The young Flohr held a belaying pin. Seeing what was about to happen to him, Abrahamson made a run and dived over the side, Rau shooting at him until he disappeared. Shaw was now ordered on deck. Flohr was given Monsson's revolver and, in order to implicate him, told to kill the captain. He fired three shots, but the kick of the gun made him miss. In contempt, Rau fired point-blank into Shaw, then ordered the body cast over the side.

Having dressed himself in Shaw's uniform, 'which revealed a cheap conceit in his character', Rau determined they must now set fire to the ship and leave her, concocting a mutually agreed story: there had been an accident on board, after which the ship had caught fire and the crew had been obliged to take to the boats. Of course, they had no idea what had happened to the other boat. Johannson and the Indian seemed unable to commit the story to memory, and Rau decided they too must die. Ordered onto the bowsprit to furl the flying jib, Johannson was shot in the stomach. In agony he worked his way back onto the forecastle head and ran aft, pleading for his life. Smit caught him and blew his brains out. Flohr was given the job of shooting the Indian, but again muffed it. The poor man leapt overboard, whereupon Rau and Smit shot at him.

Having carefully readied a boat, on 20 December the mutineers set about preparing the *Veronica* for burning, dousing the upper deck and deckhouses with Stockholm tar, linseed oil and kerosene. Having ensured the vessel was well alight, they took to the single boat and pulled away, resting on their oars until the wooden-hulled *Veronica* disappeared. Then they hoisted sail and headed south-west, landing on the island of Cajueria, off Tutoia, midway between Fortaleza and São Luís. The island was owned by a company of Liverpool merchants and was uninhabited except when regular shipments of sugar and cotton were brought down the rivers of the mainland and ferried out to it. Steamers called to load when a sufficient consignment had been amassed, and it was in these circumstances that Rau and his party were discovered by the crew of the *Brunswick* in the New Year.

Although Rau had taken care to coach his fellow mutineers, once they were held and questioned in individual custody, his statement and those of Monsson, Flohr and Smit were found to be inconsistent in detail. They attempted to insinuate that there had been trouble between the officers and the crew as a whole, a class-based confrontation between the 'British' (though in strict fact Shaw was a Canadian), and the crew of helpless foreigners. Rau added spice to this by claiming that the black man, Moses Thomas, was the leader of the mutineers. Matters had come to a head one night, and in an altercation the mate McLeod had jumped overboard to save himself from being murdered by Thomas, who had killed Shaw and Abrahamson. Not long after making his statement, Flohr asked to revise it, and told a story that corroborated the original account given to Browne by Thomas aboard the *Brunswick* and reiterated by him under interrogation.

In the preliminary hearings the Crown decided to withdraw the charge of murder against Flohr, his defence counsel arguing that he was a young man who had been utterly compromised by the others. Flohr had now turned King's Evidence and substantiated Thomas's story, so that on 13 May 1903 Rau, Monsson and Smit were brought to trial at Liverpool Assizes. A large model of the *Veronica* was placed in the centre of the court for all to see.

The prisoners Rau, Monsson and Smit were defended by counsel and pleaded 'not guilty' to the initial single charge of murdering Shaw. They persisted in their assertion that Thomas was the leader of the mutiny, that Flohr had seconded him, and that the very men whose testimony was being used to condemn them were in truth the guilty parties. The case for the Crown was led by the distinguished King's Counsel Lord Birkenhead, who asked why they had not told this story immediately they were rescued by the *Brunswick*; the inadequate explanation given was that 'they had trouble enough of their own'. As to their carrying revolvers, this was entirely for self-defence against the cook, Moses Thomas.

Systematically Lord Birkenhead and his assistant Mr Tobin demolished the case for the defence, and in his summing-up the judge spoke of the defendant's part in 'a most horrible story'. After seventy-five minutes the jury returned with a verdict of guilty, though Monsson was recommended for mercy on account of his youth and previous good character. In passing sentence on the murder of Captain Shaw the judge also referred to the defendants' almost casual killing – after that of the three officers – of 'four or five of your fellow sailors'.

They were all sentenced to death and Rau and Smit, 'maintaining their stolid, sullen demeanour to the end', were hanged at Walton Gaol on 2 June 1903; Monsson escaped death, his sentence being commuted to penal servitude for life.

Curiously, as Rau and company were seizing the *Veronica* and executing their captain, another master was conducting a spirited defence with remarkable consequences. In this case, he had been warned that one of his crew was armed. In the late summer of 1902 Captain Peattie, a Scotsman from Paisley, was preparing to sail from San Franciso with a cargo of grain in the full-rigged ship *Leicester Castle* of Liverpool. His crew complement of twenty-eight was short by fourteen men, and having drawn a blank at the British consulate Peattie was compelled to seek the assistance of the boarding-house masters to make up numbers. The waterfront had been scoured and when the men were brought off, on 25 July the runner warned Peattie that one of them had a gun. Mustering the new men, Peattie made a further unpleasant discovery: three of the men supplied had no papers, and the gun-toting Hobbs was among this trio – all of whom were American nationals. A quizzing of the three, the other two being Sears and Turner, convinced Peattie that none of them had been to sea before and he asked the runner to remove them, but the man explained that the port was utterly devoid of men and, bribes notwithstanding, he could not find any more.

Against his better judgement Peattie, who suspected the three of being 'cow-punchers', agreed to take them and gave the runner his bounty. Then he sent for Hobbs and told him he would have to deliver his gun up to safe-keeping. Hobbs refused, claiming it was his private property, but Peattie insisted and Hobbs reluctantly acquiesced, handing over a large Colt, claiming that the only ammunition he had was in the chamber. Satisfied, Peattie let Hobbs go forward, the new men signed on, and next day the *Leicester Castle* put to sea.

A 2,000-ton ship, the *Leicester Castle* was known as an able if not spectacular passage-maker, and generally a happy ship under Peattie, who was opposed to hazing and made his feelings on this score well known to his officers. That he already had half his crew on board shortly before sailing attested to this fact, for the blandishments and opportunities ashore in California at the turn of the nineteenth century were more than most seamen could resist. A month after passing the Golden Gates the new men had worked off what was called 'the dead horse' – that portion of their wages that went to the boarding-house masters for 'securing them a job' – and were now, as they said, 'working for themselves'. By this time the *Leicester Castle* had crossed the Equator and, having passed the doldrums in only three days, had picked up the South East Trades and was stretching down towards the distant Horn.

These to a sailing ship man were halcyon, 'flying fish' days. There was little sail-handling to do and the sailors indulged in the traditional pasttimes of the seaman – model-making, embroidery, knot-work and, among those with a talent, mandolin- and concertina-playing, which induced others to sing. Hobbs, Sears and Turner, though obedient to their orders and giving no trouble, took no part in these sailorizing relaxations and kept themselves apart. This brought them under some scrutiny by their shipmates, and it was noticed that Hobbs appeared to be preoccupied with some private problem.

On 2 September the man at the wheel asked the mate on watch where they were and was told that the ship was about three hundred miles north of Pitcairn, a fact which he recounted to his comrades in the forecastle during his watch below. Hobbs picked up on the fact, and seemed fired by it. That evening he, Sears and Turner were in deep conversation at the foot of the mainmast until after dark. It was a moonless and sultry night and the South East Trades were failing, a fact noted as being of more significance than their distance from Pitcairn by Captain Peattie as he paced the poop about ten o'clock. Like most of his ilk, he had the habit of walking the deck for an hour before leaving it to the officers with his night orders. Peattie discussed the dying wind with the second mate, Mr Nixon, and then went below to read in his bunk before dropping off to sleep.

At about half-past ten a knock at the door preceded the entrance of Sears, who very respectfully told him there had been an accident and a man had fallen from the foreyard. Puzzled as to why anyone should have been aloft, and by the lack of any sort of commotion, Peattie told Sears to bring the man aft, got out of bed and, pulling on shirt and trousers, went into the saloon and lit the lamp. It was a ship-master's duty to act as surgeon, and the traditional operating area was the saloon table. Men of Peattie's stamp could clean wounds, lance abscesses, set bones and stitch up gashes with crude effectiveness. But Sears remained in the saloon and Peattie asked where the injured man was, telling him to get the second mate to bring him in. Then as Sears vanished through the door forward Peattie heard a movement behind him, where the companionway from the poop came below by way of the chart room. Turning, he saw Hobbs with a levelled revolver; then four bullets hit the ship-master above the heart. Shouting an alarm, Peattie lunged forward and struck Hobbs a blow to the face, whereupon Hobbs fired again, the bullet lodging in Peattie's right biceps. Peattie bravely persisted in his attempt to disarm his assailant, but he was now suffering badly and Hobbs easily shoved him away. As the master fell back wounded, Hobbs fired three more times. One bullet splintered the mirror above the saloon sideboard, the other two hit Peattie, both in his upper chest.

The noise of gunshots and shouting brought the sleeping mate from his cabin. A man of quick wits, and well aware that such insurrections are usually initiated by a small group, the mate assessed the situation, turned and ran forward, out onto the poop, and slammed the alleyway door. Then he bellowed for all hands to lay aft. Behind him Hobbs, seeing that Peattie was not yet dead and presumably wanting to save his ammunition, struck the prostrate captain with a serving mallet he had taken from the sailmaker's shop. Peattie's initial shouts had alarmed Nixon, who had gone on a fool's errand initiated by the mutineers. He now came running aft and scrambled down into the saloon where Hobbs, swinging round from his battering of Peattie, lugged out the Colt and shot Nixon straight through the heart.

By now, however, the mate's cries had brought some help. An apprentice named Dunning and Beck the steward burst into the saloon, to be confronted with a scene from hell, lit by the swinging lamp above the saloon table from which the cloth, partially spread by Peattie at the point of Hobbs's entry, had been half-pulled. Nixon, his fist clenched, was expiring at the foot of the after companionway; Peattie lay in his own gore on the deck surrounded by broken and upset chairs; the deckhead and bulkheads of the *Leicester Castle*'s handsomely panelled saloon were spattered with blood. The author of this orgy of death had just vanished up the after companionway. To Dunning and Beck's astonishment Peattie moved, and then cried feebly for the mate.

At this point the mate arrived with most of the crew. Having largely been in the watch below, they had armed themselves with anything that came to hand. Peattie was lifted into his bunk and his wounds were dressed by Able Seaman Brennan, who had served as an ambulanceman in the Boer War. The mate took immediate charge and secured all the arms on board, which included the Colt Peattie had taken from Hobbs, and posted sentries to secure the poop as a citadel. Going on deck, the mate was told by the helmsman that Hobbs had run up from the saloon, then turned and gone forward. Uncertain of the extent to which the mutineers were armed and aware that they had deceived Peattie over this matter, and somewhat uncertain of the temper of the polyglot crew generally, the mate decided to wait until daylight, when he would have a better view of the ship which was now ghosting along in light airs, the surrounding sea perfectly calm.

There was a hiatus for some time, then, not long after midnight, the mate and helmsman on the open poop were astonished to hear abusive language, curses about 'limejuice' ships and a shout of 'Hurrah for the American flag!'

Looking over the starboard side the mate saw Hobbs, Sears and Turner drifting past them on a raft extemporized out of spare grain-shifting boards and cork fenders which they must have made earlier. The ship was hove-to in the hope of seeing the raft at daylight, but it had vanished. Later it was discovered that the three men had provisioned themselves well, including buckets full of water and a stock of clothes looted from the now empty forecastle. The calm conditions had aided this bold if desperate exodus, which had at least removed the mutineers from the ship.

Peattie declined the mate's suggestion that they put into distant Valparaiso for medical attention, despite the fact that he 'was in a very bad state, as I had five wounds from the revolver, and my scalp was terribly broken and bleeding profusely'. Under Brennan's ministrations his condition rapidly improved and he was actually on his feet the day after the mutiny and able to resume command, attending to the burial of the unfortunate Nixon.

In due course the *Leicester Castle* doubled Cape Horn, passed the Straits of Le Maire and headed for Queenstown (as Cobh was then called) to receive onward orders for her cargo of grain. When she arrived the pilot cutter took back ashore with him the news that the master of the ship just then entering the port was walking her poop with four bullets in his body! Peattie was a brief marvel to the citizens as he landed to make his statement and engage the authorities. The Royal Irish Constabulary carried out a full investigation, discovering that all three of the missing Americans were thoroughly implicated.

Hobbs had not in fact had a second gun, but had acquired one by sending Turner below to Nixon's cabin. When the mate asked what he was doing in the second mate's cabin Turner said that Nixon had asked him to pop below and bring him up some tobacco – a perfectly reasonable explanation. In fact Turner had stolen Nixon's revolver and the young man had not noticed, it was therefore with his own weapon that he had been murdered.

Extensive enquiries followed. It was assumed that the three men were fleeing the law and had sought to seize a ship with which to escape to some tropical island – shades of Comstock's dream and still, even in the new twentieth century, a possibility. Hobbs's reaction to the news of the proximity of Pitcairn seemed to point towards this, and a later report made by the master of the British sailing ship *Howth* at San Francisco on 13 February 1902 of a sighting of fire signals off Pitcairn on 25 September added to this possibility. The California authorities knew nothing of 'Hobbs', 'Sears', or 'Turner' but there was no guarantee that men without papers were who they claimed to be. The British sloop *Shearwater* was ordered from Honolulu to Pitcairn, but had found no fugitives when Commander C.H. Umfreville reported back in early February 1903.

'Cow-punchers' were perfectly capable of constructing a raft and taking food and water with them, but no seaman would have abandoned ship on a raft in that deserted region of the Pacific. Three hundred miles was an immense distance on such a fragile craft, while the difficulties of locating Pitcairn had defeated the best navigators in the Royal Navy in their hunt for Christian 123 years earlier, and were surely too much for Hobbs, Sears and Turner. They were never found, and it is entirely possible that they were dead before daylight revealed an empty sea to the watchers aboard the *Leicester Castle*.

The *Leicester Castle* herself was ordered to discharge her cargo in Manchester where her story excited a movement to end the system of 'crimping' prevalent at San Francisco. The California State Commissioner for Navigation suggested a Congressional Act to licence and regulate all boarding-house masters, but the notion was not taken up: 'The pernicious practice continued to flourish until the last square-rigger out of the port spread her white wings and sailed away.' Peattie and his mate fade into obscurity, their brief fame eclipsed by history's bigger picture, yet their survival was untypical.

In most of these largely motiveless mutinies – and there were many similar cases – the master and his officers paid, like Nixon, with their lives. So distant from the land were those who mutinied, both physically and in their thinking, that they imagined that by seizing the ship from her lawful master, they would right any real or imaginary wrongs done to them. Sadly, any master and his officers caught up in such pointless violence had nothing but their skills and their constituted right to direct their crew by articled agreement to weigh in the scales against insurrection. All too often it was insufficient to save their lives. But no two mutinies were precisely the same: infrequently, dissension arose between a master and mate, with disastrous consequences.

On New Year's Eve 1833 the British ship *Alexander* was approaching the West Indies with a cargo of Welsh coal destined for Jamaica. Captain William Herrington had shipped a tough alcoholic mate named Coulsen, who hazed the men to such an extent that eventually Herrington was forced to intervene. Fuelled by rum and hate, Coulsen brazenly murdered Herrington with a maul before the eyes of the helmsman, intending to carry the ship into port, sell her and her cargo, and vanish. Finding the crew less than tractable he tried to bribe them, but with little success; they insisted on heading for Jamaica, to which Coulsen agreed, while laying a course for San Domingo. The men were not fooled, and took over the ship once the coast and a pilot boat were in sight.

The *Alexander* was sailed to Port Royal and Coulsen found himself committed to trial before Jamaica's chief justice, Sir Joshua Rowe, who condemned him to death for murder. He was executed in January 1834, so at least Captain Herrington was avenged. A year earlier, in June 1832, the crew of the Liverpool-registered *William Little* rose against the master and threw him overboard before scuttling their ship near Fanning Island in the Pacific, not far from where Comstock had murdered Captain Worth. Four of the crew arrived at Woahoo in the Sandwich Islands in February 1833, but then disappeared.

Once again the matter of motive is lost to us, but the most common was that of instant and unimaginable wealth. In 1836 the small, fast opium clipper *Fairy*, originally built for Jardine, Matheson and Co., was in defiance of the Chinese authorities being used to distribute Malwa opium from the receiving ship *Colonel Young* moored off Lintin Island, along the southern coast of China. Under the command of a Scotsman named McKay, she was not a happy ship. Her chief mate, a man named Guthrie, was a fault-finder and habitually hazed the crew, who resented his assaults. They were a polyglot collection of Filipinos, lascars, Portuguese and Chinese. Having exchanged her cargo for silver bars the *Fairy* was returning down the China coast towards the end of August when, shortly after taking over the watch with the mate at four in the morning, the six Filipinos came aft. Opium clippers bore arms to beat off equally the interdiction of Chinese government junks or the attacks of pirate craft alike, and the hands were trained in their use. Gathering swords and pistols the Filipinos quickly slew Guthrie and immediately afterwards attacking the officers below, killing Captain McKay, the second mate and the gunner.

Returning forward, the 'Manila-men' poked their shipmates awake, then hove the *Fairy* to and at about nine o'clock set them adrift in one of the *Fairy*'s boats; they then headed for their native Luzon, where the ship was run ashore and wrecked. Stealing the $70,000 silver dollars on board, the mutineers vanished in the jungle. In the following weeks stories began to leak back to the ship's agents, Jardine, Matheson and Co., whose own intelligence service were soon able to piece together what had happened. Fourteen of the non-Filipino crew had survived when the *Fairy*'s boat capsized in heavy surf on the Chinese coast and they were examined by the Chinese magistrate responsible for the Changpuheen district. Then reports came in that a wreck resembling the well-known opium clipper had been seen on the Luzon shore, accompanied by further news that silver bars were being offered for sale in Manila. According to one authority, the perpetrators 'were duly tried, condemned and executed for murder'; others claim retribution was either non-existent or, at best, only partial.

Disaffection aboard ship might spring from one or more of several sources, most common of which was poor food, with or without poor conditions generally. Mutiny preceding piracy, or at least an intention of turning pirate, seems to have motivated a few insurrections, while tyranny on the part of commanders and officers, if not uncommon, seems never to have been the goad that romantic retrospection would have it. Quick-wittedness on the part of a master or his officers often scotched rebellion before it had taken hold and any prospective mutineers had to implicate the majority of their shipmates in order to make a success of their revolt. What is perhaps most remarkable is the number of occasions – they are indeed the majority – in which this forward thinking was entirely absent.

When the firemen aboard the Holland-Amerika steamship *Obdam* laid down their shovels and slices on the night of 20 July 1891 the ship slowed down, warning Captain Bakker and Chief Engineer Bol of trouble. Bol attempted to placate his men, but met only derision. Bakker went below into the men's accommodation armed with a revolver and, confronting the crowd, ordered those on watch back to the stokehold. Contemptuous solidarity was the response, and then they closed in on him. One of the men, Pieter Duzen, leapt forward and Bakker shot him, an act which not only saved his life, but cowed the rest. By this time all the officers were armed, and the mutiny fizzled out. When Bakker's conduct was examined in court in Amsterdam, he was exonerated. The mutineers proffered no charges, and in recognition of their subsequent good conduct none were offered against the remainder of the crew. Duzen was said to have been a 'socialist agitator', influenced by English activists who were on strike in London.

Such a motive introduces as a factor the then rising tide of the working-man's struggle for better recognition of his worth and value to his economic masters ashore. In the preceding half-century national authorities had increasingly regulated conditions aboard merchant ships, and the lows of ship-board unrest began to shift away from individual acts of mutiny towards a more general – and gentle, if such an adjective can ever be used to describe social division in a small societal unit – concept of withdrawal of labour, or strike.

Nevertheless, any defiance of a master's lawful order, howsoever mild that defiance, remains mutinous. If, as occurred in 1925, a depression of wages below the level of subsistence forced the crews of hundreds of British ships in ports throughout the British Empire to walk ashore, that corporate act could be re-defined as a 'strike'; at sea, such disobedience, no matter what the provocations, remained mutiny, particularly if the safety of the ship was involved. Pragmatism rules this issue; only one man can command a ship – it cannot be run by a committee – and a ship-master has as much right as the captain of a man-of-war to the full protection of the laws of his flag-state, irrespective of his personal character or whether he has a proclivity to despotism. It is for the courts to decide the *degree* of guilt exhibited by the accused, and courts were, as we have noted, quite capable of discharging men whose culpability was dubious or insufficiently proven, and of commuting death sentences. Nor did those administering the law invariably smooth the path of a master, for whom command was always a wearisome burden.

On Sunday 12 September 1880 the auxiliary steamship *Bengal* sailed from Penarth in South Wales towards New Orleans with 60 tons of sand ballast and 860 tons of steam coal. The *Bengal* was commanded by Captain C.E. Stewart, an experienced master who held a commission in the Royal Naval Reserve, and his crew consisted of Indian lascar seamen and firemen. Perhaps significantly, Stewart had left the *serang*, the lascar boatswain, sick in hospital. In ships manned by Indian, Malay and Chinese crews, orders were always passed via the senior petty officer, in this case the *serang*, who had immense prestige and influence with the crew. Such men were usually fiercely loyal to the hierarchy, and were treated accordingly. With her *serang* ashore, the *Bengal*'s sailors were under the junior petty officer, or *cassab*, and he seems to have had less influence. The firemen were under a petty officer known as a *tindal*.

Next day, having cleared Lundy Island, the *Bengal* was heading west when the wind began to increase in force from ahead during the forenoon. It began to rain, and in the evening, with the barometer falling, Stewart recorded his ship labouring in a 'heavy gale from South and S.W. with Lightning'. By midnight the gale was accompanied by 'fierce squalls and rain and [a] high sea'. As the *Bengal* was 'labouring heavily' Stewart had securely battened down all hatches, the engine room and stokehold, and a reefed main trysail was set to steady her.

By early morning the 'heavy gale' had veered into the 'WSW with furious squalls of wind and rain and a high and fierce sea, the ship labouring and pitching heavily and the engines racing in a dreadful manner for when she pitches into the head sea the whole of the propeller seems to come out of the water.' At four in the morning Stewart wrote that the ship was

> paying off and coming to the wind as she likes for the Engines are useless to her. The seas breaking on board from end to end. At 6 a.m. the whole of the Lascars and Firemen came aft and using most threatening language demanded the ship should be run back, that if

I did not do so they would do no more work, &c, &c. After talking to them for some time without any result, I consulted with the Officers and Engineers and they all thought it best to turn back for shelter. After thinking calmly over the turn affairs had taken, I decided to go back and at 8 a.m. in a lull managed to put the ship before the wind and sea.

Shortly afterwards the *Bengal* 'split the foretopsail in trying to reef and so set the foresail to run with'.

The ship was now running before a 'high dangerous sea' which increased with more 'furious squalls and rain' during the afternoon, and at 8 p.m. the seas were 'really tremendous'. At midnight it was 'just the same and the ship [was] rolling and lurching [so] that one can only hold on. At times the seas break against our stern and come on board with great force.' Having altered course to clear the Scillies, Stewart was making for Falmouth with her propeller still racing and the *Bengal* rolling her rails under as green seas swept her decks. With a moderation in the weather on the afternoon of Wednesday the 15th, the *Bengal* burnt blue lights for a pilot off Falmouth that night. None came out to the ship, so she was anchored to await daylight.

Next morning Stewart steamed into Falmouth, which was crowded with sheltering shipping, and on Friday a Mr Campbell, representing his owners, came aboard. Stewart and Campbell mustered the crew and

ordered the crew to return to duty and continue [the] voyage to New Orleans to which they *All* refused, cooks, servants and all adding at the same time they would go to Prison and suffer any punishment sooner than go to the Westward. At Noon [we] went on shore and consulted a Magistrate who said if we landed the men for punishment we should still be answerable for them when the term of imprisonment was over. Several telegrams passed between Campbell and the Firm and at 3.40 he returned to London by the express train, and at 8 p.m. I returned on board.

Next morning, with the entire crew idle, Stewart 'stopped their food and locked up the water tanks'. Then at eleven he 'took the Lascar Cassab and the Fireman Tindal on shore to see a Magistrate and even he could not induce them to work – all they wanted was to leave the ship and go to Prison. This continued for some time when a Telegram came from the Firm with orders to proceed to Cardiff and load there. This had the desired effect and after some trouble with the rest of the crew we got [up] steam and [weighed] our anchors . . .'

The *Bengal* returned to Penarth Dock, near Cardiff, where Stewart learned that the *serang* had died the day the crew refused duty. The news seems to have quietened the crew for the voyage to New Orleans was cancelled and the *Bengal* rapidly loaded more coal and sailed for Port Said, where the coal was discharged to bunker other ships. Thereafter the ship was engaged for some time on the 'Hadji-run', taking Muslim pilgrims to and from Jeddah, from where they walked to Mecca.

By diverting their ship, Stewart's 'Firm' cut their losses and avoided a painful and expensive process. They also preserved their crew's integrity, though the degree to which this encouraged protest can only be guessed at. The evidence of Stewart's personal log suggests that the conditions the *Bengal* encountered were extreme and that after the ordeal his crew eventually returned to their duty. One cannot but consider what spice the lascar's action adds to the oft-quoted remark of Dr Samuel Johnson, who said that 'No man will be a sailor who has contrivance enough to get himself into a jail; for being in a ship is being in jail with the chance of being drowned . . . A man in a jail has more room, better food, and commonly better company.' Stewart's lascars clearly thought so.

12

'WATERED BY OUR TEARS'

LADEN with Muslim pilgrims homeward bound to Singapore from the *Hajj*, Captain Stewart's *Bengal* anchored off Colombo to ship a new crew. As the old one signed off its petty officers attempted to persuade Stewart to alter their discharge papers, but he was a 'by-the-book' ship-master and refused the petition. Although their revolt had been bloodless it *had* been mutiny, leaving Stewart and the *Bengal* exposed to the full malice of the elements. Although a modern sociologist might argue the case for it having been a mere strike, to strike when a ship is beset by bad weather is a crime at sea. In this respect the mutiny of the *Bengal*'s crew was unusual, for a ship's company rarely mutinied when all faced a common danger; they might not believe in God, but they all recognized an Act of the Almighty when it was before them, and they all knew, as the under-writers and the loss-adjusters knew, that no captain was to blame. Even Bligh, in his pig-headed attempt to round the Horn to the westwards, failed to raise the ire of his crew during that month of high endeavour and ultimate failure.

Apart from the vicious, malicious and utterly criminal risings detailed in the last chapter, rising in which the act itself seemed to be the objective, most major mutinies continued to arise from poor food, poor conditions and poor pay, with unjust punishment also a powerful motive. The seaman, whether naval or merchant, lived a life which he largely accepted as being outside societal norms and in which he forfeited individual liberties. In light of the thousands upon thousands of merchant voyages and naval commissions made during the last five hundred years it is clear that he usually knuckled down and got on with it, and in return he had his pay, his food and his small privileges – shore leave and a list of conditions of one sort or another. If these were tampered with, however, trouble was almost bound to ensue. As we have seen, even curtailed meal times could be a cause of dissent. Wise officers and commanders had a regard for such simple 'rights' and, far from the eighteenth century providing signal examples of tyrannical and stupid leadership, it is the twentieth which excels.

During the period following the conversion of Britain's economy from agrarian to industrial, social and political reform had followed. Though often too tardily to match the desperate needs of vast numbers of people moving into the new and rapidly expanding manufacturing towns, the nettle had at least been grasped. At sea, in the merchant service, regulation had slowly increased during the first two-thirds of the nineteenth century and accelerated somewhat after the seaman's cause was espoused by Samuel Plimsoll and accepted by some patriarchally-inclined shipowners. As steam slowly superseded sail this increased with the formation of larger and larger liner companies. One effect of this was to allow maritime labour to begin to organize itself formally, following the lead of tradesmen and craftsmen ashore, and to confront the ship-owner with a militant and articulate opposition which demanded an increasing share of profits for its own legitimate improvement. These aspirations were echoed, though less stridently, in the Royal Navy and dramatically increased in volume in time of war, when mobilization added numerous civilians to the muster roll.

These changes were found in both the mercantile and naval forces of other countries, but because of Great Britain's unique position in the years before the First World War, with the world's largest navy and its largest mercantile marine, they had their most profound impact within the twin sea-services of the British Commonwealth and Empire. As we shall see, however, it was in neither the Royal Navy nor the British merchant fleet that the most dramatic events occurred.

While Georgian society was marked by a highly stratified class system, it was not entirely an exclusive one, and certainly not at sea. In contrast the Victorian era, during which the navy was largely untroubled by great wars, saw an increase in the social divisions between the classes. It also disparaged trade, opening a gulf between the naval and merchant services which was never to close again, though it came near to it during the second half of the Second World War. The lack of real battle testing also ossified the Royal Navy, to an extent that even the experience of the First World War failed entirely to undo, so that this conservatively-commanded force, in failing to move with the times, was bound to experience a clash of class interests. Although the lash had been abolished, degrading and humiliating punishments remained: birchings and canings were common in naval training establishments up to about 1935, and corporal punishment lingered until 1950.

Over-zealous insistence on formal respect and often excessive insistence on 'good order and discipline' fomented much trouble. In 1902, at the height of British naval power when the 'bluejacket' was an iconic image whose costume was aped by the sons of the crowned heads of Europe, there were 321 court martials of ratings, most of which were for physical or verbal offences against superiors – which of course included officious petty officers receiving 'cheek' and 'lip' from young sailors. When the lower deck considered that one of their number had been given an excessive punishment, it could still combine and cause such disturbances as wracked HMS *Furious* in 1909, HMS *Leviathan* in 1910, HMS *London* in 1913, and HMS *Zealandia* in 1914. In the war years that followed, disturbances occurred aboard HMSs *Teutonic*, *Fantome* and *Amphitrite*. Few of these mutinies were publicly known: the Royal Navy was the nation's bulwark, and the nation's confidence in it must not be shaken. It was only in foreign navies that mutiny disturbed the tranquillity of naval power – and none more so than in Russia.

By 1905 the Imperial Russian Navy was a relatively potent force, possessing a powerful battle fleet and with auxiliary squadrons disposed in the farthest dominions of the Tsar. In February 1904 the Japanese attacked the Russians in the Liaotung Peninsula where, in ports leased from the Chinese, they over-wintered their Pacific Fleet. This the Japanese swiftly defeated, and gained the ascendancy, besieging Port Arthur and compelling the Russian High Command to dispatch Admiral Rozhdestvensky's Baltic Fleet half-way round the world to recover the initiative. Unfortunately Rozhdestvensky was annihilated off the island of Tsu Shima by Admiral Togo in May, and the resulting national humiliation further inflamed an already simmering social unrest in Russia itself.

The defeat of Rozhdestvensky's fleet was attributed to in-efficiency inherent in the privileged system over which the Tsar presided. Because of the war Russia's finances were in a mess, and hundreds of thousands of lives had been squandered. The civil disturbances occurring throughout the country attracted a severe backlash from the representatives of autocracy, and encouraged those in Russia who sought an overthrow of the traditional and outmoded system of government, any opposition to which was pitilessly crushed. Significantly, the ranks of the navy included a large number of political activists mostly belonging to the Social Democratic Party. A substantial proportion of these were in ships belonging to the Black Sea Fleet, which had taken no part in the Russo-Japanese War and whose morale was already low in consequence of the monotony of their duties and the long periods they lay inactive at their base at Sebastopol. At the end of June the news of Tsu Shima cast a further gloom over this squadron, which was then ordered to sea for gunnery exercises.

The first ship to leave, ahead of the others though escorted by the torpedo boat *N267*, was the *Kniaz Potemkin Tavritchesky*, better known to history as the 'Battleship *Potemkin*'. Kapitan II Ranga Evgeny Golikov headed from Sebastopol for Tendra Bay, close to the Romanian border and not far from Odessa, where he anchored his ship. On Tuesday 27 June Golikov was enjoying his lunch when he received a report from his executive officer, Kapitan III Ranga Ippolit Giliarovsky, that the men were in a mutinous mood. The political activists had been seeking a pretext to foment trouble, and it had come to hand in the form of stinking, maggot-infested meat which the men refused to eat. This had been taken on board shortly before the battleship sailed in circumstances which bred a swift-travelling rumour that the contractors were corrupt and the captain and officers had profited from the swindle.

Golikov cleared the lower deck and, having learned that the meat was certified fit for the consumption of the sailors and stokers by Surgeon Smirnov, addressed the crew. Smirnov apparently agreed that the meat had attracted the eggs of some flies, he told them but there were only on the surface and after proper cooking the meat was edible. Golikov concluded by recalling his ship's company to their duty to the Tsar, and then dismissed them. All might have passed off peaceably, for the majority of the *Potemkin*'s crew were long-service men who if not docile were certainly not radicals, had not Giliarovsky recalled the muster. Golikov meanwhile had retired to his cabin, unaware that his younger second-in-command had decided to take a harsher line with the mutineers.

Giliarovsky now paraded the ship's marines under arms, and it is alleged that he ordered a tarpaulin to be spread on the sacred planking of the quarterdeck. Neither the purpose of the tarpaulin nor indeed its actual presence is clear; the horrors of this insurrection were much embellished by the later effects of Sergei Eisenstein's film, purporting to be documentary in intent but in fact perverse and propagandist. Whether the tarpaulin was there or not, the presence of the marines suggested to the returning seamen that bloodshed might ensue; certainly coercion seemed to be intended. Seeing only Giliarovsky and the armed marines, with no sign of their captain, the men drew the conclusion that some among their number were to be taught a lesson in the prescribed Tsarist manner.

Among them was Afanasy Matushenko, a revolutionary who had been working on a plot to suborn the entire squadron when it arrived at the anchorage. The present situation was clearly too good to waste, and Matushenko called out to the marines not to fire on their shipmates. Others, thought to have been members of Matushenko's revolutionary cell, tried to disarm the gunners. As they surged forward, Giliarovsky allegedly compounded his high-handed stupidity by firing at one of them, Gunner Grigory Vakulenchuk, who fell mortally wounded. There followed a confused struggle in which a midshipman beside Giliarovsky was also mortally wounded, and an attempt by the gunnery officer, Lieutenant Tonn, to mediate and avert the frightful carnage that seemed about to ensue resulted in his death. With the men's blood-lust provoked, all sense of reason vanished; revolt against generations of acquiescence, fawning and victimization spread through the *Potemkin* like fire. As other officers appeared they were shot at; Some who attempted to escape by jumping overboard where exposed to opportunist rifle fire. A handful was picked up by the *N267* but most were massacred. Captain Golikov was apprehended and executed; Smirnov was caught in his cabin trying to kill himself. After being brutalized he was killed and thrown overboard. Lieutenant Alexeyev, the navigating officer, was found attempting to reach one of the magazines. Pleading that he was only obeying Golikov's last orders, he begged for quarter and threw in his lot with the mutineers. He was granted his life on condition that he handle the *Potemkin* according to the instructions he would receive.

As Kapitan III Ranga Baron von Jurgensburg attempted to steam the *N267* out of the Bay and out of range, his vessel received a shot from the *Potemkin*'s secondary armament. Intimidated, he brought his torpedo boat back alongside the battleship where he, his own officers and those he had rescued were secured in custody aboard the *Potemkin*.

The vast majority of the *Potemkin*'s crew had taken no part in the mutiny, though many were mute and astonished witnesses. As the situation gained momentum they stood stupefied by Matushenko's oratory. From atop the capstan so recently vacated by Golikov, the revolutionary harangued them: they were heroes; they had lit the torch of revolution and were the first to throw off the chains of slavery. Soon they would carry the whole squadron with them, and then join their comrades ashore. It was heady and inspiriting stuff.

Matushenko was now in command, with Alexeyev ready to navigate the ship towards Odessa, a few miles along the coast, and Engineering Lieutenant Kovalenko, a Marxist sympathizer, keen to provide the motive power. At Odessa it was planned to make contact with revolutionary elements which were fomenting daily confrontations between strikers and the Tsarist forces. In addition to the police, the latter included Cossacks under General Kokhanov, the local military commander.

The arrival of the *Kniaz Potemkin Tavritchesky* off Odessa that evening flying the red flag encouraged the forces of reform and revolution. A student leader named Constantin Feldmann came aboard at the head of a group of ardent socialists. Learning of the death of Gunner Vakulenchuck in the night and of the desire of his shipmates to give him a suitable funeral, Feldman suggested that his body be landed as a symbolic act about which the revolution might coalesce. Most of the *Potemkin*'s bewildered crew merely wanted Vakulenchuk properly buried. As happened in most mutinies, once the heat of the insurrectionary moment had passed, there was a sense of rudderless impotence. If not exactly a political reaction, it was enough to persuade a disappointed Feldmann and his colleagues not to expect much from the *Potemkin*. The battleship's presence offshore was stimulating enough, however, and when Vakulenchuk's body was landed next day at the foot of the Richelieu steps it attracted sufficient popular attention to provoke Kokhanov into ordering the Cossacks to clear the crowds. Eisenstein is believed to have grossly exaggerated what followed; nevertheless few authorities entirely write off the event as anything other than 'a massacre'. (In the so-called 'Boston massacre' of March 1770, be it recalled, British infantry actually killed only three and wounded two people.) Dismounting from their ponies, the Cossacks descended the wide steps firing over the heads of the assembly and then, as the populace appeared defiant, into the body of the crowd. Kokhanov claimed the dead to number 500, while the total number killed in Odessa over several days is put ten times higher.

Throughout the 28th Matushenko received demands from the shore that the revolutionaries aboard should assist the towns-people by opening fire with their guns, but he demurred. All would be well when the rest of the squadron arrived, he assured them though what exactly he meant by this he did not say. In the meantime the *Potemkin* had been taking coal aboard; that done, her crew had been subjected to further haranguing by Feldmann. As time passed, none of the rest of the Black Sea squadron arrived – only the solitary auxiliary *Vekhia*, bearing Golikov's widow and heir. In a hiatus that day, Vakulenchuk's body was buried by a dozen unarmed seamen, who were fired at by the Cossacks as they made their way back to the *Potemkin*'s boats; three of them were killed.

Matushenko's confidence in his fellows aboard the other ships of the squadron was misplaced. At Sebastopol, in the temporary absence of the Commander-in-Chief, Admiral Chukhnin, Vitse Admiral Krieger had learned of the defection of the *Potemkin* and ascertained the loyalty of the rest of the squadron. Ordering one ship to remain at her moorings, Kontr Admiral Vishnevetsky was to take three battleships, one cruiser and four torpedo boats to Odessa to overwhelm the mutineers, Krieger prepared to follow in his flagship, the *Rostislav*.

Off Odessa the loss of some of the burial party focused the attention of the *Potemkin*'s crew on the shore. Feldmann's blandishments were one thing, the death of their own comrades quite another. Informed that a meeting of the Tsarist military was to take place in the theatre at 19.30 that evening, the *Potemkin*'s secondary armament fired two blank warning shots and two live rounds. The latter landed wide and killed only more citizens; it was bathetic. Word had also arrived that the Black Sea Fleet was on its way.

Next morning Matushenko and his committee, along with Feldmann, saw the smoke of the approaching squadron. The hands were piped to their stations and the anchor was weighed. Alexeyev was ordered to head towards Vishnevetsky and the *Potemkin*'s guns were manned. Whether the Russian admiral doubted the temper of his men or feared the potence of Matushenko's gunners is unclear. What is certain is that he turned away and headed for Tendra Bay 'to await reinforcements', presumably Admiral Krieger and his flagship. He earned himself a severe reprimand, but he met Krieger, who had brought another man-of-war with him in addition to the *Rostislav*. Forming two divisions, the Black Sea squadron next headed back towards Odessa. Here its approaching smoke signalled the end of a performance by the ship's band on the quarterdeck of the *Potemkin* which, having seen off Vishnevetsky, had re-anchored off Odessa.

Once again the mutineers weighed anchor, manned their guns and steamed towards the advancing columns. Receiving a radioed demand to surrender, Matushenko told Alexeyev to maintain course and speed, sweeping aside the cruiser *Kazarsky* which was acting as advanced picket. What happened next was worthy of Eisenstein's drama; the men on most of the opposing ships poured out of their gun turrets and abandoned their battle stations to cheer the *Potemkin* as she passed between them. Krieger, Vishnevetsky and the other captains and officers could only wring their hands in frustration. When the *Potemkin* had passed through the lines, Alexeyev turned her about and overtook the squadron, heading back towards Odessa. As Krieger ordered the squadron to turn away, the battleship *Georgi Pobjedonosets* (*George the Conqueror*) followed in *Potemkin*'s wake, anchoring in company off Odessa a little later.

Matushenko and Feldmann went aboard her only to find that the mutiny aboard the second battleship was incomplete: parts of the ship were in loyalist hands and the petty officers were resisting the demands of the revolutionaries. Feldmann talked himself hoarse convincing the waverers, and by the following dawn the revolutionary 'fleet' appeared to consist of the two battleships, the *N267*, the storeship *Vekhia* and a collier from which the *Potemkin* had bunkered.

This was an illusion. The following morning the *Georgi Pobjedonosets* was in fact uncommitted, and further attempts to suborn her failed. In the end her anchor was weighed and she headed for the inner harbour of Odessa, only to ground on a shoal, and afterwards to beg forgiveness from the Tsar. By now General Kokhanov had called up artillery and the heights above the town were invested with heavy guns. Taking the city was impossible, and with every hour that passed the men aboard the *Potemkin* became increasingly disillusioned. They knew what the regime would do to them if they submitted. For those in any doubt there was the example of the fate of the protesters of Bloody Sunday, who in the previous January had gone peacefully to present a petition to the Tsar at the Winter Palace in St Petersburg. They had been shot down for their pains, and 130 of their number killed. While unwilling to prosecute the revolution so fervently called for by Matushenko and Feldmann, the majority knew that surrender meant death, or exile in Siberia. Not even rotten meat could persuade them to martyr themselves; instead they would head for the Romanian port of Constanza.

Hearing of Krieger's humiliation on his return to Sebastopol, Admiral Chukhnin complained that 'the sea is full of rebels' and sanctioned Lieutenant Yanovitch's wish to lead an attack by volunteer officers in the destroyer *Stremitelny* to avenge the deaths of their colleagues. Filled with zealous young bloods, the *Stremitelny* left after dark on 1 July but arrived off Odessa to find that the *Potemkin* and the *N267* had slipped away some hours earlier.

On their arrival off Constanza the mutineers aboard the *Potemkin* appealed to the Romanian authorities for water, fuel and stores, but King Carol's government repudiated any notion of offering them sanctuary. Disappointed, the *Potemkin* and the *N267* put to sea again, avoiding the approaching *Stremitelny* and the battleships *Sinop* and *Tri Sviatitelia*, whose officers had persuaded their crews to remain loyal and do their duty.

Enclosed in a land-locked sea as she was, the *Potemkin*'s fate was now sealed, but Matushenko and his men were not yet ready to give up. Short of water they headed out to sea, bypassing Sebastopol and their hunters. In company with the little torpedo boat *N267* they headed for Feodosia, on the far side of the Crimean peninsula from the Russian naval base. On board the daily routines went on, supervised by the petty officers, while Feldmann dreamed up revised plans for taking the revolution to the Chechens of Caucasia. When the battleship arrived off Feodosia, the ship's ruling committee was welcomed, but only fresh water was offered them. Matushenko responded by demanding coal and food as well, or the battleship's guns would blow the small town off the face of the globe. As the townsfolk fled to the hills Matushenko and Feldmann took a party of men to seize a coal hulk, and were fired upon by an infantry foot patrol. Three seamen were killed as the rest leapt back into the *Potemkin*'s picket boat and headed for their ship. Rifle-fire followed and another man was hit and fell into the water with a cry; courageously Feldmann dived after him. The picket boat steamed on, and a few minutes later a boat was pulled out from the shore to capture Feldmann and the wounded sailor.

For Matushenko and the others hell-bent on revolution the game was all but up, for now the *Stremitelny* arrived: failure, exile and death confronted them. Their vision of social justice was extinguished, and the Black Sea was 'watered by our tears'. Only a breakdown in the *Stremitelny*'s steam-turbines prevented the affair ending then and there, but once again an element of farce prevailed. The *Potemkin* and her consort again escaped, weighing anchor and steaming away, to arrive off Constanza again on 8 July. Here the committee decided to scuttle the ship, and those of her crew who wished to do so were allowed to land, and gave themselves up to the Romanians. About five hundred were suffered to stay, and the Romanian government eventually rejected Russian attempts at extradition, on the grounds that the seamen's act had been political, not criminal.

Some of these men found themselves caught up in a Romanian peasant revolt in 1906 and were subsequently deported to Russia, where the authorities promptly sent them into exile; some returned to Russia under an amnesty, only to find themselves tried, condemned and exiled like the others; a few emigrated to Britain and Argentina. But not all the *Potemkin*'s crew had followed Matushenko: about three hundred surrendered to the Russians, who almost within hours finally caught up with the *Potemkin*. Courts-martial condemned seven of those remaining to death; nineteen others received life sentences in Siberia, a further thirty-five long penal sentences. Incredibly, Alexeyev and the handful of surviving officers, pleading that they had been obliged to do as they were bid to save their lives, were exonerated. Feldmann later escaped from prison to Austria, and is today remembered in Odessa, where after the successful Bolshevik Revolution of 1917 the Nikolaevsy Boulevard was renamed in his honour. As for Matushenko, he evaded the Ochrana's agents in Romania and headed for New York where he worked for some time, associating with Russian émigré radicals and caught up in revolutionary fervour. In 1907 he foolishly returned to Russia using false papers, only to be recognized, tried and hanged at Sebastopol.

As for the ship whose name is better remembered than those of any of the human participants, except perhaps the 'martyred' Vakulenchuk in Russia, the tragi-farcical nature of the mutiny aboard the *Kniaz Potemkin Tavritchevsky* was not at an end with her scuttling. Even this was botched. By 11 July the water had been pumped out of her, she had been refloated, and the Imperial Russian naval ensign of St Andrew's cross was rehoisted. Taken in tow by the *Tri Sviatitelia* (the *Holy Trinity*) she was taken back to Sebastopol, where in October she was renamed *Pantelymon* – meaning a peasant of the most humble stock – and remained inactive throughout the First World War. Then, in

1919, as the tide of revolution closed on the Crimea, Tsarist officers scuttled her a second time, to prevent her falling into the hands of the Bolsheviks. Her final and lasting resurrection was in 1925, when to celebrate the twentieth anniversary of what Soviet historians came to call the First Bourgeois–Democratic Revolution Sergei Eisenstein made his celebrated film of the incident, dramatizing the events in five sequences that have, like his storming of the Winter Palace, come to be regarded as reality itself.

In reality there was no stirring climax, only the end common to most mutinies – failure. Such is the power of the moving visual image, however, that the mutiny aboard the 'Battleship *Potemkin*' is as well-established a myth as that aboard the *Bounty*. Perhaps the most interesting fact about the mutiny aboard the *Kniaz Potemkin Tavritchesky* is that it established itself as a key event solely because it coincided with the civil unrest in Odessa, circumstantially linking mutiny with social change. What had its genesis in a specific, traditional ship-board complaint about bad food has become a defining moment in the great move for social change and the advancement of the less well-off. The first mutinies, those against Magellan and Drake, were about command, fomented among those vying for high office. Later, exemplified by the masterly revolt at Spithead, they concerned genuine grievances, only to be followed by a degenerate series of cathartic expressions of discontent, envy and malice on the path of minorities challenging an inadequate command structure backed by law and usage, neither of which proved of the slightest use when mutiny actually occurred. With the possible exception – which if anything proves the general rule – of *some* evidence of political agitation at the Nore, the mutiny aboard the *Potemkin* marks another shift in gear; it is the first mutiny to become indissolubly linked with a greater social movement and a more general aspiration for real change, as opposed to a redress of complaints.

Had not the ship anchored off Odessa, and had not the indefatigable Feldmann and his associates clambered on board full of revolutionary zeal, it is unlikely that the *Potemkin* mutiny would have acquired this iconic status. As was so often the case in earlier mutinies, it is clear that Matushenko and *his* colleagues had little idea what to do once they had seized the ship, committed murder and placed themselves outside the law. Any ray of hope that might have been kindled by the ambiguous conduct of the Black Sea squadron under Kontr Admiral Vishnevetsky soon evaporated. The indifference or confusion of the majority of the *Potemkin*'s crew as to what was going on suggests that in due course the affair would have fizzled out, as it did on the *Georgi Pobjedonosets*.

Not that political agitation was absent from other navies; far from it – but an awareness of the situation of those who made up the so-called 'lower-deck' had begun to permeate the social consciences of American and British society at large, and the work of communist and anarchist activists was to some extent countered by such organizations as the American Navy Relief Society and the British Sailors' Society, and the work of the Misses Wintz and Weston in establishing the British Sailors' Rests. Both the first and the last of these also founded magazines of interest to and dealing with the life of the blue-jacket, and these combined measures did much to prevent the great majority of reasonable men being stirred up by hot-heads. The irony of the *Potemkin* affair was that moderates in other navies could point to its conspicuous failure as a measure of the folly of attempting to create a Utopian Workers' Paradise this side of the grave.

As has already been mentioned, the Royal Navy was shaken by a number of relatively minor mutinies in the first years of the twentieth century. The affair on the *Leviathan* in 1910 was attributed to what the then First Lord of the Admiralty, Reginald McKenna, called 'mischievous socialist literature that our men had been flooded with', and as a consequence four sailors were convicted of 'mutinous assembly'. McKenna may well have been correct in part, but in addition that old pot-boiler, inadequate pay, was beginning to simmer. The vastness and apparent wealth of Britannia's empire was obvious not least to the Royal Navy's globe-trotting sailors; equally, the obvious distinction between their own conditions and those of their officers was a daily reminder of their inferior situation. And while the naval blue-jacket was rarely a revolutionary, he did feel that the nation and its empire owed him and his estranged family a decent living. He was not able to perceive the subtle difficulties experienced by a gradually bleeding Britain with a slowly ailing economy in propping up this vast accumulation of territory, or the cost of defending it in the face of other rising industrial powers by means of the home-funded and over-extended navy of which he was a vital if tiny part. It was all very well for McKenna to blame 'the socialists' – by which he meant every radical political group – but by ignoring the fundamental grievances of the lower deck he and his successor, Winston Churchill, were merely postponing trouble. To his credit, however, Churchill had in fact been instrumental in securing a pay rise for the ratings, though one smaller than he had applied for. It was the first they had had for some sixty years and it failed to dissipate discontent, for this was rooted deeper. When the crew of the *London* was reported as being in a state of 'incipient mutiny' it was blamed on the conduct of the battleship's captain, who was 'blinded with his own self importance . . . '

Not even war deterred the blue-jackets from showing their feelings if excessive punishment stirred discontent. In 1917 the hands aboard the cruiser *Amphitrite* simply remained in their messes as a sign of disapproval and resentment. Similar non-violent mass protest had taken place a few months earlier aboard four other men-of-war, including the sloop *Fantome*.

In the prolonged stalemate after the pyrrhic British victory at Jutland in the spring of 1916, both the British Grand Fleet and the German High Seas Fleet swung idly at their moorings, the former at Scapa Flow in the Orkney Islands, the latter in the Jade and Weser estuaries off Wilhelmshaven. The men proved to be, as Admiral Sir Charles Napier had long before warned, 'the devil in harbour'. The stultifying routine was bad enough, a ceaseless round of spit-and-polish with no perceptible purpose other than to keep numerous men occupied, broken mainly by the demands of the officers' social lives; but it was also in stark and demoralizing contrast to the immense losses of life among the soldiers fighting amid the horrors of the trenches on the Western Front. There was, withal, a sense that the empire's bulwark was not pulling its weight. A confidential memorandum warned the Admiralty in London that lower-deck sentiment was like a 'combustible mass'. Informed opinion believed that between the strain of a protracted war, idleness and a lack of a sense of victory, ignition was imminent.

The Admiralty had enough problems: added to the immobility of the Grand Fleet was the realization that the Royal Navy had lost the war at sea. Such had been the onslaught of the German submarine offensive against British trade that the nation had been brought to the very brink of collapse. In 1917 the Admiralty Board gloomily informed the War Cabinet of David Lloyd George that the game was up. Losses of ships and men in the mercantile marine had been immense, almost beyond accurate computation. By and large the mercantile marine took the attrition and did its duty, though it suffered badly – not least from the fact that in most cases, when a ship was destroyed by the enemy, the crew's pay stopped. There had been no corresponding reform in the merchant service to that which had followed the *Wager* mutiny in the Royal Navy. Mercifully the Prime Minister was advised to over-ride all objections and introduce convoy with immediate effect, a policy which stemmed the tide of defeat at the critical moment and for which Lloyd George afterwards took most of the credit. Whether he deserved it or not, the measure saved Great Britain from a national humiliation of almost unimaginable proportions; but it did not alter the grievances of its naval ratings.

Similar problems seethed in the Russian fleet, particularly the Baltic Fleet wintering in early 1917 in the naval base at Kronstadt and in Helsingfors harbour – Finland being then a province of the Russian Empire. The February revolution that broke out in St Petersburg quickly spread, and the sailors at Kronstadt rose in revolt. Thereafter the disaffection of the Russian sailor played a major part in the overthrow of Tsar Nicholas II and the end of the Romanov dynasty, merging indistinguishably with a greater rebellion that had little to do with ships and more to do with an outmoded social system. The commander of the Baltic Fleet, Admiral Nepenin, sought to contain the trouble and tried to hand his fleet over to the provisional government, but the news of the Tsar's abdication was greeted with an outbreak of vengeful violence that ended in the death and mutilation of many officers. The fates of many of these unfortunate men vividly exposed the vulnerability of a small number of officers on any ship, and ought to have persuaded any naval authority of the wisdom of co-operation and the cultivation of good relations between officers and ratings. Unfortunately, among naval officers of the day there was a perception that their ships' companies were provided for the benefit of their own way of life, a point of view lent credence when there was little for a moored ship's company to do. Few senior officers bothered to recall the inherent wisdom of Drake's sermon at Port St Julian and his insistence that the gentlemen and the mariners should work together. While the Tsarist navy was tearing itself to bloody pieces the lesson continued to be disregarded among the two contending fleets at opposite extremities of the North Sea.

Despite the combustible nature of the great grey ships at Scapa Flow, it was aboard their enemies at Wilhelmshaven that the spark flashed first. For a few months after the collapse of Tsarist Russia in the east and the return of Lenin and his communists in a special train provided by the Germans, Berlin had been sanguine that its arms would prevail in the west. Under the pressure of revitalized German offensives the Anglo–French on the Western Front had seemed likely to break. But the timely reinforcement of the Western Allies by General Pershing's American army corps had halted the Germans, and defeat of the Central Powers now seemed imminent. Aboard the German High Seas Fleet at Wilhelmshaven or at anchor in the Schillig Roads, the prospect was fearful. Its commanders determined to make one last, decisive move against the Royal Navy.

The German navy had acquitted itself quite well during the early years of the war. It had fought the Royal Navy to a standstill off Jutland but, crucially, had failed to dominate the North Sea afterwards, thus leaving its opponents in technical possession of the battlefield. Modelled largely on the Royal Navy, of which the Kaiser was an honorary Admiral of the Fleet, the German Kriegsmarine, having begun its existence as an enlightened force with a professional middle-class officer corps, had in the age of Tirpitz and the arms race with Great Britain attracted an increasing number of the Prussian *jaeger* class. These men brought with them the worst presumptions of aristocratic superiority, the effect of which was to produce an endless insistence on blind obedience, exaggerated respect for rank and the consequent dull, repetitive drills, and routines of cleaning and polishing. Unsurprisingly this exacerbated class distinction and demotivated the majority of sailors to the point of apathy. Such corrosive conditions bred more than disaffection; they also nourished organized opposition. As in the Tsar's navy, small cells dedicated to social reform began to form within the High Seas Fleet. As the British blockade began to bite and to affect the families of the sailors and stokers, and as idleness worked its mischief among them, the Germen ratings grew increasingly resentful of the way of life enjoyed by their officers.

For many years, almost since its unification and establishment as a modern state, Germany had had a left-wing movement, the Socialist Workers Party, dating from 1875. The inflammatory literature produced by such organizations was banned, and many officers belonging to right-wing *brüderbonds* took a severe view when tracts and newspapers emanating from leftist sources were discovered on board ship. As there had been rumblings in the British Navy, so mass disobedience had taken place in the German. When on 6 June 1917 poor food was served to the stokers aboard the battleship *Prinzregent Luitpold,* the men refused to eat it. Other agitations followed, stirred up by anarchists, socialists and communists, their task made easier because in many cases the German capital ships lay alongside and their ships' companies were allowed ashore into large canteens and beer-halls where they were exposed to oratory or more subtle influences.

On 2 August a party of stokers walked off the *Prinzregent Luitpold* because a promised film show had been cancelled. That evening as one of these stokers, Albin Köbis, persuaded six hundred men from other men-of-war, including several battleships, to strike, Kapitän zur See Karl von Hornhardt had eleven of the stokers arrested as they came back on board the *Prinzregent Luitpold*. Hornhardt was a hard liner and took the customary course of action based on the assumption that a challenge to discipline was a greater misdemeanour than the authorities' blindness to the men's complaints. One of the *Prinzregent Luitpold*'s men asserted that he wanted his rights rather than a revolution, but Hornhardt blamed 'widespread agitation and recruitment' by the socialists. His views were endorsed by the fleet commander, the doyen of Germany's naval officers, Konteradmiral Reinhard Scheer, who oversaw the interrogations of the four ring-leaders, including Köbis, who were among two hundred others arrested in the aftermath of these disturbances. Seventy-seven men were convicted of mutiny, nine of whom were sentenced to death, though Scheer commuted all but two. Köbis and another man, Max Reichpietsch, were shot near Cologne on 5 September. Sachse, a third in the quartet, survived to be executed for complicity in von Stauffenburg's attempt to assassinate Hitler at Rastenburg in June 1944.

Scheer promulgated a secret order to his commanders to be on their guard against any further outbreak of mutinous combination. In October, to exorcise the demons of mutiny, the High Seas Fleet was ordered to carry out a raid on Russian islands in the Baltic. This was successful thanks to the 'melting away' of the disaffected defenders. It was the very eve of the Bolshevik 'October Revolution', facilitated by the Germans' return of Lenin.

The Russian seamen quartered in the Kronstadt naval base and the Petrograd naval barracks played their part in the

Revolution, as did the crew of the *Aurora*, a survivor of Rozhdestvensky's fleet. The cruiser was scheduled for power and gunnery trials but her crew had voted to join the Revolution, and under the direction of a revolutionary committee she entered the river Neva. The blank shot fired from the *Aurora* that signalled defiance and the storming of the Winter Palace marked the end of Aleksandr Kerensky's democratic government and the beginning of the Soviet Union. It is for this, rather than the act of mutiny on the part of her crew, that the *Aurora* lies today at her moorings opposite the great palace of the Tsars.

Mutiny was widespread elsewhere that winter, and the spectre of revolution in countries other than Mother Russia haunted governing circles. The appalling losses of the Great War had it seemed unhinged much of the so-called civilized world, whose institutions appeared to be under direct threat as a consequence. There were disturbances among German infantry units, French soldiers threw aside their rifles, and British soldiers 'did not know whether to first shoot their officers or the enemy'. In the Adriatic, discontent infected the Austro–Hungarian cruiser squadron, manned by a mixed-nationality force of seamen drawn from all the ethnic variety of the Hapsburg dominions. On 1 February 1918 the executive officer of the *Sankt Georg* was shot when he went on deck to see what was troubling the cruiser's crew. The mutiny spread quickly, and leadership was asserted by a junior lieutenant named Anton Sesan, who ordered the squadron anchorage in the Gulf of Kotor (Cattaro) on the Montenegrin coast to be sealed by the guns of the old battleship *Kronprinz Erzherzog Rudolf*. Sesan assured loyalists in the fleet that the purpose of the revolt was a demonstration in favour of peace. The authorities ashore took little notice of this assertion, and as the battleship's guns traversed the adjacent coastal railway line, artillery fire opened up from the shore, killing two men aboard the *Kronprinz Erzherzog Rudolf*. This demonstration of force quickly ended the mutiny as officers regained control of their ships. The aftermath was one of arrests and executions. After the Romanovs, the Hapsburgs were the most reactionary European monarchy.

Perhaps it was this that served as a warning to the German Admiralty, who made a belated attempt to modify the extremes in their behaviour of the officers of the Kriegsmarine, but it was too little, too late. As the Western Allies, rejuvenated by the addition of the Americans to their Order of Battle, began a last push in Flanders, the High Seas Fleet was ordered to sea.

Curiously, the urge for peace, or at least for peace with honour, had stirred something in the very officers whose conduct so disgusted their men. Alarmed by the potential consequences of continued inactivity, in particular for themselves and their splendid warships, the senior officers at Wilhelmshaven and in Berlin were meditating a mutiny of their own. By early 1918 Scheer was Chief of Staff, and in concert with his successor von Hipper was proposing a naval offensive that would draw Jellicoe and Beatty out of their Scottish fastnesses and destroy them in the 'single afternoon' in which Jellicoe had long since foreseen that he might lose the war. It was a bold plan, but lacked the sanction of the combined High Command and the government of Prince Maximilian of Baden, though Scheer claimed it had the Kaiser's secret, tacit approval.

But the plan foundered on the failure of Scheer, Hipper and their subordinates to consider the state of mind of their men. It was impossible for the plan to be executed without certain preparations, not least the loading of munitions, especially mines, fuel and other stores. All leave had to be stopped and a thousand and one other minor indications that something was afoot warned the men that the fleet was preparing for sea. No attempt was made to explain to the sailors what was being done; instead, rumour worked its electrifying way through the fleet: they were to go to sea to die for the Fatherland, the Kaiser, and the honour of their officers. Twenty years earlier the clarion call might have worked; in late October 1918 it fell upon deaf ears. As the first executive orders were passed for the ships to get under way on the 29th, mutiny broke out and spread rapidly. First to be affected was the SMS *Markgraf*, then the *Kronprinz Wilhelm*, the *König, Thüringen* and *Helgoland*. By nightfall more than thirty battleships and cruisers were involved, red flags flying defiantly from their mastheads. Despite this Hipper held a final council of war aboard his flagship, SMS *Baden*, which lay surrounded by fog. At daylight next morning he was made aware that his fleet was in open and defiant mutiny. Hipper's only success was in ordering one of his squadrons home to Kiel, where it went willingly, turning its back on the North Sea. He then tried to muster a small force of loyal minor warships to assist him in reasserting his command, and in this he was partially successful. A force of marines boarded several of the battleships, arresting large numbers of mutineers at bayonet point.

Meanwhile, at Kiel, Hipper's ships arrived and simply downed tools. The port admiral ordered them to sea again, but to no avail. Attempts were made by Berlin to defuse the situation by sending Gustav Noske, a former editor of a left-wing newspaper and a member of the Reichstag, to mediate. By the time Noske arrived the captain and two officers on the *König* had been shot in an attempt to prevent their ship's company from hoisting the red flag. Noske insisted the 'bloody business must end'. The naval authorities wanted the Kiel fiord blockaded, and the mutineers punished with 'blood and iron'. But as Noske's negotiations secured pardons and Kiel subsided to a kind of normality, the action of the Imperial German Navy had been spreading not only to other ports, but throughout the German people. The end of the war and the abdication of the Kaiser were called for, and as a direct consequence the German government sued for peace. The Armistice came into force at 11.00 on 11 November 1918.

The High Seas Fleet did proceed to sea once more under its old, imperial ensign, but only to surrender ignominiously under the guns of the British Grand Fleet and a squadron of the United States Navy. And it did obey one last order from its hated officers. Mutiny still simmered in the German ships interned in Scapa Flow, where a repatriation scheme moved with demoralizing tardiness. Disrespect was now routinely shown to the officers, and a plot in one ship to murder her commander had been betrayed. By May 1919 the terms of the peace agreement reached Admiral von Reuter, nominal commander of this imprisoned fleet: the German navy was to be emasculated. In the wake of this news came the removal and return to Germany of a large number of the men. On 17 June von Reuter quietly promulgated orders for the destruction of the High Seas Fleet, which as its remaining members recalled unhappily had never been defeated. On the warm, sunny morning of the 21st, as a North Sea har obscured the gaunt grey captives of the Royal Navy, the German admiral and his staff paraded on the *Emden*'s quarterdeck, and at 10.00 the signal was passed. Before the British knew it, the remnants of the High Seas Fleet, their cooling water pipes smashed and opened to the sea by their inlet valves, with water pouring into their hulls, sank to the bottom of the Flow, scuttled by their skeleton crews.

13

'SUSPICION AND RESENTMENT'

FOLLOWING the Armistice of November 1919, the consequences of the Bolshevik Revolution two years earlier began to preoccupy the governments of the victorious Western Allies. Bolshevism was seen as a recrudescence of the free, fraternal, egalitarianism of the French Revolution, and therefore as appealing to the increasingly organized, important and empowered masses. As such it posed a direct threat to the status quo, and as such it was in the interests of those in power to scotch it at source. This was perceived as a priority because the Bolsheviks, not content with having assumed power in the most repressive state in Europe, were openly declaring their desire to export revolution, exactly as their predecessors in Paris had 130 years earlier. To counter this, the Western Allies acted to support the White Russian counter-revolution, engaging in military operations under the blanket of 'Intervention'.

In the wake of the Kaiser's abdication communism was becoming a force in Germany too. It was active in Great Britain, where Marx had conceived his political theory and where he thought it best applied. In France it had formed a part of the political tapestry since the defeat of Napoleon, rising into dreadful prominence in the wake of the Franco–Prussian war in the Paris

Commune of 1870. Rooted deeply in the psyche of the French sailor, the ideals and aspirations of 1789 surfaced naturally in favour of the Russian working classes in 1919, provoking disobedience aboard French battleships that were anchored off Sebastopol in support of their government's part in the Allied Intervention. A prolonged detachment and a perceived discrepancy between life on the lower deck in comparison with that in the wardroom provided the *casus belli,* and on 12 April the sailors of the *France* refused to coal ship. Admonished by their flag-officer, they continued their refusal, only to have five of their number killed by a party of Greeks commanded by a junior officer from the flagship, the *Jean Bart.* Disaffection now began to ferment aboard the *Jean Bart* as the *France* was withdrawn and twenty-three of her crew were convicted of mutiny at Toulon. Public opinion modified their sentences and the matter slowly cooled down as, shortly afterwards, the *Jean Bart* followed her home. French interest in Intervention was effectively at an end.

In the Royal Navy the bluejackets despaired of having any of their grievances attended to if they were passed up the chain of command by way of 'the usual channels'. Such complaints were anathematized as 'trouble' and, unwisely, little notice was taken of them. Following the demonstrably successful formation of trades union by other workers, the sailors and stokers initially sought to form a 'Lower Deck Union' to articulate their grievances and negotiate with the Admiralty. Dissatisfaction with government policy in continuing warlike activities against a former ally only added to the simmering of socialist ideology, and in January 1919 the crew of a small warship, the patrol vessel *Kilbride* then stationed at Pembroke Dock in Milford Haven, struck for an increase in pay. This was the main grievance in the fleet but the 'non-violent' action was treated as a full-blooded mutiny and the perpetrators received prison sentences of up to two years' detention, plus loss of privileges and seniority.

Worse still, widespread disaffection was being reported in the squadron deployed directly against the Soviet Russians in the Baltic. Its Commander-in-Chief, Rear Admiral Sir Walter Cowan, had experienced earlier disturbances aboard the *Zealandia* in 1914, and as a man normally disposed in favour of his seamen found their disobedience hard to manage. He was not helped by the requirement of Lloyd George's government to prosecute warlike operations against the Bolsheviks, with whom the men had a genuine if naïve sympathy, but without the usual wartime pension provisions for the dependants of any men killed. Real trouble broke out aboard a number of ships, and Cowan was driven to appeal to his men by an order of the day. Perhaps the most disturbing incident for Cowan was the refusal of a party of men aboard his own flagship, the *Delhi*, to do their duty. The disobedience earned the hard core of these men eighteen months' penal servitude and a dishonourable discharge from the navy. In September 1919 a detachment of Royal Marines, whose loyalty was traditionally held to be unbreakable, refused to undertake further duties after covering the withdrawal from Murmansk. On top of all this, a hundred men from three destroyers at Rosyth, under orders to join Cowan, 'deserted'. These men, from the *Versatile*, *Velox* and *Wryneck*, actually entrained *en masse* for London and were forming up at King's Cross to march in good order to petition the Admiralty, when they were ambushed by the police. Most were formally arrested, and in due course a handful was court-martialled for 'desertion and non-violent mutiny', dismissed the service and jailed.

In the months that followed the failure of Intervention the Royal Navy was savaged by the effects of post-war reductions and compliance with the Washington Treaty. Britain was the only maritime power to conform fully to her obligations under this arms limitation agreement, and it almost emasculated her naval power at a stroke. The enormous reduction in manpower diminished the political muscle of the lower deck and thus the volume of its agitation. As the world slid into the Great Depression those still serving as ratings thought themselves well-off by comparison with their former shipmates ashore, who with other workers suffered great hardship in the severe down-turn in the world economy.

As has been mentioned earlier, the men of the merchant service struck in 1925 over the issue of pay, which was barely adequate to furnish their families with the means of subsistence. The severe fall in post-war freight rates made it difficult for British ships to carry the world's goods and make a profit, to which the ship-owners' reaction was to lower the seamen's wages. Widespread strikes occured on British merchant ships in ports in South Africa, Australia and New Zealand, but these were increasingly understood as being part of the organized labour movement, and less and less thought of as mutiny. One or two masters tried to get their ships to sea with the help of their officers and cadets, in order to entrap their disobedient crews into committing mutiny by subsequently refusing to carry out sea-going duties, but these attempts were largely ineffective. There were also disturbances in Dutch and American merchantmen but these often involved stowaways or strike-breakers, for it was a period of universal hardship and turmoil. It is possible to class these incidents too as strikes rather than mutiny, which in its classic sense seemed to be sliding into the past, at best a part of the long and unhappy struggle of ordinary people to benefit from the fruits of their labours, at worst a destruction of civilized order without which no progress was possible.

As socialism reached intellectual and political maturity it became increasingly recognized as a potential force for widespread good and the cementing of a cohesive society, rather than as the agent for its destruction, for it blurred the distinction between reasonable political protest and absolute lawlessness and sought to address, *inter alia*, the fundamental cause of ship-board mutiny: the absence of an effective means of expressing a grievance.

Indeed, mutiny *might* have been consigned to history had the reasonable aims of the middle-of-the-road socialists not still been seen in some corners of hidebound institutions like the British Admiralty as 'red plots'. During the ferment among Cowan's ratings, when superannuated admirals like Fisher were sounding perceptive warnings of potential trouble, Their Lordships had initiated a series of enquiries under Rear Admiral Sir Thomas

Jerram. The findings of the Jerram Committee led to some excellent reforms in pay and allowances, which, combined with the post-war reductions in the fleet carried out under the First Lord, Sir Eric Geddes and known as the 'Geddes Axe', had, as has been noted, postponed agitation among those still serving afloat for a decade.

However, by 1931 the Depression that had followed the Wall Street Crash was biting hard, and the British government was compelled to seek economies. One of these was a reduction in the pay of the armed services. The pay of the humblest seamen and stokers in the fleet was to be reduced by 25 per cent. Naval pay had not risen much since 1919, and the recommendations of the Jerram Committee, having been implemented, were then rescinded for new recruits in 1925, so that by 1931 what remained of their benefits had been eroded. To embitter this pill further the army and air force were far less severely affected, while naval officers' pay was subjected to a cut of only 11 per cent. The effect of this appallingly tactless and severe reduction was to reduce the men's pay to below the cost of living. In other words, to add to the enforced estrangement inherent in the sea-life, the dependants of a man serving the state were now to be driven into debt.

As the decision and the extent of the percentage reduction were emerging from Whitehall, the ships of the Atlantic Fleet were leaving their base ports along the south coast of England, assembling in the North Sea and making their way towards Invergordon on the Cromarty Firth. The Atlantic Fleet's Commander-in-Chief was seriously ill and had been temporarily relieved by Rear Admiral Wilfred Tomkinson whose command was divided into two. On the passage, these two 'opposing' forces carried out an exhausting and demanding exercise. While this was in train, the Admiralty mishandled the manner by which the cut in pay was promulgated to the fleet.

During the run-up to the announcement in Parliament, the Admiralty had presciently warned the government that so severe a reduction in pay was likely to result in trouble within the fleet.

Although during the 1920s secret intelligence reports had indicated that communist subversion was active in Britain and in the navy itself, the ratings of the Royal Navy had never excited any real apprehensions of revolution in the breast of the most paranoid flag-officer. What troubled some of the more peppery admirals was the sympathetic conduct of the first Labour Government, which understandably had favoured meeting the grievances of the 'other ranks' in the armed services. A no-concession policy gripped the more reactionary members of the Admiralty Board, especially when a dispute erupted aboard the submarine depot ship HMS *Lucia* at Devonport in January. This had its origins in a refusal to allow Christmas leave, accepted reluctantly on the grounds that home leave would be given prior to joining the Atlantic Fleet. Bad weather delayed the ship's programme and the promise was reneged upon instead, the men found themselves painting ship. Then, owing to the imminence of the *Lucia*'s departure, ordinary Sunday leave was cancelled. It was precisely this obsession with 'tiddley-work' taking precedence over welfare that the ratings saw as an abuse of power, and what made this general grumble worse was the loss of the modest freedom of Sunday afternoon shore leave. The ratings 'disobeyed the order, remained on the mess deck and symbolically lowered the hatch'. *Culloden*'s crew had done exactly that a century and a half before. The *Lucia* had suffered a series of changes of captain and her first lieutenant was afterwards described as possessing 'an unfortunate manner . . . which was deeply resented'. The sit-down strike was ended by an armed detachment escorting the arrested protesters, whose action was entirely non-violent, ashore in a peaceful manner. Despite the cautionary tone of the enquiry's findings, which drew profound lessons for the future handling of such disputatious misunderstandings, 'the affair was pursued to a bitter conclusion'. Twenty-six participants were court-martialled and 'dealt with summarily. Sentences ranged from six months' hard labour to six days.' Mercifully for the four ring-leaders, the socialist First Lord Mr A.V. Alexander (later to serve Churchill as First Lord in the Second World War) would not countenance the extreme nature of the severer penalties. Instead the men were charged with 'wilful disobedience', jailed, and dismissed the Service. Alexander went further and terminated the careers of the captain, first lieutenant and boatswain without a court martial, concluding that their leadership had been at fault. Leading petty officers were also criticized for having failed to inform the first lieutenant of the mood of the men. This outcome made many senior officers distinctly unhappy, and unsettled many senior rates' messes.

Shortly afterwards, with the country 'living beyond its means', the Labour administration collapsed and a National Government, under the same prime minister but with Alexander removed from the Admiralty Board, implemented the findings of a Royal Commission and announced the cuts in the pay of the armed services. On leaving office Alexander had warned the Prime Minister, Ramsay MacDonald, that the Royal Navy could not be relied upon to accept such swingeing pay cuts as were proposed. He was proved right. Jerram's reforms, already weakened by their partial dismantlement in 1925, were undone at a stroke.

As the Atlantic Fleet underwent its manoeuvres, with the 'unhappy' *Lucia* among the transports and depot ships acting as a convoy, Tomkinson received a signal notifying him of the imminent cut in pay. After this, in David Divine's phrase, 'The Admiralty appears to have sunk into an elegant torpor', entirely forgetting its own 'Delphic prophecy'. As for the men in the warships, the 'News reached the Fleet in various ways – by wireless on 10 September [the afternoon the Chancellor of the Exchequer, Philip Snowden, announced the cuts to Parliament, along with extensive rises in taxation], and from newspapers on the arrival of the Fleet at Invergordon. The newspapers forestalled the Admiralty Fleet Order, which caused suspicion and resentment.' Evidence was afterwards produced that on the passage north there was widespread concerting of action for when the fleet anchored off Invergordon. Despite this, Lieutenant Commander J.H.Owen, who afterwards prepared an examination of the sequence of events, added in his 'small masterpiece of commonsense' that 'The mass of the men knew nothing of it.'

Official notification together with the reasoning and explanation behind it was certainly sent directly to the Commander-in-Chief of the Atlantic Fleet – but the fleet was at sea, so it could not therefore reach Tomkinson and his senior officers before they arrived at Invergordon. It is true that BBC broadcasts were making no secret of the state of affairs, and the unhappy situation of the country as a whole was known on the lower deck. Unfortunately, however, the Admiralty letter failed to arrive at Invergordon before the fleet, for it was sent to Portsmouth where the former, and nominal, C-in-C lay in hospital. At Portsmouth it was neatly pigeon-holed against such time as his flagship, the battleship *Nelson* – which was just then approaching the Scottish coast – should return to her base port. Someone realized what had happened and a second copy was hurried north but arrived too late for promulgation on Saturday 12 September, by which time the Atlantic Fleet lay at anchor in the Firth and its ships' companies were going ashore to fill the base's canteen and read the newspapers accounts of what they had heard was rumoured.

There is little hard evidence to suggest that what followed owed anything to any third party. The outbreak of this mutiny seems to have been entirely spontaneous and entirely understandable, based on the ratings' anger and frustration. The fruits of the Saturday-night meeting seem to have been a hardening of attitudes and a determination to strike. Moreover, no one knew anything about the Admiralty Fleet Order the BBC was telling them had been 'published yesterday'. Only Tomkinson had detailed prior knowledge by virtue of the Admiralty signal.

By midday on Sunday 13 September the captains of the assembled battleships, battle-cruisers, carriers, cruisers and their attendant destroyers were aware of reports about 'a meeting ashore' that evening. The duty ship was the battleship *Warspite* and her shore parties were readied in case of disorderly behaviour. Sunday afternoon was taken up with inter-ship football matches and a slow drift towards the beer pumps in the canteen. What began as chat developed as the evening drew on to a full-scale political meeting led by Able Seaman Len Wincott from the cruiser *Norfolk*. A system of delegates from each ship was worked out with a moratorium on any action until after the other watches had had their runs ashore the following day, Monday.

The meeting was dispersed by a shore patrol without much apparent rancour beyond some beer-inspired stroppiness. The patrol was led by *Warspite*'s executive officer, a commander, and reports that he was roughed up were untrue, subsequent embellishments of the class-war gloss put upon the event. As the men were shepherded back to the pier and the liberty boats returned them to their ships, this officer reported to Tomkinson aboard HMS *Hood*. What had taken place appeared to have been a noisy disturbance, fuelled by alcohol and a grievance, and was seen by the patrol as a cathartic letting-off-of-steam. Tomkinson agreed.

On Monday the *Warspite* and *Malaya* proceeded on gunnery trials without any trouble. By midday the official Fleet Order regarding the detail of the reductions had arrived, and efforts were made to promulgate it swiftly. They were frustrated by insufficient copies being available, which delayed the final broadcast until Tuesday morning in some ships. This general tardiness, due entirely to administrative incompetence, was seen by the men as suspicious. According to Owen, the 'final meetings were held in the canteen and on the recreation grounds on the Monday to perfect the organization, but also to instil the belief that only concerted action would save the families of the men from ruin.'

Having met his subordinate admirals and some senior captains, Tomkinson now decided to report 'a slight disturbance in the Royal Naval canteen Invergordon yesterday . . .' It was not normal for the acting C-in-C of the Royal Navy's most powerful battle-fleet to inform the Admiralty of 'a slight disturbance', and it ratter looks as though Tomkinson was suspicious of coming trouble and sought to protect himself. It is also likely that he was sending a warning for, significantly, the signal was encrypted and categorized as 'Important'.

Neither the Admiralty Board nor any of its individual members took any action at all. Tomkinson's isolated plight went as unrecognized as the plight of the many sailors now condemned to an immediate 25 per cent cut in pay. Insulated from the outside world, the Admiralty remained aloof.

Aboard the ships at Invergordon some captains were anticipating trouble and attempting to head it off. For example Patterson, Tomkinson's flag-captain, addressed the *Hood*'s company on that Monday forenoon wisely emphasizing 'the importance of their putting forward any representations they had to make, through him'.

The Monday afternoon meeting in the canteen was distantly witnessed by the shore patrol from the duty battleship *Valiant*, led by Lieutenant R.F. Elkins. Observing that the meeting was listening to a speech by a rating standing on a table, Elkins got inside and refused to leave until he was 'satisfied that what is being discussed is not to the prejudice of discipline'. Amid catcalls he was forced out of the canteen 'by some sailors and marines . . . bent down in the form of a rugger scrum. The door was shut and locked behind me.'

Elkins tried to get in again, but his intervention had disrupted the meeting and some men began to leave. Several tipsy sailors apologized for his man-handling and explained that 'they were doing this for you [meaning the officers generally] as well as for ourselves'. Not convinced that the meeting was over, Elkins sent a message for reinforcements, observing that another speaker was now on his feet, and then another. It was quite clear that the assembled men were planning action against the pay cuts, calling for leaders who would be prepared 'to go to the wall' if necessary.

Having agreed to 'pack up . . . after breakfast . . .', the meeting was on the point of dispersing when Elkins's reinforcements arrived from the *Hood*. Leading them, Lieutenant Commander Beresford explained that there was no harm in discussing the pay reductions, but that an organized meeting would be broken up – he was rather late for that, and amid general good humour the men went back to their ships. The *Rodney*'s watch ashore sang

The Red Flag as the liberty boat puttered back across the waters of the Firth.

Elkins's and Beresford's reports reached Tomkinson as he was finishing dinner with a number of his senior officers. There was a rowdy noise from *Rodney*'s forecastle, but the belief that this was still a letting-off-of-steam persisted. Insofar as he himself was concerned, Tomkinson seemed content to let matters take their course, though he sent two signals to the Admiralty. One reported 'further disturbances' the cause of which 'appears to be the drastic reduction in pay rates'; the second repeated a signal to his ships in which he had requested individual cases of hardship resulting from the pay-cuts to be reported to him without delay, 'in order that I may bring the matter at once to the notice of the Admiralty.' The following morning the fleet was due to proceed to sea for further exercises.

At 05.20 on Tuesday 15 September the hands were piped to turn out. The response varied but many men refused, simply absenting themselves from duty by remaining in their hammocks. Others refused to turn-to about 06.00, still others had breakfast and then milled about on the forecastle of their ship. In some ships the stokers raised steam and then left the boiler rooms. As these groups were seen from the other ships, their example was followed. At 06.30, as scheduled, the battle-cruiser *Repulse* got under weigh and proceeded to sea to join *Warspite* and *Malaya* for gunnery exercises, to barracking from some of the other warships as she glided through the mist and headed for the open Moray Firth beyond the neck of the Cromarty Firth. The *Valiant* was due to leave at 08.00, followed at intervals by *Nelson*, *Hood* and *Rodney*. As the time passed the men grew bolder, though in most ships the officers were waited on as usual by their stewards at breakfast. Shortly before 08.00 the *Valiant*'s Captain Scott was informed that his stokers were vacating the boiler rooms. HMS *Nelson*'s men, initially obedient, gradually stopped work as the time for unmooring drew near. The first lieutenant and some petty officers sought to weigh anchor without the men, but a mass of ratings emerged to squat on the cable like so many migrating swallows. Similar incidents were taking place on all the fifteen capital ships, until 12,000 seamen and marines had refused duty.

Aboard the cruiser *Norfolk* Wincott dictated a manifesto which began with a declaration of loyalty and sought to 'implore them [the Admiralty Board] to amend the drastic cuts in pay . . . inflicted upon the lowest paid men . . .' In essence, the men were 'refusing to serve under the new rate of pay', and the manifesto not unreasonably stated that 'The men are quite willing to accept a cut which they, the men, consider in reason.'

The Admiralty did not acknowledge receipt of this paper, which was almost identical in tone, down to the request for the confirmation of Parliament, to the Spithead delegates' petition, but stirred itself into action around noon. Their Lordships had received Tomkinson's signal that the ships' companies were refusing duty, and underwrote his decisions. Officers were adjured to 'take every opportunity of laying stress on the fact that great sacrifices are being required of all classes of the community and that unless these are cheerfully accepted . . . the financial recovery of the country will be impossible. Similar changes of pay have been made in the Army and Royal Air Force.' Similar, perhaps, but not identical. And that was all.

Stalemate ensued. The afternoon dragged on, the business of striking becoming monotonous after the heady excitement of revolt. Bored officers wandered ineffectually about their quarterdecks. The men leaned on the forecastle rails and smoked. *Warspite* and *Malaya* returned to the fleet anchorage as men in the other ships shouted insults.

In view of his slightly anomalous position as acting C-in-C, Tomkinson might have expected help from London. In 1797 members of the Admiralty Board had posted to Portsmouth and Sheerness; in 1931 they remained detached, as though suspended above the mucky affair they had created. The First Sea Lord, Sir Frederick Field, neglected even to telephone Tomkinson. At 13.40 Tomkinson sent another signal which detailed the men's grievance over pay, in particular pointing out the impact of the

25 per cent reduction: 'I do not consider that the men will feel they have received justice unless reductions are more in proportion to their pay . . .' Tomkinson urged an early decision, which was the only sensible thing he could do, and the only sensible thing the Admiralty could do. There was essentially no difference between Tomkinson's analysis and the men's manifesto, and neither was unreasonable in the circumstances.

After six hours the Admiralty replied that they would consider any representations of hardship, but stated that the new rate of pay remained in force and 'confidently expect[ed] that the men of the Atlantic Fleet will uphold the tradition of the Service by loyally carrying out their duty.' A detailed and nit-picking signal sent half an hour later argued that the men's petition was unreasonable, and a 25 per cent pay cut perfectly acceptable. Moreover, it began with the Board's expectation that the Fleet would return to its duty immediately Tomkinson's 'investigations' into individual hardships had been completed. Clearly the Admiralty appreciation was way off the mark, and Tomkinson was expected to work miracles. Either that, or he was being set up as a scapegoat.

Shortly after midnight Tomkinson responded emphatically: 'the situation at Invergordon will not be met until definite decisions have been communicated.' The 'Exercise programme is out of the question . . .'

By the following morning Tomkinson had begun to perceive the Admiralty's failure to grasp the seriousness of the position, and his own isolation. Shortly before noon on the 16th he sent a signal which '*recommended*' – a strong word in naval parlance – that a 'representative of the Board visit me to discuss matters on the spot.' It was in effect as forceful a demand as a Commander-in-Chief could make of the Board of Admiralty. In mid-afternoon Tomkinson was ordered to disperse the fleet to its home ports 'to enable personal investigation by C-in-Cs and representatives of Admiralty with view to necessary alleviation being made. Any further refusals of individuals to carry out orders will be dealt with under the Naval Discipline Act . . .'

It was, as far as the ratings were concerned when it was 'promulgated to the Fleet forthwith', a declaration of war; but, ship by ship, the ratings were persuaded by their officers to sail – and they did. The strike, or mutiny, at Invergordon appeared to be over. On Thursday 17 September the House of Commons was assured that the First Lord of the Admiralty, Austen Chamberlain, was 'not going to look back . . . to what has happened on this occasion . . .' In the debate that followed, the country's elected representatives seemed to be forgiving the sailors, thanking Admiral Tomkinson and declaring – with a sense of relief – an amnesty. The navy was the nation's bulwark, and one did not destroy the fence just because a few planks were loose.

At the beginning of 1931 a mutiny aboard a Chilean battleship had been scoffed at in the British press, though the Chilean authorities blamed it upon their sailors' contact with British communist agitators during the *Almirante Lattorre*'s refit in Devonport Dockyard. Mutiny in South American navies – there had been two tragically messy incidents in the Brazilian navy, one in 1911 the other in 1925 – was seen as of no consequence. When the news of the mass revolt at Invergordon broke in London, the shock was therefore profound.

As a result of the Admiralty's muted press release on Wednesday there was a run on gold: five million was removed from the Bank of England. On Thursday a further ten million was withdrawn, and on Friday another eighteen. Such was the prestige of the Royal Navy and its standing in the world that 'Europe thought that revolution had started, that troops were unpaid, and mobs starving.' By Monday 21 September 1931 that canteen meeting of disaffected sailors in Invergordon the week before had forced Great Britain off the gold standard. While the press was accused of rumour-mongering, the run on gold was a measure of the perceived importance of the Royal Navy as a stabilising influence on a troubled world. As the Frenchman Lemierre had perceptively written: 'the trident of Neptune is the sceptre of the world'. The events at Invergordon suggested it was no longer in safe hands.

In fact this economic consequence did little damage, though its abstract effect was powerful. The following Monday the government announced that since there were 'classes of persons' who were 'unfairly affected' by the proposed cuts in public service pay, 'the simplest way of removing just grievances is to limit reductions . . . to not more than ten per cent.' The decision was communicated to the Royal Navy by Admiralty signal. In addition to the clause mentioning 'just grievances', the signal reassuringly concluded: 'The balance of the Budget will be maintained.' It seemed as though the matter had been laid to rest.

As the Atlantic Fleet's battle squadrons broke up and returned to the Nore, Portsmouth and Plymouth, the secret services went to work on the Admiralty's behalf. Fears of a renewal of the revolt at Portsmouth proved groundless, however, and the fruits of a myriad grubby investigations bolstered by the substantial theoretical value of *in vino veritas*, were meagre. No red plot was discovered, no grand plan had been mooted. The worst that might have ensued was a vast expenditure of hot air and a sullen disposition to keep the Atlantic Fleet idle off Invergordon until the Board of Admiralty should come to its collective senses. Apart from widespread disobedience there had been no real violence, apart from the accidental hitting of an officer's head in the Invergordon canteen by a flying beer glass – and that had been apologized for. There had been no bloodthirsty intention, only typical and predictable bloody-mindedness.

By late October the results of the secret service investigations were coming to hand. Disappointingly for the Board, the Admiralty had gathered some evidence from interrogated sailors that was 'reliable, but not in the legal sense'. A small left-wing publishing house was closed down under dire threats of the consequences of an attempt to seduce members of the armed forces from their allegiance, but little of real substance could be found to indict the sailors in the fleet. Instead of convictions, all that could be obtained were grounds for some dismissals, though the net had swept well beyond Invergordon. A total of 397 men were finally kicked out of the navy, though only about 110 came from the Atlantic Fleet; most of the others were either members of the *Delhi*'s crew (which had caused trouble in Canada when they heard of the pay cuts), or men with a reputation for trouble-making elsewhere in the wider fleet. Wincott and a handful of other central and identifiable figures from Invergordon were sent for a 'disciplinary course' indistinguishable from penal servitude, and then dismissed from the navy with loss of pay and pension.

But the Admiralty were aware that as the days following the indiscipline at Invergordon lengthened into weeks and then months they were increasingly being suspected of mismanagement. Certainly they were entirely ignorant of the conditions under which the long-serving ratings subsisted, despite several attempts to enlighten them made by various parties, including an anonymous sailor who assumed the pen-name 'Neutralis'. The Board sought to restore its image, in its own eyes if not the nation's, smarting in the knowledge that its powers had been usurped by the politicians and that Chamberlain had been acting more as a Cabinet member than as political head of the Board of Admiralty. In short, it had suffered a 'dangerous infringement of its privileges'.

A little later this situation was suddenly blown apart following Admiral Sir John Kelly's appointment as Commander-in-Chief of the Atlantic Fleet. As Tomkinson reverted to command of the battle-cruisers, Kelly was charged with fully examining the causes of the 'mutiny' at Invergordon. He was not to carry out a formal enquiry, but to pursue the Admiralty's objectives by subtler methods. He was also given *carte blanche*. In a private letter to Field he confessed that he found himself in 'a very delicate, even a very unpleasant situation', for he had concluded that opinion was unanimous 'from the highest to the lowest' that the cause of the fleet's mutiny was 'the action of the Admiralty in accepting the "Cuts" as at first promulgated. Furthermore,' Kelly went on with ruthless honesty and no little courage, 'my enquiries lead me to believe that complete confidence . . . will not be restored so long as the present Board of Admiralty remains in office. The bitterness of adverse opinion and its entire unanimity against the Admiralty has astonished me. It transcends anything I have ever known . . .'

Kelly's findings generated a storm of fury in the Admiralty, which turned its ire upon the unfortunate Tomkinson. In the immediate aftermath of the mutiny Field had written a personal letter of congratulation to Tomkinson praising him for his tactful handling of the crisis. The rear admiral had also received the formal approbation of the Board. Executing a shameless volte-face the Board now censured Tomkinson, but without actually telling him. At an extraordinary meeting of senior admirals chaired by an unhappy Field, Tomkinson's future was now linked with that of the Board itself. In other words, Field was advised that Tomkinson's disgrace must be conditional upon the Admiralty Board admitting its share of the blame.

Field's Board declined to do this and on 1 January 1932 it achieved its ambition. Unable to bear the blame itself, it formally censured Tomkinson for failing to realize the gravity and purpose of the canteen meetings, for failing to close them, for continuing to attempt to get the Fleet to sea as proposed, and for failing to address the men himself 'although he must have realized that the men's grievances had at any rate considerable justification.'

In the light of Kelly's findings and its own conduct at the time these were extraordinary conclusions, extraordinarily expressed – particularly the last two, which would have run contrary to Board orders. Other careers were to also affected, among them those of Tomkinson's flag-captain, Patterson, who was to be relieved, as was Bellairs of *Rodney* and Dibben of *Adventure*. Two Board members were also quietly censured, but another, the Fourth Sea Lord Vice Admiral Preston, sagely summed up the Board's collective error: 'that the main root of the trouble lay in the Navy's lack of appreciation of the . . . lower-deck mind.'

The Admiralty now buried the entire matter along with Tomkinson, who was promoted vice admiral and relieved of his command. He was with his battle-cruisers in the West Indies when the letters informing him of both changes in his circumstances arrived in the same post. The British public had been informed five days earlier. All Tomkinson's subsequent pleas for a proper inquiry fell on deaf ears: the British could still 'kill' an admiral *pour encourager les autres*. As for the Atlantic Fleet, it was expunged from history. As the successor of the Grand Fleet it had never fought a battle, and it never did. Instead it was reincarnated as the Home Fleet. Tomkinson's flagship, the mighty *Hood*, was blown up in action with the German battleship *Bismarck* in 1941.

Comparisons with the events at Spithead in 1797 are inevitable, as is the conclusion that Bridport and Howe acted with more courage, energy and common sense than Field and his Board. They did not duck the ultimate responsibility of high command, for in spite of the yawning gulfs in Georgian society, the flag-officers of George III were in closer touch with their men than were those of George V. While hotheads may have orchestrated the upsurge of rebellious sentiment resulting from the awesome pay reductions announced by MacDonald's government that autumn weekend at Invergordon, many hundreds of sensible, long-service ratings were moved by a genuine and quite understandable concern for their families' welfare. So punitive and consequential a drop in pay was unacceptable even to faithful men, and the question they faced was, what were they going to do about it? It was what had troubled Elkins as he surveyed that crucial canteen meeting and noticed the number of vociferous long-service men. The *Nelson*'s captain, Captain F.B. Watson, understood the reasons for the mutiny and the impact of the pay cut: 'It is no exaggeration to say that in many cases it is not hardship they [the ratings] are facing but the ruin of carefully and thriftily built up homes. These men literally budget their commitments in pence. What little margin they have disappears under the new scale . . . [they] never expected a cut and arranged their manner of living accordingly.'

They had placed their trust in the Board of Admiralty to look after them and it had failed them. This, and this alone, was the cause of the mutiny at Invergordon.

14

'A PRETTY SORRY LOT'

As a matter of interest, Invergordon *had* possessed its equivalent to Matushenko and Feldmann: able Seaman Les Wincott and his associate Fred Copeman *had* sought to mobilize more than a simple strike, but they had failed. Both men later joined the Communist Party, and Wincott made his home in Moscow. The operations of Naval Intelligence found some evidence of communist agitation among the ships of Britain's Mediterranean Fleet, but these were opportunistic attempts to capitalize on the instability arising from the world-wide depression and, like so many revolutionary moves, occurred as things began to improve. Poor conditions sparked disturbances aboard the net-layer HMS *Guardian* and the battleship *Warspite* in the mid 1930s, but low pay was almost always the real mainspring of trouble. Just as it had fuelled the mutiny in the Chilean battleship *Almirante Lattorre*, it had provoked disorder at Invergordon. Two years later, in 1933, it was the issue of pay that affected the sailors and stokers aboard the Dutch battleship *De Zeven Provincien*. From *Potemkin* to this Dutch man-of-war, trouble tended to break out in big, capital ships where the crews were large and could be dominated by pedagogues and 'lower-deck lawyers', where the petty officers were usually senior men working their time out and less inclined to take their pastoral duties seriously, where the men were most isolated from their officers, and their officers found it difficult to carry out divisional duties without efficient support from the petty officers. Often, too, the segregation of the officers created, a 'them-and-us' atmosphere which was inherently inimical to the maintenance of discipline and to that essential cohesiveness that made a true ship's company to which, as Drake had so eloquently stated more than four centuries earlier, they all belonged. While the little *Kilbride* marks the exception to this rule, she may also be seen to follow it, since a local disaffection among a correspondingly *small* crew can seize hold of a ship with equal ferocity. On the other hand, small ships tend to be commanded and officered by young men, are kept busy, and are generally happier.

To what extent Invergordon and Eisenstein's film influenced the ratings aboard the Dutch East Indies flagship it is impossible to say; both were adduced as causes, to which may be added the unpopularity of Dutch colonial rule, and a rising independence movement in the East Indies. The announcement of a cut in pay of between 10 and 17 per cent first initiated trouble in the cruiser *Java* on 3 February, but this was quickly suppressed by armed force. It was known about aboard *De Zeven Provincien* by the night of the 4/5 February, when the warship lay at anchor off Kutaraja (Banda Aceh) on the north-east tip of Sumatra and Captain Eikeboom and several of his officers were ashore in the colonial club.

The crew of *De Zeven Provincien* was made up of Dutch and Indonesian ratings and the news of the pay cuts combined with that of the arrest of their colleagues aboard the *Java* provoked an immediate insurrection. The mutiny quickly took hold, the officers being overwhelmed and confined to the upper bridge. The executive officer had sent word ashore the moment he heard of trouble, but Eikeboom was later alleged to have laughed and remarked that the native ratings could not weigh anchor unsupervised. He gave the messenger a note instructing the executive officer to contain any problems and confine the Javanese ratings.

Having thus dismissed the matter, Eikeboom was therefore surprised when his executive officer appeared, dishevelled and anxious, to report that the battleship was in the hands of her mutinous crew, and that Captain Eikeboom had lost his ship. Eikeboom, a victim of hubris, watched as the mutineers not only got *De Zeven Provincien* under weigh, but broadcast their intentions to the colonial government at Batavia (now Djakarta). Her native stokers below in her engine and boiler rooms, and her sailors on deck happily confounded their commanding officer. *De Zeven Provincien* steamed south-east along the west coast of Sumatra, demanding abolition of the pay cuts and release of the *Java* mutineers. Meanwhile Eikeboom had commandeered the steamship *Aldebaran,* and with a small detachment of infantry followed his runaway ship.

At The Hague the Dutch government were aware of a rising tide of socialism across Europe, and that it was accompanied by more sinister Communist agitation. Like the British Admiralty, the Dutch were aware of attempts to suborn the loyalty of their sailors. Consequently they ordered the mutinous man-of-war intercepted, and on 7 February announced to the population of The Netherlands that strong measures were to be taken. Meanwhile, in pursuit in the wake of *De Zeven Provincien,* Eikeboom and his party had transferred to a faster vessel, the *Eridamus,* which was soon joined by the mine-layer *Gouden Leeuv.* Ahead of the mutinous battleship, the now loyal cruiser *Java,* two destroyers and two submarines were ordered to sail from Batavia, pass through the Sunda Strait and intercept her as she steamed down the west coast of Sumatra. This squadron were supported by three flying-boats from Tanjong Pandan on the island of Belitung, and one of them located *De Zeven Provincien* as she approached Bengkulu on the 8th.

On 10 February the opposing forces closed one another and the *Java* ordered the unconditional surrender of *De Zeven Provincien,* to which the mutineers responded by declaring their peaceful intentions and demanding a fair hearing. The Dornier flying-boats now overhead were ordered to drop bombs ahead of *De Zeven Provincien*, but this produced no result except that the ship herself was bombed. The explosion did considerable damage, starting a fire, killing a score of men, and causing many of the mutinous Javanese to jump overboard. After this *De Zeven Provincien* slowed to a stop and was boarded by armed seamen who repossessed her as the squadron's boats picked the terrified mutineers out of the water.

Then came the reckoning. With a preliminary investigation completed, the first court martial sat at Sourabaya in November. The legal process dragged on for more than a year. In December eight Dutch sailors were sentenced to prison for between one and seventeen years. A further 115 prisoners were arraigned in the New Year, and on 27 January 1934 the officers held on board were put on trial for failing 'to do their utmost'. Most sensationally, in February Eikeboom surrendered his sword and had his conduct examined at The Hague. He was found guilty of gross negligence, which had resulted in his ship falling into the hands 'of a mutinous crew', and sentenced to be discharged from the Dutch naval service and to serve a four-month prison sentence. His only appeal was to Queen Wilhelmina, who rejected it, along with all other pleas for clemency.

While the problem of communication between the Dutch and the several ethnic minorities manning Dutch colonial warships was undoubtedly a contributing factor to the ignorance of Eikeboom and his officers as to the temper of some of their men, it was not an absolute excuse, as the defending lawyers sought to attest. Invergordon might have inspired the mutineers in the Dutch East Indies squadron, and the appeasing attitude of MacDonald's British government might have inspired Queen Wilhelmina's to adopt an opposite, no-compromise, policy, but British commanders had learned their own lesson. There was in the Royal Navy following Invergordon a greater readiness in officers to understand lower-deck attitudes, albeit imperfectly and through the patronising filters of class-consciousness. This

minor advance in social integration was set against the wider
fears of the world-wide communist revolution proclaimed by
Moscow as the ultimate goal of the Marxist–Leninists, and most
western governments were quietly establishing Draconian
measures to deal with insurrection, both civil and naval/military.
As Spain was torn apart by civil war between the left and right,
the latter was rising in central Europe. Italy was already fascist,
and as the sailors of *De Zeven Provincien* steamed past
Bengkulu, Hitler was repudiating the Treaty of Versailles and
reintroducing compulsory military service in Germany.

When the Second World War broke out the dreaded spectre of
red revolution began to recede. Although Joseph Stalin had
ordered the Soviet Army into Poland from the east as the
Wehrmacht invaded from the west, by the summer of 1941 the
unlikely allies had split and Hitler was at war with Russia: the
dreaded Reds were now allies and, as Allied men-of-war and
merchant ships delivered *matériel* to the ports of north Russia,
the seamen could observe for themselves the grim reality of
'Uncle Joe's Workers' Paradise'.

Under wartime conditions neither men-of-war nor merchantmen were kept much in port, and mutiny once more seemed
unlikely. It was true that there were disturbances aboard many
merchant ships, but these were largely over poor conditions; and
the authorities were by now more accustomed to unionization
and the 'right to strike', less apt to regard every dispute with
fractious seafarers as 'mutiny'. One of the least glorious of these
incidents was the refusal of the civilian crew of the landing-ship
Royal Ulsterman to take their vessel to Norway, where the
Anglo–French intervention in support of the Norwegians against
the invading Germans was reaching its disastrous climax. The
Royal Ulsterman was swiftly remanned with a largely naval crew
of ratings, and sailed as planned.

Although such anomalies arose from misunderstandings about
the role of merchant seamen in what were effectively warships,
most of these disputes were less complicated and were settled
rapidly, since the machinery to deal with them as industrial

disputes had been developed and was more or less mutually acceptable to both sides. Although by 1944 war-weariness had begun to manifest itself in the Allied merchant services engaged, in particular, in the Battle of the Atlantic, such incidents were not serious and rarely constituted mutiny. In the worst of them, the premature evacuation of two merchantmen in convoy followed by the refusal of the crews to leave their lifeboats and return aboard, it was the masters who suffered most.

Two significant exceptions did occur, however, and they were almost predictable. Suffering from a lack of personnel to man merchant ships, the British Ministry of War Transport adopted the foolish expedient of releasing men from prison if they 'volunteered' for service in the Merchant Navy. Many did, especially hardened criminals from Glasgow's notorious gangs incarcerated in the city's infamous Barlinnie Gaol. Trouble among these men was fomented aboard an ageing transport with a chequered history, the former American liner *George Washington*. The old passenger ship was commanded by a distinguished master, Captain David Bone, and in 1942 it was intended that she should become one of the increasing number of liners co-opted as troopers, ferrying thousands of soldiers across the Atlantic to Britain. In the event the trouble-makers aboard her were frustrated by the failure of the old ship's boilers and the *George Washington* was returned to the American flag.

The Barlinnie Gaol alumni made one spectacular attempt at mutiny which might have had disastrous consequences had it not been swiftly suppressed. In late December 1942 convoy JW51B left Loch Ewe bound for Murmansk. It consisted largely of American freighters laden with munitions for the Red Army but was led by a British ship, the newly-built – and newly manned – *Empire Archer*. This ship bore the convoy's commodore, who was responsible for the collective conduct of the merchant ships. As a gale continued to rage on the 29[th,] Commodore Melhuish attempted to reassemble his disrupted convoy. At the same time the commander of the naval escort, Captain Rupert Sherbrooke, informed him that JW51B was liable to come under attack from

German capital ships. It was at just this time that Melhuish was told by the *Empire Archer*'s own master, Captain Maughan, that there was trouble in the ship's engine room.

Several of the firemen shipped aboard the *Empire Archer* had been released from Barlinnie only a few weeks earlier. Discovering that the *Empire Archer*'s cargo included a consignment of naval rum bound for the small flotilla of Royal Naval minesweepers stationed in north Russia, they broached it and became drunk; they then refused to turn-to. With the ship at sea under imminent threat of attack this was mutiny at its most blatant. Captain Maughan and his officers were faced with a real problem, and it is to their credit that the matter was so swiftly dealt with, especially as it was compounded by one of the perils of the sea: 'In the ensuing violence two men were knifed. This fight occurred simultaneously with the threatened break-adrift of a railway locomotive which, among a deck cargo of eight heavy tanks, had parted some of its lashings.' In due course the drunken firemen were overcome by Maughan and his officers in a spirited if minor suppression of mutiny that eventually resulted in the offenders being returned to prison.

War-weariness not only characterized the last two mutinies of any note in the Royal Navy but imbued the entire operation of Force X. In the summer of 1944 the Admiralty had received several secret memorandums advising them that Their Lordships must take 'energetic steps to improve the morale of the Navy . . . so as to create a will to continue the fight until Japan is defeated.' A convoy escort group commander signalled that 'if, however, the Lower Deck gradually discovers for themselves that there is going to be little or no demobilization after Germany is defeated, grave discontent may occur in ships . . . which do not possess the best officers.' By this time the bulk of the Royal Navy was manned by conscripts, 'Hostilities Only' ratings whose service to their country was deemed to be over when the direct threat to Great Britain and to their families had been removed by the defeat of Nazi Germany.

The Prime Minister, however, was anxious to re-establish the prestige of the British Empire in the Far East, where it as much as

British pride had been wounded by the success of Japanese arms, and in particular the humiliating surrender of Singapore by General Percival in 1941. As a consequence of Churchill's lobbying of Roosevelt, the President had brow-beaten the Anglophobic commander of the United States Navy, Fleet Admiral Ernest King, into allowing British participation in operations in the Pacific against the Japanese. King condescended to permit a force of landing-ships to join the American navy as a task force under American command.

Accordingly, in the late summer of 1944 Rear Admiral A.G.Talbot, whose distinguished career had hitherto culminated in D-Day operations directing amphibious forces off Sword Beach, hoisted his flag aboard HMS *Lothian*. Formerly the *City of Edinburgh*, this vessel was one of six converted cargo-liners which had been especially fitted out for amphibious operations. As Talbot's flagship, HMS *Lothian* was grossly overcrowded, some 750 men aboard a cargo-liner designed for a tenth of that number; she was burdened with an excessive staff and numerous communications 'numbers' with poor crew accommodation carved out of her cargo spaces. There was limited water capacity to support so large a crew, but worst of all was the indifferent food her company were compelled to eat. These basic deficiencies were in marked contrast with conditions aboard similar American ships, and predictably proved a cause of trouble, among both American personnel assigned to the *Lothian* and her young British crew, who 'were all about eighteen or nineteen'. Few of these were regular sailors, and all of them considered 'their' war over.

Nor could Talbot, his staff, flag-captain and officers have regarded their task as glorious. The war, as far the Royal Navy was concerned, was ending with a whimper.

As Force X sailed from New York, where leave for the crew had been limited, it headed into the Tropics. Conditions aboard the *Lothian* 'became . . . unbearable. We had rats, thousands of cockroaches, weevils in the food . . . [which] was bad and inadequate . . . The water . . . was foul. Then there was the intense heat and the putrid, fetid atmosphere in the mess deck. I remember', recorded Ordinary Seaman Bill Glenton, 'how exhausted I felt . . . the conditions had totally run us down. We couldn't go on living a tough naval existence without good food.'

On the passage to the Pacific the *Lothian* left the Panama Canal and paused at Balboa for repairs, all but one of the other vessels in the force going ahead under Captain Hutchison and HMS *Glenearn*. Here in Balboa, on 1 September, matters aboard *Lothian* came to a head: in echoes of Invergordon, the men announced that they were 'not going to sail across the Pacific until the Navy' did something about their grievance, which they had properly expressed to higher authority. 'The Navy' did nothing. When the men were ordered on deck after the morning stand-easy, shortly before the *Lothian* was due to sail, they refused to obey. When the first lieutenant, Lieutenant Commander Buckel, came below, they defied him. Buckel had the messdecks secured and went to report to Captain Petrie; Talbot was at the time hosting a lunch for a number of American officers. The situation was very embarrassing. Just as the Americans left the ship prematurely, the men burst out of the stinking messdecks and stormed ashore. Captain Petrie addressed them and attempted to recall them to their duty, with no success. He later tried to coerce them with armed marines and a detachment of soldiers on board, but the young ratings just laughed, well aware that neither of the armed groups would open fire on them, or indeed be ordered to do so in full view of the local Panamanians and American service personnel. Most of the ratings wearied of the ensuing stand-off and wandered back on board; the ring-leaders remained on the quay, where they were eventually arrested by the *Lothian*'s marines and locked up.

During the long Pacific crossing the seventeen ring-leaders were kept under guard and the rest of the mutineers lived in an uneasy limbo, uncertain of their future, grudgingly going about their routine tasks. Petrie had mentioned 'mutiny', and it had begun to sink in that those who sowed the wind usually reaped the whirlwind. As the *Lothian* headed east to join the American

Seventh Fleet, Talbot relieved Buckel of his duties as the *Lothian*'s executive officer and initiated an inquiry. Aboard his flagship Talbot's reputation slumped as he put the crew through a series of exercises designed to expunge the mutiny and prepare the Force for battle. He had previously commanded three aircraft carriers, so he was well qualified to ready *Lothian* and her sisters for 'assault operations'; it is clear that he was unsympathetic to any suggestion that they were at best only auxiliary warships. Talbot's regime and the unchanged conditions ensured that the ratings remained unhappy, particularly with half of them under threat of some form of disciplinary action. In the wardroom the rumours that Buckel was to be court-martialled for his manner of handling the breakdown of order upset many of the officers, few of whom were regulars.

Once the *Lothian* had rejoined the rest of Force X a series of courts-martial was held, the first at Bora Bora in the Society Islands, the second at Finschaven in New Guinea. During the latter, the majority of the mutinous men were ordered ashore for recreational exercise while on board the ring-leaders were tried by a court martial presided over by Hutchison of the *Glenearn*. One of the causes of the disaffection produced by the defence was that the men's water ration had been severely constrained owing to the numbers of men on the ship, which made it difficult to keep up the required appearance of the white uniforms Talbot insisted upon all hands wearing in the Tropics. Although the *Lothian* was fitted with evaporators designed to produce fresh from salt water, these were often defective. Moreover, what water was available was usually foul, since the cement-wash lining the ship's tanks had been disturbed, and the pumps operating the system frequently failed. All this was exacerbated in the men's eyes by Talbot's habit of taking a daily bath. The fact that this was in salt water was of little consequence: the mere implication of unreasonable privilege worked unfavourably upon the impressionable minds of young men. Hutchison, though he was a regular naval officer, had had extensive experience of merchant ships converted to men-of-war, having distinguished himself when in command of the *Breconshire*, a sister-ship of the *Glenearn*. He knew that flexibility and adaptation were necessary in such vessels, and that punctilious insistence upon naval forms was an aggravation. (He had in fact been considered as senior officer for Force X, but an admiral had been insisted upon.) 'When the court heard the whole story they came to the conclusion that the accused had been severely provoked.' The fact that they were 'Hostilities Only' seems to have mitigated the sentences, but naval discipline 'had to be preserved and they were duly found guilty'.

All but three were sentenced to ninety days' detention. The three that had seized weapons were given a year's hard labour and locked up aboard the *Glenearn*. The sentences were light, but several petty officers and leading hands were demoted for not having done their utmost in heading off what Talbot, perhaps mindful of Tomkinson's fate, was now playing down as 'a strike against bad living conditions'. After the trials of the mutineers, Force X weighed anchor. On its departure Talbot was acquainted with the deployment of Force X: 'almost continuous[ly] in forward operational areas participating in training and assault operations . . .' The attack on Leyte in the Philippines was imminent.

On 2 October Force X arrived off Hollandia, the assembly anchorage for the invasion of Leyte, and Talbot reported to Rear Admiral Daniel Barbey, who was in charge of the amphibious assault force. Barbey later summed up Force X as 'a pretty sorry lot. They are not prepared for tropical duty . . . their material condition [is] poor.' Moreover, their 'cleanliness and sanitation' were ' . . . not up to the standards maintained by ships of the US Navy.' It was damning stuff, and while it did not apply to *Glenearn*, it did to *Lothian*. To Talbot's intense chagrin Barbey relegated Force X to training duties, on the diplomatic grounds that although it was fitted with landing-craft these were not of an American pattern, and adaptation of the davits to accommodate the American craft was impossible. Once this decision had been reached, Force X was disbanded as auxiliary to American operations. It was a profound humiliation, but it was not the end of the drama.

Lothian was moved away from the main anchorage to a more secluded bay and the court martial flag was again hoisted as Captain Lord Ashbourne, captain of the fast minelayer *Ariadne*, came aboard to preside over another. This time the prisoner was an officer, Buckel, who faced several charges, chief of which was that he had not used his utmost endeavours to quell the mutiny. Buckel had risen from the lower deck, a not unusual occurence in wartime, but one that may have counted against him in his attitude to the lower deck, at least in the eyes of Talbot. Whatever influence this fact had upon the court, Buckel stated afterwards that the circumstances surrounding his trial had been weighted against him. He only received the letter enumerating the charges against him a bare twenty-four hours before the court sat, scarcely time for him to cobble together a defence. Then, that very same day before the trial, he had been requested to give up his 'Prisoner's Friend' or defending officer, who was wanted to appear as Deputy Judge Advocate! Buckel and his substitute 'Friend' then had to sit up all night preparing the defence.

Furthermore, the principal charge was grossly unfair, for while Buckel was accused of not having done his utmost to suppress a mutiny, the mutinous ring-leaders, in a damage limitation exercise by Talbot, had been charged with the lesser act of insubordination, notwithstanding the fact that three of them had tried to secure arms. The verdict of the court was a foregone conclusion, even though, at the last minute, Petrie spoke up eloquently for his much-put-upon first lieutenant. In the end Buckel was found guilty of the lesser charges of 'tardiness in singling out the ringleaders and of attempting to appease them'. In some mitigation, the court's sentence was minimal: Buckel was dismissed his ship, but not the Service. None the less, it was enough to ruin his career.

After the American Seventh Fleet and Barbey's amphibious assault force had sailed from Hollandia, the remnant of Force X was ordered to Australia. On the way south Petrie mustered the ship's company in a tropical downpour which added its dreadful gloom to the captain's portentous words as he read the provisions of the Naval Discipline Act, ending '. . . shall suffer death by hanging . . .' After a pause Petrie concluded, 'or such other punishment . . .', and the men heaved a collective sigh of relief. The ring-leaders were to serve their hard labour in Australia; the rest of the men who had disobeyed the order to muster on deck in Balboa, and who were already under three months of punishment drill, were given 'two and two', which meant their conduct record would show they were of the second class, and they would take the second place for leave. Petrie then gave way to Talbot, who delivered himself of a harangue in which he told the *Lothian*'s assembled ne'er-do-wells that they had disgraced the white ensign.

Several ships from Force X, especially the *Glenearn* and briefly the *Lothian* herself, subsequently played their part in the British Fleet Train and in due course even earned King's praise. A year later, a new captain who joined the *Lothian* in Sydney was appalled by her condition. He also had two-thirds of his crew in Australian hospitals with tuberculosis, picked up in their infamous and putrid messdeck.

When a return to civilian life was daily expected, such punctilious insistence upon rules and respect for rank was equally difficult to accept for its own sake elsewhere in the fleet. Unfortunately there was a perceptible tendency, not just in admirals like Talbot but also among some of the young commanders, to insist that although the war was over, naval service was not. One of the worst instances of this occurred aboard the fleet destroyer *Javelin*.

At the end of the war in Europe this destroyer was in the Mediterranean. The news of Germany's surrender was welcomed on the lower deck but greeted with disbelief by Lieutenant Commander Marjoribanks. The *Javelin* was Marjoribanks's first command and it was clear that, war or no war, he intended to make his mark on the ship. Although she bore a large number of 'Hostilities Only' ratings, many of them and a few regular naval sailors had seen long and arduous service and they found their new captain difficult to stomach, for Marjoribanks was 'a regular naval officer with pre-war experience in big ships. Clever, precise and petulant.'

Marjoribanks seems to have been obsessed with the assertion of discipline, insisting on the strict observance of a series of petty regulations 'enforced with neurotic punctiliousness'. Any infringement attracted the severest penalties. When a sentry refused an order to turn a fire hose on Greek bum-boatmen coming alongside to peddle their wares – a practice of ancient precedent, and in any case an undignified response to former allies who had not only endured German occupation but whose exiled men-of-war had fought beside the Royal Navy – the man was severely punished. The multitude of such petty tyrannies that bore down upon the ship's company's tolerance might have been mitigated by a good first lieutenant, but *Javelin* was doubly unfortunate because this officer was 'intense and gloomy', an introvert unlikely to plead the men's cause in front of the new captain. When the defaulting sentry was paraded, Marjoribanks swore at the Duty Officer who was pleading good conduct in mitigation.

Marjoribanks was given to handing out generally insulting remarks as to the ship's company's abilities, which most of the men found intolerable. The irony of it was that, in the words of one of his officers, Lieutenant (later Admiral of the Fleet Sir) Henry Leach, Marjoribanks was 'unsure of himself and . . . lived on his nerves and was not a natural ship-handler.' As one crew member afterwards wrote, 'Pinpricks at first merely irritating made for a cumulative resentment . . . aggravated . . . by the need to hide it by a show of outward docility and . . . the unspoken, ever more insistent feeling "Why do we put up with this?"'

Life under such a regime would have been bad at the best of times, but it was made worse by the desire of most of the men to be demobilized. One such was Leading Seaman Leverett, 'a gentle and quietly unassuming person . . . the best seaman on the ship', who wrote daily to his wife and lived for when the *Javelin* would be paid off. On Sunday 16 September the *Javelin* was lying at anchor off Rhodes awaiting inspection by the flotilla commander at 09.30 the following day. To the sailors' incredulity it was announced that in order to have the ship ready for this visit the crew would turn out at 04.30, a ludicrously early hour. When the pipes shrilled through the messdecks next morning 'there was no concerted disobedience but nobody obeyed promptly'. Such tardiness soon brought Lieutenant Leach onto the messdecks 'shocked and white faced', generally chivvying the men and taking some names for form's sake. Marjoribanks saw the crew's action as wholesale disobedience. He ordered the lower deck cleared, but only a few men mustered on the upper deck as required. 'Some few hours later' the ship's company did parade, but only after Leverett had turned his back on an officer who was telling him personally to 'fall in'. In fact, as Duty Boat Coxswain Leverett was one of the few men excused a general muster, but he was arrested, and as a consequence most of the rest of his shipmates refused to turn out until he was released. They barricaded themselves below, though 'No violence was used or so much as hinted at.' Nevertheless, this was mutiny.

As is the case with most mutinies, however justified the rebellion, it had no future. Having made their quiet protest in support of Leverett the ship's company could do no more, and in the end had to come to heel. HMS *Javelin* accordingly weighed anchor and proceeded to Malta, where on Friday the 21st a court of enquiry investigated the incident, followed by a series of courts-martial. Due process took its unremitting course. Among those arraigned, eight petty officers were deprived of their rank, denied their gratuities for long service and good conduct, and dismissed the service despite their hitherto first-class conduct and war records. In addition, they were to serve one year in a civilian prison. Other able and ordinary seamen were found guilty of 'mutiny not accompanied by violence' and of 'wilful dis-obedience', for which custodial sentences varied, though among the junior rates these were partially suspended. It was the trusted petty officers who had most offended the sensibilities of naval justice.

When it became known about in Britain the affair assumed some prominence, and the newspapers called it 'The Spit-and-Polish Mutiny'. It ran counter to the mood of the nation which had had enough of war and militarism, and aspired to better times. The 'Spit-and-Polish Mutiny' was an embarrassment to Attlee's Labour government. Sensing this, Mr A.V. Alexander, still First Lord of the Admiralty, attempted to mitigate the severity of the court's sentences, which bore heavily upon the petty officers. The year's imprisonment and dismissal from the navy were 'not excessive', he told the House of Commons, but having 'taken into account the former good record of these men, and their mistaken sense of loyalty to another rating', that is to say Leverett, it was his opinion that the petty officers should not be dismissed, but immediately released from the service as 'an act of grace'. Nevertheless, all their hard-won campaign medals were forfeit, and all eight were reduced to the ranks before discharge.

Marjoribanks was replaced and given a desk job, but he had irreparably damaged *Javelin* for the remainder of her commission. Their Lordships now sent the destroyer 'an entirely new captain . . . who was the opposite of Marjoribanks. Shabby and sometimes reputedly drunk at sea . . . he was as slack as his predecessor had been over-strict.' As a consequence of this, 'the ship presented a Hogarthian Spectacle on Christmas Day, with men "flaked-out" here and there all over the lower deck.'

As Sir Henry Leach later commented: 'The situation was simply that of men being driven too far too long, often without real need and with a complete absence of encouragement. Most of those concerned were wartime only; the war had been won and they yearned for release . . . it was too much, and the camel's back quietly broke.'

Leach exposed the heart of the matter: most of the mutineers were not vocational sailors but, psychologically, civilians; and they deeply resented first Marjoribanks and his ridiculously punctilious antics, secondly the humiliation such folly subjected them to, and thirdly what they felt was unreasonable detention in their country's service. Such war-weariness was widespread among the amateur sailors called-up by the exigencies of war, and equally rife in the United States Navy. If Admiral Barbey in leaving Admiral Talbot behind at Hollandia had felt any sense of *schadenfreude* at the humiliation of Britain's once proud and pre-eminent Royal Navy, he came to regret it. Once word reached the dough-boys on the lower decks of the Seventh Fleet operating in support of the invasion of the Philippines that home leave would be severely curtailed in the face of operational demands, there was widespread 'discontent and a general lowering of morale'. Trouble broke out in several ships, especially a naval auxiliary, the USS *Kilty*, whose anxious medical officer reported that 'prolonged combat experience' had produced 'an increasing number of disciplinary problems'. Yet again, 'the men feel no one is vitally interested in what happens to them'. Something had to be done before there was 'serious damage to the ship', aboard which mental disturbances had reached 'alarming proportions'.

Part of the sloth of which both the American and British naval authorities seemed guilty was a result of fears of a resumption of war, this time with Soviet Russia, for the world was sliding into the Cold War and the nuclear age.

15

'POOR BLOODY MANAGEMENT'

THE long confrontation with the Soviet Union known as the Cold War once again sparked fears among the high commands of the two most powerful western navies that communist infiltration and agitation were at work among the ratings of both fleets. This anxiety seemed congruent with the rise of trade union power ashore and the wider aspiration for social equality expressed at the democratic ballot box. It was also underlined by a series of spy scandals affecting both the Royal Navy and the United States Navy.

As we have repeatedly noted, mutiny could be the manifestation of both a rebellion against real or imagined injustice and in favour of political change. A violent example of this had occurred in the Royal Indian Navy in February 1946 when a British officer at the Signals School at Bombay (Mumbai) once again insisted upon a strict observance of regulations and acted in a thoroughly disgusting manner. The unrest began ashore, but the Signals School ratings had to hand the means of transmitting the news both to the Indian fleet and to the world at large. The insurrection quickly spread, and became part of the move for Indian independence. Admiral Sardarilal Nanda, who as a young officer was present, afterwards thought the men 'didn't see it so much as mutiny but as an expression of feeling against the British'. There had been an undeniably racist atmosphere in the Indian Navy during the war, not helped by the unwise recruitment into the volunteer reserve of a number of former tea planters which created a 'masters and slaves' institution. This combined with poor pay and conditions to foment a dangerously explosive situation. In all, 56 ships' companies mutinied, some 10,000 men, and were ruthlessly suppressed by armed force. Disorder spilled outside the confines of the naval dockyards and barracks, and more than two hundred had been killed before matters simmered down again. All the forces of imperial law and order had achieved was a speeding up of the process of parturition: within two years India had been granted full independence. Although it was not seminal in securing this independence, it might be argued that the Indian Naval mutiny, though viciously put down, had been as effective as that at Spithead. If this is so, then the fact that it began with the senseless abuse by one officer of a handful of ratings eating their midday meal who refused to stand up respectfully in his presence, may be an object lesson in the real responsibilities of command.

Unlike Great Britain, the United States was not in retreat from the status of a 'Great Power'. To the paranoid public servants of the Great Republic, subversives were communists, and anyone who might be likely to fall under the influence of such 'masters of deceit', as Edgar Hoover, the then head of the FBI, called them. Susceptible individuals were defined by a concerned official as recent European immigrants, Negroes, certain Jews, former academics who were 'now commissioned as officers'. He also added to the list of potential defectors 'officers who have inherited money and who have never, through their own ingenuity or effort, earned any other than what the Navy has offered them', and 'officers who are in debt'.

In the event, however, it was in Canadian warships that mutiny reappeared. In 1949 a small non-violent protest erupted aboard the destroyer *Athabascan,* which was escorting the

Canadian aircraft-carrier *Magnificent* in the Caribbean. The disturbance was caused by the ancient grievances of poor-quality food, long working hours often dedicated to pointless tasks lumped under the heading of 'bullshit', a lack of shore leave and – perhaps worst of all to a sailor during the working day – curtailed meal times. These were exactly mirrored aboard another Canadian destroyer, HMCS *Crescent*, then in the Far East, provoking another minor mutiny. Although it may have comforted Ottawa, and confirmed Washington's anxieties, to ascribe this discontent to agitators, one Canadian officer was more forthright and more accurate, blaming 'poor bloody management by the officers'. The subsequent enquiries revealed little, and their findings were hushed up. Significantly, not one of the mutineers was punished.

Elsewhere, however, the communists were successful. In the aftermath of the expulsion of Chiang Kai-shek's Kuomintang from China by the Communists in 1949 there occurred a serious mutiny among the crew of the cruiser *Chongqing*. This warship was the former British cruiser *Aurora,* and although her crew were nominally Nationalist, corrupt government and military defeat had weakened Chiang's hold over the hearts and minds of his followers. The crew of the *Chonqing* mutinied and defected to the Communists, an act which demoralized the Nationalists, facilitated the crossing of the Yangstze River by the forces under Mao Tse Dong, and hastened the end of the civil war. Perhaps this mutiny, little known of in the West, had the most profound consequences of any in the whole of naval history.

Elsewhere, post-war turmoil had a less revolutionary effect. Return to a peace-time establishment persuaded the British Admiralty to turn the clock back. As competent reserve officers returned to the merchant service or their civilian careers and the up-and-coming generation of regular naval officers, to which Henry Leach belonged, had yet to make their mark in the Royal Navy's policy-determining hierarchy, reaction seemed to dominate Admiralty thinking. Some disillusioned officers on the threshold of high command gave up and resigned from the service; others were persecuted for their unorthodox views or their perceived wartime 'failures'. Others, with limited experience, rose rapidly. One of these admitted he had spent the war in big ships and 'knew nothing of the Battle of the Atlantic'. Ultimately, however, the rising and more enlightened generation prevailed. Most of the divisiveness and purblind obduracy that ran counter to the reinvention of Britain in her retreat from imperial pretension were swept from the corridors of the Admiralty as it was subsumed into the Ministry of Defence.

Elsewhere in the country, however, reaction began to ossify the very agent of change as trade union power overstretched itself and made serious inroads into the international viability of the British economy. Barely twenty years after it saved the nation and Mr Alexander declared in Parliament that the nation must never forget the debt owed to it, the British Merchant Navy was almost entirely paralysed by a widespread strike among its seamen. It was the culmination of a period of industrial unrest which had, ironically enough, produced significant improvements in pay and conditions in merchant ships. Most British ship-owners decided that enough was enough and 'diversified' their interests – a euphemism for pulling out of shipping. In the twenty years that followed the seamen's foolish action the British merchant marine simply bled to death. The 1966 seamen's strike was not a mutiny in legal terms, but it had the most far-reaching political and economic impact of any action taken by British seamen in seeking redress for perceived – and largely imagined – grievances.

By contrast, the Royal Navy had become sufficiently sensitive to human relations to be able to ward off potential discontent. To some extent this was helped by its inevitable reduction in size, but more significant was the fact that its increasingly technologically advanced ships demanded educated ratings whose cast of mind was not very different from that of their officers. However, as in the case of the *Kilbride*, trouble could still simmer particularly aboard small and busy ships. In 1970 a mutiny broke out aboard HMS *Iveston* in Ullapool, where the minesweeper was acting as a fisheries protection vessel. She had suffered a succession of changes in her commanding officer – always an unsettling matter – and seems not to have been a happy ship. For reasons that remain unclear, a group of able seamen disobeyed orders and one struck an officer attempting to assert authority. They were court-martialled and sentenced to disgraceful dismissal, but the case was hijacked by the press who attempted to exploit class divisions between officers and ratings. In a damage-limitation exercise the Ministry of Defence reduced the sentences to unqualified dismissal.

Nor was the United States Navy, now the world's pre-eminent naval force, immune from indiscipline. The social turmoil produced by the twin influences of the Civil Rights Movement and the protracted humiliation of the Vietnam War inevitably impinged upon the armed forces in the field. The first disturbance had about it elements of farce, however, and harked back to an earlier age, evoking images of tyrannical, or at least odd, behaviour on the part of a commanding officer. This curious affair erupted in 1966 aboard the USS *Vance*, an elderly and much-altered destroyer whose captain, Lieutenant Commander Marcus Arnheiter rapidly acquired the soubriquet 'Mad Marcus'. From the moment he ordered the seat of his water-closet changed from black to white, it was clear that he was an oddball. Quite unfitted to command, he treated the *Vance* and her crew as his private fiefdom, seeking action in defiance of orders and creating deep unhappiness among his officers. His erratic actions resulted in a complaint from the commander of another American warship whose operations off the coast of Indo-China Arnheiter had compromised, and after ninety-nine days in command, he was removed from the *Vance*. One of his officers wrote that 'this guy is paranoid'; Arnheiter countered that the officers had instigated a 'conspiracy to mutiny'. While the *Vance* affair exposed the continuing possibility of unsuitable men being posted to command men-of-war, it also emphasized the difficulties loyal officers experienced in resolving such a problem. The failure was, of course, the responsibility of the respective appointing authority embedded in the high command, but the burden of it fell on the put-upon officers under their unsuitable captains.

'Mad Marcus' Arnheiter was a post-war exception. Late twentieth-century mutinies have tended to be linked with political upheaval, usually motivated by a desire for change on the part of the underdog, as with the crew of the *Chongqing* – but not exclusively so: in 1973 the captain and officers of the Greek destroyer *Velos* 'mutinied' in favour of their exiled monarch. King Constantine XIII had been dethroned by a military coup in 1967 and the action aboard the *Velos* was intended as part of a widespread revolt against the usurping generals' government on the past of a navy loyal to the King of the Hellenes. The plan was to blockade the ports of Piraeus and Salonika in a revolt coinciding with a left-wing underground student insurrection ashore – an unlikely combination that failed to mature. The plotters at the naval base at Salamis were arrested, the plot was exposed and only Ploiarkhos (Captain) Nicholas Pappas and his ship declared for the king. At the time the *Velos* was engaged in a NATO exercise off Sardinia and on the forenoon of 25 May, to the surprise of the mixed-nationality force, she broke away from the formation, signalling her loyalty to the NATO Alliance and her intention to restore democracy to Greece. As far as the seizure of the *Velos* was concerned, Pappas had committed mutiny against his ship's 'owners' – but since the Greek government was self-appointed we teeter on the edge of a legal quagmire. Had she been a commercial vessel the action of Pappas and his officers would have been barratry; they clearly thought of themselves as patriots, and patriots of an ancient tradition.

Arriving off an Italian fishing port, two officers tried to contact King Constantine at his villa near Rome; but by now the higher NATO command and the Italian *carabinieri* were involved, and the *Velos* was gently taken into custody as Athens demanded the return of the *Velos*, her captain and ship's company. In the event the *Velos* and her crew went home, but

Pappas and his officers claimed political asylum and were permitted to remain in Italy. In due time, of course, the Greek generals' regime was ended, though it was not succeeded by a restoration of the monarchy.

Idealism also motivated the only confirmed mutiny in the large Soviet Navy, in which rumblings of discontent in other Russian warships (including at least one nuclear submarine) have from time to time been heard. Operating in the Baltic, on 7 November 1975 the powerful guided-missile frigate *Storozhevoy* was moored near Riga in modern Latvia. The demand for weapon space and the consequent poor living conditions in many Soviet warships had for some years combined with poor food to produce low morale. However, the loyalty of all crews was monitored by the political officer assigned to each warship, and this system kept most in thrall. The situation aboard the *Storozhevoy* was in stark contrast to the norm, since the political officer or *zampolit*, Kapitan Lietenant Valery Sablin, was something of a purist. Bablin considered, not unreasonably, that the Soviet Politburo had betrayed the pure idealism of Marxist-Leninism, and was unusually sympathetic to the grievances of the crew of the *Storozhevoy*. At about 20.00 that evening, while many of the ship's crew were enjoying a run ashore, in a bold, foolish and quixotic act of deception Sablin managed to secure the *Storozhevoy*'s commander and the most loyal of his officers. The sailors remaining on board, mostly of whom were conscripts, were confused and did what they were told, which was to get the *Storozhevoy* under way, clear the Daugava estuary and head for the Swedish coast. In the few moments it took Sablin and his accomplices to take over the ship – and thereby commit mutiny pure and simple – a petty officer escaped ashore and attempted to alert the authorities, only to be frustrated by delays and disbelief. But on board the frigate as she made her way to sea, another loyalist got inside the communications flat and transmitted a message which was taken more seriously. Consequently, as the *Storozhevoy* began her passage west she rapidly attracted a hostile escort of warships and aircraft which ordered her to stop. Sablin was undeterred until shells and bombs began to explode around the frigate. None were targeted to hit the errant *Storozhevoy*, but a near-miss damaged her rudder and Sablin, who appears never to have wished to defend the ship nor to cause bloodshed, surrendered. As armed boarding parties approached the frigate, the *Storozhevoy*'s commander was released by her boatswain and the ship was swiftly retaken.

The Swedish naval authorities, who had had several brushes with Soviet warships during the protracted stand-off of the Cold War, monitored the radio traffic with interest. By contrast Tass, the Soviet news agency, remained utterly silent. After some months the *Storozhevoy* made a quiet passage by way of the Suez Canal to the remote waters of the Sea of Okhotsk. In May 1976 Sablin and fourteen fellow mutineers were tried in Moscow; the fourteen were sent to the Gulag, and on 3 August Sablin was shot. He was by all accounts content to die in vindication of his dramatic protest. Less candid than Sablin, the Soviet naval authorities denied there had been any mutiny in the Baltic Fleet, though they hurriedly replaced its commander-in-chief.

The command structure of a man-of-war, far more than that of a commercially regulated merchantman, reflects the political architecture of the state to which she belongs. It also mirrors the defects inherent in that state's society. Moreover, since by being at sea a warship becomes an isolated, hermetic unit, there is no space for the easing of constraints. Thus it is not only a microcosm of human existence, it is also a forced environment where dissension naturally comes to a quick climax, a situation that may be further exacerbated by the failure, or total absence, of a policy or means by which any grievance can be properly addressed – the root cause of so many mutinies at sea.

In the early 1970s there were serious and incapacitating incidents of mass disorder aboard at least two large United States aircraft carriers, the USS *Constellation* and USS *Kitty Hawk*. Both arose from racial inequities which in turn had their origin deep in American society, and in the in aftermath the authorities were anxious to limit the extent to which they were seen as mutiny. The huge crews, long deployments and lack of proper shore-leave common to these 'troubled carriers' caused conditions in which ethnic rivalries simmered to the boil, and in the boiling produced ugly scenes of disorder, disobedience and violence. History will confine both to a wider social aspiration associated with the black Civil Rights Movement, and while a Congressional Report described events aboard the *Constellation* as 'a carefully orchestrated demonstration of passive resistance', that is unlikely to be how it appeared to Captain John D. Ward or his officers. The cause was better put by Leonard Guttridge in his study of naval insurrection: 'Command rooted in tradition faltered before a contumacy born of social flux and racial discontent.'

It was an unfortunate irony that the USS *Kitty Hawk* had as her second-in-command the first black executive officer to be appointed to a United States aircraft carrier. But even his presence was not enough to stem a serious outbreak of disorder on so vast a ship, with her flats and passages, companionways, hidey-holes, and trunkings, her large open hangar decks with their lethal cocktail of parked jet aircraft, fuel and ammunition. The threats and confrontations that occurred aboard these two mighty men-of-war were serious, compromising the operational abilities of both carriers and resulting in their temporary removal from the front line. Yet despite the extreme nature of the incidents there were men on both ships who remained in ignorance of the affairs as they took place, while their commanders initially remained preoccupied with operational duties, until the gravity of the situation in their respective ships was drawn to their attention. While the disappearance of His Britannic Majesty's Armed Transport *Bounty* into the then unknown wastes of the vast Pacific was an act with no truly shattering consequences, the disruption caused to the United States Navy of the accident aboard these two large capital ships was, at the very least, an embarrassment, and one that arose directly from a dislocation of command.

EPILOGUE

PERHAPS such circumstances as prevailed aboard the USS's *Constellation* and *Kitty hawk* point most cogently to the root cause of all mutinies: a detachment of the captain of any vessel, irrespective of size, from the mood of his crew, *all* of his crew, not just those with whom he has most in common or sees most frequently. It is a complex necessity for the commander of a ship to maintain a certain detachment from the daily round of his ship. Not only must he bring to any disciplinary matter, or any dispute requiring resolution, an unimpeachable impartiality, but he must always be giving his full consideration to the fundamental business of his ship, to its role, conduct, safety and navigation – matters which are, as it were, exterior to the vessel herself. Within the hull, however, the blood and bone, the sinews and power of his command lie in part in machinery and electronics but also in the human component, and are largely in the hands of the executive officer. He must possess an intuition as keen as his commander's and enjoy a close and confidential relationship with him. No matter how much technology may reduce the human presence, it remains essential to the function and efficiency of a ship. That is why proper food, set and respected meal times, adequate if not lavish living conditions, and reasonable rates of pay remain important to seafarers. Most of the commanders who were faced with mutiny had either lost sight of these fundamentals, or had no control over them. In the former case they were wilfully inviting mutiny as a consequence of long-term, pent-up frustration; in the latter, it was the captain who suffered the consequences of a ship-owner's greed, or a commander-in-chief's incompetence.

No captain can command without order and discipline, but if he ignores the simple provisions that common decency demands in return for labours undertaken, he courts disaster. Today this principle is at least understood by the high commands of most major navies who invest large sums in the training of individuals for service aboard modern, highly technical and complex warships. The same cannot be said to prevail in the commercial sector where, ironically, the opposite is true. After a century of slow and painstaking reform and sensible regulation, matters are sliding backwards into a morass of almost paranoid over-regulation imposed by the International Maritime Organisation, a United Nations agency, and the bureaucracies of individual nations. This situation has been exacerbated by the perception of merchant ships as potential carriers of terrorists and terror weapons into the heart of a community in the wake of the events in the United States of 11 September 2001.

Such paper-government of international shipping is not simply an over-reaction to the events of 9/11; it is seen as the only way to halt the downwards spiral in pay and conditions, and in the material state of a good deal of modern merchant shipping. Sadly, the best intentions of regulators fail to affect the unscrupulous, and only succeed in hampering and inconveniencing the better-regulated ships belonging to properly-run shipping companies. Nevertheless, a significant number of vessels fall within this category because in today's global free market the conditions aboard flag-of-convenience merchant ships are again deteriorat-ing to nineteenth-century standards, with crews recruited from third-world nations being paid at low rates. This is because owners seek their profits on the margins of operational costs, and the beneficiaries of cheap shipping – the public – expect cheap goods and foodstuffs in their local supermarkets. An over-capacity of ships, along with men and some women willing to risk a great deal to escape poverty and civil unrest in their own counties, to better enable some owners to make significant profits. This is bad enough, but there have been several incidents in recent years where at the conclusion of a voyage the ship-owner is found to have vanished and a ship and her crew have been left penniless, to fend for themselves far from home on a coast where their plight is held to be someone else's responsibility. Quite whose is unclear, but with flag-of-convenience registration in countries which provide open registers, the seafarer is auto-matically cast as the loser in a bargain which may turn rotten. Usually in such deplorable circumstances the ship's master and his officers are as destitute as their humblest rating, but as the absent owner's representatives they may become the focus of hate and revenge tomorrow, just as they were in the past.

It is a curious but worrying reversion, a symptom of our unstable and unpredictable world, and its consequences may yet be as sanguinary and as disruptive as anything history has yet recorded. Just as piracy has re-emerged bloodily onto the world's stage, so too may mutiny: for mutiny is not an historical curiosity, it is a simple expression of human discontent.

BIBLIOGRAPHY

All titles published in London, unless otherwise stated.

Aiken, A., *In Time of War*, published by the Author, Glasgow, 1980

Barrow, J., *A Chronological History of Voyages into the Arctic Regions*, John Murray, 1818.
——*The Eventful History of the Mutiny and Piratical Seizure of HMS 'Bounty' its Causes and Consequences*, John Murray, 1831

Barrow, T., *The Whaling Trade of North-East England, 1750–1850*, University of Sunderland, Sunderland, 2001

Baynham, H., *From the Lower Deck, The Old Navy, 1780–1840*, Arrow Books, 1972

Bell, C.M., and Elleman, B.A., [eds], *Naval Mutinies of the Twentieth Century*, Frank Cass, 2003

Berckman, E., *Nelson's Dear Lord; A Portrait of St Vincent*, Macmillan, 1962

Bergreen, L., *Over the Edge of the World, Magellan's Terrifying Circumnavigation of the Globe*, HarperCollins, 2003

Biden, C., *Naval Discipline in the Merchant Service*, J.M. Richardson, 1830

Blake, R., *Jardine Matheson, Traders of the Far East*, Weidenfeld & Nicolson, 1999

Bligh, W., *An Account of the Mutiny on HMS 'Bounty'*, Alan Sutton, Gloucestershire 1981

Bone, Sir D., *Merchantmen Rearmed*, Chatto and Windus, 1949

Bullocke, J.G., *Sailors' Rebellion, A Century of Naval Mutinies*, Eyre and Spottiswoode, 1938

Clowes, W. L., *The Royal Navy*, 6 vols, Sampson Low, Marston, 1899
Corbett, J.S., *English Men of Action: Sir Francis Drake*, Macmillan, 1890
Cotton, Sir E., *East Indiamen, the East India Company's Maritime Service*, The Batchworth Press, 1949

Danielsson, B., *What Happened on the 'Bounty'*, Allen and Unwin, 1963
Dash, M., *Batavia's Graveyard, the true story of the mad heretic who led history's bloodiest mutiny*, Phoenix, 2002
Dening, G., *Mr Bligh's Bad Language*, Cambridge University Press, Cambridge, 1992
Divine, D., *Mutiny at Invergordon*, Macdonald, 1970
Dobrée, B., and Mainwaring, G.E., *The Floating Republic*, Pelican Books, 1937
Domville Fife, C.V. (ed), *Square Rigger Days*, Seeley Service, 1938
——*Epics of the Square Rigged Ships*, Seeley Service, 1958
Dugan, J., *The Great Mutiny*, André Deutsch, 1966
Dyall, V., *A Flood of Mutiny*, Hutchinson, 1957

Ellacott, S.E., *The Seaman*, 2 vols, Abelard-Schuman, 1970

Forester, C.S. (ed), *The Adventures of John Wetherell*, Michael Joseph, 1954

Glenton, B., *Mutiny in Force X*, Hodder and Stoughton, 1986
Gruppe, H.E., *The Frigates*, Time-Life Books, Amsterdam, 1979
Guttridge, L.F., *Mutiny, A History of Naval Insurrections*, Ian Allan, 1992
——*The Commodores*, Peter Davies, 1970

Hadfield, R.L., *Mutiny at Sea*, E.P. Dutton, New York, 1938
Haine, E.A., *Mutiny on the High Seas*, Cornwall Books, 1992
Haining, P., *The Jail that went to Sea*, Robson Books, 2003
Heaps, L., *Log of the 'Centurion'*, Macmillan, New York, 1973
Heffernan, T.F., *Mutiny on the 'Globe'*, Bloomsbury, 2002
Hirson, B., and Vivian, L., *Strike Across the Empire*, Clio Publications, 1992
Hope, R., *Poor Jack, The perilous history of the merchant seaman*, Chatham, 2001
——*A New History of British Shipping*, John Murray, 1990
Hough, R., *The 'Potemkin' Mutiny*, Hamish Hamilton, 1960
——*Captain Bligh and Mister Christian; The men and the Mutiny*, Cassell, 1972
——*The Blind Horn's Hate*, Hutchinson, 1971

Hoyt, E.P., *Mutiny on the 'Globe'*, Random House, New York, 1975
Humphries, S., *The Call of the Sea*, BBC Books, 1997
Hurd, A., *The Merchant Navy*, Vols I, II and III, John Murray, 1923
Hurd, D., *The Arrow War*, Collins, 1967

Jackson, G.V., *The Perilous Adventures and Vicissitudes of a Naval Officer, 1801–1812*, William Blackwood, 1927
James, W., *The Naval History of Great Britain*, 6 vols, Richard Bentley, 1847

Kemp, P. (ed), *The British Sailor, A Social History of the Lower Deck*, Dent, 1970
——*The Oxford Companion to Ships and the Sea*, Oxford University Press, 1988
Kindleberger, C.P., *The World in Depression, 1929–1939*, Allen Lane, The Penguin Press, 1973

Lavery, B., *Nelson's Navy*, Conway Maritime, 1989
Lehane, B., *The North West Passage*, Time-Life Books, Amsterdam, 1982
Lewis, M., *A Social History of the Navy, 1793–1815*, Allen and Unwin, 1960
Lloyd, C., *The British Seaman, 1200–1860, A Social Survey*, Associated University Presses, Cranbury, New Jersey, 1968
Lubbock, B., *The Last of the Windjammers*, Brown Son, & Ferguson, Glasgow, 1927
——*The Opium Clippers*, Brown Son, & Ferguson, Glasgow, 1933
——*The Colonial Clippers*, Brown Son, & Ferguson, Glasgow, 1948

Macdonald, Sir R., *The Figurehead*, Pentland Press, Durham, 1993
Marcus, G., *The Age of Nelson*, Applebaum, Sheffield, 1971
——*Heart of Oak*, Oxford University Press, 1975
Marshall, J., *Royal Naval Biography of Peter Heywood, Esq.*, Longmans, Green & Co, 1825
Mitchell, M., *Elcano: The First Circumnavigator*, Herder, 1958

Neale, J., *The Cutlass and the Lash: Mutiny and Discipline in Nelson's Navy*, London, 1985
Nicol, J., *The Life and Adventures of John Nicol, Mariner*, Cassell, 1937 (reprint of 1822 edition)
Northcote Parkinson, C. (ed), *The Trade Winds*, George Allen and Unwin, 1948
——*Trade in the Eastern Seas*, Frank Cass, 1966

Pack, S.W.C., *The 'Wager' Mutiny*, Alvin Redman, 1964
Pigafetta, A., *Magellan's Voyage*, The Folio Society, 1975
Plimsoll, S., *Our Seamen, An Appeal*, Virtue and Co., 1873

Pope, D., *The Black Ship*, Weidenfeld and Nicolson, 1963
——*The Devil Himself*, Secker and Warburg, 1987

Rawson , G., *'Pandora's' Last Voyage*, Longmans, Green & Co., 1963
Reisenberg, F., *Cape Horn*, Robert Hale, 1950
Rodger, N., 'Mutiny or Subversion? Spithead and the Nore', article
   in Bartlett, T., Dickson, D., Dáire, K., Whelan, K. (eds), *1798,
   A Bicentenary Perspective*, Four Courts Press, Dublin, 1998
——*The Admiralty*, Terence Dalton, Lavenham, 1979
——*The Wooden World, An Anatomy of the Georgian Navy*,
   Collins, 1986

Sanderson, M., *Sea Battles, A Reference Guide*, Purnell, Abingdon,
   1975
Stackpole, E.A., *Mutiny at Midnight*, Frederick Muller, 1944
Stammers, M.K., *The Passage Makers*, Teredo Books, Brighton, 1978

Vigneras, L.A., *The Discovery of South America and the Andalusian
   Voyages*, The University of Chicago Press, Chicago, 1976
Villiers, A., *The Way of a Ship*, Hodder and Stoughton, 1954

Walter, R., *A Voyage Round the World*, Heron Books, 1968
Watkin, R.C., *Mutiny on the 'Bounty'*, Manx Antiquarian Society,
   Douglas, 1969
Wilcox, L.A. *Anson's Voyage*, George Bell, 1969
Woodman, R., *Arctic Convoys, 1941–1945*, John Murray, 1994
——*The Victory of Seapower, 1806–1814*, Chatham, 1998
——*The Sea Warriors*, Constable, 2001
——*The Real Cruel Sea*, John Murray, 2004

Yule, H., and Burnell, A.C. *Hobson-Jobson, The Anglo-Indian
   Dictionary*, Wordsworth Reprint 1996, original publication 1886

(Author Unspecified), *Outline History of the USSR*, Foreign
Languages Publishing House, Moscow, 1960

Additional information has been culled from various articles in *The Mariner's Mirror*, the journal of The Society for Nautical Research, specifically: Volume 1, 1911; Volume 13, 1927; Volume 21, 1935; Volume 22, 1936; Volume 33, 1947; Volume 41, 1955; Volume 42, 1956; Volume 44, 1958; Volume 46, 1960; Volume 53, 1967; Volume 54, 1968; Volume 65, 1979; Volume 70, 1984; Volume 79, 1993; and Volume 85, 1999. Further original material has been found in *The Naval Chronicle, The Mariner's Chronicle, Lloyd's List* and selected documents in the Library of the Honourable Company of Master Mariners.

GLOSSARY

Admiral   a senior officer in charge of a group of ships (a squadron or fleet). Sometimes referred to as a flag-officer, and subject to grades: full admiral, vice admiral and rear admiral. The most senior is an Admiral of the Fleet (British) or Fleet Admiral (American). Other nations usually follow a similar practice.

'All hands!'   the summons for the entire company of a ship to muster on deck, often for a major manoeuvre, or under duress when a special effort is required.

barge   on a warship, a boat reserved for the carriage of the captain or admiral.

bargeman   a member of a barge's crew, usually hand-picked and therefore privileged and loyal.

battle-cruiser   a capital ship mounting heavy guns but sacrificing armour for speed.

battleship   a capital ship, heavily armoured and mounting heavy guns.

beat (to windward)   to work a sailing ship upwind by a series of tacks made sailing as close to the direction of the wind as possible.

boat   a widely abused term often used to mean a ship, which it is not. A boat is commonly open and is a relatively small craft, auxiliary to a ship – which may carry several – and may be used as a working craft to support the ship or, as is more usual today, as a lifeboat.

bow the foremost part of a ship.

bow-chaser a gun mounted in a sailing warship as far forward as possible so as to point at a vessel being chased.

bower a heavy anchor carried at the bow.

bark in the eighteenth century, a plainly-built merchantman without a figurehead. In the nineteenth century, the American equivalent of the English 'barque'.

barque a nineteenth century English expression for a three-masted vessel having the third, or mizzen, mast rigged with fore-and-aft sails. Later in the century four- and even five-masted barques were built.

bear away to alter course away from the wind.

bowsprit a spar extending from a ship's bow to which the forestays are taken and from which the jibs are set.

brace a rope or wire purchase which alters the angle of a yard and thus trims the sails.

brig a two-masted sailing vessel having a fore and main mast, square-rigged on both masts.

brigantine a two-masted sailing vessel having a fore and main mast, of which only the foremast is square-rigged.

cable a heavy rope or, after about 1830, a chain which is secured to an anchor.

cable tier a platform in the hold upon which the heavy anchor cables were coiled. A small natural ampitheatre was thus formed, and within this enclosed space unlawful congregating might take place. Gambling was the most common form of meeting, but any 'combination' found in the cable tier was likely to arouse at least suspicions of 'mutinous assembly'.

captain the commanding officer of a ship. In the Royal Navy the proper title of a full captain was 'post-captain'.

cast (of the lead) a measure of the depth of water under a vessel taken by throwing a lead weight secured to a marked line.

caulking the stuffing forced between the planks or strakes making up a ship's side to keep her watertight.

charter, to the hiring of a merchant ship for commercial purposes.

clew up, to to draw the corners of the lowest sails (the courses) up prior to their being furled. The ropes which do this are called clewlines.

colours the ensign of a naval ship denoting her nationality, or the national mercantile flag of a ship's owners.

course (1) the direction or heading on which a ship is proceeding, usually expressed by reference to the compass.

course (2) the lowest and largest sails on each mast.

cruiser in the days of sail, a generic term referring to a vessel operating independently, harrying enemy trade or reconnoitering. Such duties were usually carried out by frigates or sloops-of-war. After the introduction of steam power the cruiser became a specific type of warship with a medium calibre armament, a long range and little armour. Essentially her duties remained unchanged.

cunning an obsolete word for 'marine knowledge'.

doldrums an area of calms and light and unpredictable winds lying in the tropical belt.

eight bells the four double strokes on a ship's bell that mark the end of every four-hour watch period.

ensign the appropriate national flag of a ship, see **colours**.

fathom an obsolescent measurement of depth, equating to six feet or a little under two metres.

fireman in a merchant ship, a rating who tends the boilers.

First Lord (of the Admiralty) the political head of the Royal Navy; a civilian post that was also a Cabinet post, but nevertheless often held by an admiral.

First Sea Lord (of the Admiralty) the leading sea officer, always an admiral, who was the operational head of the Royal Navy and advisor to the First Lord. There were subsidiary Sea Lords with departmental responsibilities.

fish, to, to support a fractured spar such as a mast or yard by placing other timbers alongside it and lashing the whole together.

flag-officer a synonym for an admiral, from the fact that admirals were distinguished by flying a distinctive flag from the masthead of their flagship.

fluke   that part of an anchor designed to bite into the sea-bed.

flying jib   the outermost *jib* (which see) set at the extremity of the bowsprit.

foremast   the leading mast in a ship.

fore-and-aft rigged   the rig of a sailing ship in which the spars stretch the sails in line with the hull. All modern yachts are fore-and-aft rigged. See *square-rigged*.

frigate   a sailing warship of upwards of twenty-eight guns designed for extended operations and having a single deck of guns; a captain's command. The term was resurrected in the Second World War to describe a small anti-submarine convoy escort.

greaser   in a merchant ship, a rating who assists in the engine room but is distinct from a *fireman* who tends the boilers.

green sea   a seaman's term for a wave which washes aboard ship.

gun-port   an aperture, closed when necessary by a hinged lid, through which a gun is pointed and fired.

hammock   the removable canvas bed of the common seaman.

haul one's wind, to   to swing a sailing ship onto a course as close to the wind as possible.

heave-to   to bring a sailing ship as close to the wind as possible and then to check her forward motion so that she rides easily and without strain in heavy weather. As far as it was possible to do so, this was effectively to stop the ship but to keep her under control. See also *lie-to*.

hold   in a merchant ship, that lowest part of the hull which contains her cargo. In a sailing man-of-war the hold was the lowest part of the ship in which her stores were kept.

hulk   an old, de-rigged ship reduced to a harbour installation for holding coal or other commodities such as opium, gunpowder. A vessel which has lost its masts through heavy weather or enemy action is often referred to as a hulk, and the word once meant a particular type of medieval merchant ship.

jib   a triangular sail carried in the forepart of a sailing ship on the bowsprit.

jury rig   an extemporized arrangement of masts and sails following heavy weather or enemy damage.

latitude   measurement of distance north or south of the Equator, expressed in degrees. Lines of equal latitude run parallel to the equator and are referred to as 'parallels'.

lazarette   a securable locker containing valuables or, sometimes in a merchantman, ammunition.

lead see *cast.*

leeward   the direction away from that of the wind.

leeway   the inevitable sideways drift made by a sailing ship when she is sailing in any direction other than directly before the wind (called 'running'). It varies with the angle to the wind and is greatest when a sailing ship is steering as close to the wind as possible.

lie-to, to   to haul some of the sails aback to that the wind acts on their leading surface: the means by which a ship may be held stationary, subject to some leeway and tidal or current-drift. A ship lies-to to pick up a pilot, to send away a boat to communicate with another ship, or, in the case of a whaler, to await the return of her whaling boats. It differs from heaving-to in that the latter normally applies to the conduct of a ship in heavy weather.

line of battle   in the days of sail, the conventional formation for fighting with the massed broadside guns of a squadron or fleet deployed most advantageously and the vulnerable bow and stern protected by neighbouring ships. See *rake.*

line-of-battle ship   a vessel mounting more than sixty guns on several decks and deemed powerful enough to lie in the line of battle. A frigate was not so deemed.

log (1)   the written record of the conduct of a ship.

log (2)   a device, altering over time, by which a ship measures her speed through the water.

longitude   the east or west measurement, by international convention from Greenwich, measured in degrees and delineated by 'meridians', all of which run through the poles. Before the invention of the ship-board chronometer, longitude was very difficult and in many cases impossible to determine with any accuracy. Until the prime meridian was established at Greenwich, longitude was expressed from a known location.

'lower deck, the'   deriving from the berth or accommodation deck of a frigate, 'the lower deck' is a term used to describe its inhabitants: in other words, a warship's crew.

luff, to; luff up   the alteration of a ship's head closer to the wind. To luff up meant that a vessel lost her forward motion through the water, and by this means a sailing ship was slowed down.

mainmast   the principal mast, the middle and highest in a three-masted ship, the second from forward in a four- or five-masted vessel.

Master   the proper term for the commanding officer of a merchant ship, who is 'Captain' by courtesy.

Master's Mate   a non-commissioned rank in the sailing navy, ranking above a midshipman and attached to the *Sailing Master*.

Mate   in a merchant ship the officer next below the Master in rank. He is usually referred to as *the* Mate and may be supported by other officers, at least a Second Mate and often a Third Mate. The term is synonymous with Chief Mate, rarely First Mate. Large passenger ships often used intermediate ranks to confuse the issue and some liner companies called their mates 'officers', so that 'Chief Officer' was also synonymous with *the* Mate. The Mate was always responsible for the cargo, the ship's maintenance and the crew, and stood a watch except in the largest ships.

merchantman   a merchant ship.

messdeck   in a warship, the accommodation for the ratings where they slung their hammocks, ate their meals and took their leisure.

midshipman   a minor non-commissioned officer in a warship. Occasionally used in merchant ships to describe a cadet or apprentice officer.

mizzen, mizen   the third mast in a sailing ship.

orlop   an arrangement of platforms above the hold in a sailing man-of-war which accommodated the warrant officers, midshipmen and marines along with several store-rooms, etc.

people, the   an obsolete expression for the crew of a man-of-war, as opposed to the officers.

pink   a sixteenth- and seventeenth-century term for a small ship having a distinctively narrow and over-hanging stern.

pitching   the longitudinal motion of a ship in a seaway.

privateer   a privately owned and armed vessel licensed by a letter of marque and reprisal, issued by her nation state to make war upon an enemy's trade.

posted missing a vessel long overdue at her destination is 'posted missing' at Lloyd's. Interested parties may then advance claims against her loss.

quarterdeck the portion of a sailing warship's deck abaft (behind) the mainmast, and the preserve of the officers, except for those working or fighting the ship.

quartermaster a petty (or non-commissioned under-) officer who supervised the steering under the officer of the watch. In a merchant ship he usually undertook the actual steering.

rake (1) the angle of a vessel's masts to the vertical.

rake (2) the manoeuvre by which a sailing warship passed across the bow or stern of an enemy and fired her broadside the length of her opponent's decks, with devastating effect.

rear that third of a fleet or squadron that lay at the end of the line of battle and from which the term Rear Admiral derives.

repay to cover the underwater body of a ship with various mixtures designed to inhabit the growth of weed and to prevent, usually unsuccessfully, penetration by the ship worm *Teredo navalis*.

radoub to re-fit or overhaul a vessel.

road an open anchorage.

rolling the sideways motion of a ship in a seaway.

royal Apart from skysails flown from clippers, the uppermost sails on a sailing ship above the topgallants.

Sailing Master a senior warrant officer who was charged with the safe navigation of a sailing warship and the stowage of her stores in the hold. The Sailing Master had unique access to the Captain of a man-of-war and often stood nursemaid to young and relatively inexperienced commanders. The rank was a very responsible one and Sailing Masters were often former merchant ship-masters. The rank had fallen into disuse by about 1840, when naval lieutenants were expected to be proficient in such tasks.

scuttle to deliberately sink one's ship to prevent her falling into the hands of an enemy.

sea, a seamen rarely refer to 'waves', usually calling them 'seas', thus 'a *green sea*'.

seaway   the seaman's expression for the state of the sea as it moves, and moves his ship.

semaphore   a form of pre-telegraphy long-distance signalling using swinging arms from standards mounted on towers. The Royal Navy had a system that radiated from the Admiralty in London to the main coastal ports. Also a means of flag signalling by hand using prescribed positions for two flags which can rapidly indicate alpha-numerics.

shallop   an early term for a small ship's boat rather like a jolly-boat or dinghy.

sheet   a rope which controls the lower corners of square sails.

ship   a widely misused generic term meaning a vessel. Strictly speaking, a ship is a three-masted, fully square-rigged sailing vessel.

ship's head   the direction in which a ship is pointing at a given moment.

sky-light   a small glazed hatchway admitting light into accommodation below.

slop-chest   the supply of oilskins, clothing, soap and other comforts available on board ship for purchase by members of the crew.

squall   a sudden, often vicious increase in wind speed, usually short-lived but sometimes highly destructive.

square rig   the original form of deep-sea sailing ship rig in which sails are extended athwart (across) the ship's fore-and-aft line and most effective when sailing with a favourable wind, as was the case when large sailing vessels harnessed the global wind system until the middle of the twentieth century. It was not impossible to tack to windward in such a ship, but she was far less efficient at doing so than a fore-and-aft rigged vessel.

stand, to (a watch)   the act of carrying out a watch on deck in a merchantman or warship, in the course of which a seaman's duties might be to haul the sails, keep a lookout, or steer the ship under the supervision of the officer of the watch. A watch lasted for four hours, and if a two-watch system was worked this meant only four hours were spent off duty before one turned-to again. Modern practice generally provides for three watches with a regime of four hours on and eight off. However, many merchant ships still run single watches, with fatigue an increasing evil at sea.

stand-to,   to be called to stations for a manoeuvre.

stand, on or off   a warship may be said to stand on or off a coast if she is cruising on the lookout for an enemy.

stations   the prescribed place for any officer or rating on any ship for an intended evolution or manoeuvre. A ship's company went to stations for leaving harbour, for taking another vessel in tow, for lowering a boat, for tacking or wearing ship, as well as for going into action.

stern   the back of a ship.

stoker   the naval term for a rating who tends the engines.

tack, to   a ship is said to be tacking when working to windward by a succession of zig-zags as close to the wind as she can go. She is said to tack, or 'go about', when she changes this direction by luffing up and passing her bow through the wind.

terral   a nighttime offshore land breeze. The term is usually used in tropical latitudes.

top   in the days of sail, ship's masts were made out of two or three separate spars, the lower mast, topmast and topgallant mast. At the doubling and joining of the first two of these a platform called a *top* extended the supporting rigging and in warships provided a fighting platform for snipers. It also provided the topmen with a little privacy – a place where invasion by an officer was unlikely, and therefore a good place to discuss matters such as mutiny.

topgallant mast or sail   the mast or sails above the topsails. By about 1870 the topgallant sails were often divided into upper and lower topgallants.

topmast   the second section of a ship's mast set above the lower mast.

topsail   the second sails upwards from the deck. By the mid-nineteenth century they were split into upper and lower topsails for ease of handling and reduction in crew size.

traverse   the record of course and distance kept by the officer of the watch, upon which basic dead-reckoning navigation was based.

trimmer   a rating who shovelled coal from the bunkers to the firemen at the boiler fronts.

under way   a ship is said to be *under way* when she is moving through the water.

under weigh   a ship is said to be *under weigh* when her anchor has been broken out of the sea-bed.

van   the leading third of a fleet, from which the term Vice Admiral derives.

wardroom   in a warship, the officers' common room.

watch   that portion of a ship's crew who are assigned duties to rotate throughout the tewnty-four hours and who may be called upon to handle the ship during their duty period.

wear ship   a similar manoeuvre to tacking, but instead of turning the ship's bow through the wind, a vessel swings right round and passes the wind from one side to another by turning her stern through the wind's direction. It was a more certain manoeuvre, but lost ground to leeward.

weather gauge, or gage   the doctrine of fighting with the weather gage was held as absolute naval orthodoxy for many years and required an admiral or a captain to keep to windward of an enemy so that he could dominate an engagement and dictate the course of the action.

weigh anchor   to heave on the cable of an anchored ship so that the anchor is broken out of the sea-bed and is lifted to the ship's bow.

windward   the opposite of *leeward*; upwind, in the direction from which the wind is coming.

yard   an adjustable spar slung across a ship from which square sails are set.

Index

In this index the following abbreviations have been used: HEIC for Honourable East India Company; RIN for Royal Indian Navy; RN for Royal Navy; USN for United States Navy.